P9-DOC-193

# *Nōmai* Dance Drama

**Recent Titles in**
**Contributions to the Study of Music and Dance**

Jazz Poetry: From the 1920s to the Present
*Sascha Feinstein*

Whose Master's Voice?: The Development of Popular Music in Thirteen Cultures
*Alison J. Ewbank and Fouli T. Papageorgiou, editors*

The Piece as a Whole: Studies in Holistic Musical Analysis
*Hugh Aitken*

Mythology as Metaphor: Romantic Irony, Critical Theory, and Wagner's *Ring*
*Mary A. Cicora*

Wagner's *Ring* and German Drama: Comparative Studies in Mythology and History in Drama
*Mary A. Cicora*

Tchaikovsky and His Contemporaries: A Centennial Symposium
*Alexandar Mihailovic, editor*

Chopin Through His Contemporaries: Friends, Lovers, and Rivals
*Pierre Azoury*

Otto Laske: Navigating New Musical Horizons
*Jerry Tabor, editor*

Perspectives on the Grateful Dead: Critical Writings
*Robert G. Weiner, editor*

The Cultivation of Body and Mind in Nineteenth-Century American Delsartism
*Nancy Lee Chalfa Ruyter*

Domenico Cimarosa: His Life and His Operas
*Nick Rossi and Talmage Fauntleroy*

The Writings and Letters of Konrad Wolff
*Ruth Gillen, editor*

# *Nōmai* Dance Drama

## A Surviving Spirit of Medieval Japan

Susan M. Asai

Contributions to the Study of Music and Dance, Number 47

GREENWOOD PRESS
Westport, Connecticut • London

**Library of Congress Cataloging-in-Publication Data**

Asai, Susan Miyo, 1952–
Nōmai dance drama : a surviving spirit of medieval Japan / Susan M. Asai.
p. cm.—(Contributions to the study of music and dance, ISSN 0193–9041 ; no. 47)
Includes bibliographical references and index.
ISBN 0–313–30698–2 (alk. paper)
1. Nōmai (Dance drama) I. Title. II. Series.
PN2924.5.N65A82 1999
895.6′2009—dc21 98–14243

British Library Cataloguing in Publication Data is available.



Library of Congress Catalog Card Number: 98–14243
ISBN: 0–313–30698–2
ISSN: 0193–9041

First published in 1999

Greenwood Press, 88 Post Road West, Westport, CT 06881
An imprint of Greenwood Publishing Group, Inc.
www.greenwood.com

Printed in the United States of America

The paper used in this book complies with the Permanent Paper Standard issued by the National Information Standards Organization (Z39.48–1984).

10 9 8 7 6 5 4 3 2 1

This book is dedicated to Ōta Zennosuke, a master *nōmai* singer, dancer, and drummer of Shishipashi village, whose tireless efforts to preserve *nōmai* have helped this tradition to withstand the test of time.

# Contents

**IV. Epilogue**

# Illustrations

# Preface

*Nōmai* dance drama is an artistic expression that combines the sacred, communal, and cultural spheres of life in communities in the northern Japanese district of Higashidorimura. It is a performing tradition that provides an identity to agriculturally based villages and represents a traditional way of life.

*Nōmai*'s importance lies in its retention of features characteristic of music, drama, and sacred practices in medieval Japan (12th to 16th centuries). Its evolution outlines an art form that combined a diverse number of performing traditions that flourished during this time. *Nōmai* singing exhibits a direct link to Buddhist chanting, while the instrumental music is of folk Shinto origin. The song texts of the ceremonial and prayer pieces reveal the sacred nature of this dance drama. In addition to bringing to light *nōmai*'s medieval roots, this work highlights the social and cultural value this tradition has for residents in villages who retain it.

Other aspects addressed in this work include (1) the interchange and borrowing of art forms between classes, (2) the role of *yamabushi* (ascetic mountain priests) and the Shugendō religion in the creation of *nōmai*, and (3) the adaptation and change of a tradition striving to survive in modern society.

Works in English on Japan's folk performing arts are greatly needed. In the field of ethnomusicology, few studies on traditional Japanese music by Western scholars deal with folk performing traditions. A wide-ranging number of studies of such traditions by folklorists and musicologists in Japan do exist, but the language barrier prevents many interested readers from access to this information. This book makes available data translated from Japanese sources, as well as firsthand knowledge extracted from interviews with *nōmai* performers. Its intended design gives it the potential to reach a broader readership and provides a basis for further studies on ritual in theatre, the role of art in religion, as well as comparative topics, such as the triplet rhythmic figure of the *taiko* drum in *nōmai* music and its possible connection to the triplet rhythm heard in Korean drumming styles. There are a number of findings which this book suggests with ramifications for various fields such as theater, folklore, anthropology, Asian studies, religious studies, in addition to ethnomusicology.

## RESEARCH

I lived in Japan from September 1983 to August 1984 researching *nōmai*. In that year I translated a broad spectrum of information pertaining to *nōmai*, documented performances, interviewed master performers, and observed training sessions as well as cultural and community events of the area.

My fieldwork coincided with the period before, during, and after the new year, since the most important and complete *nōmai* performances occur during this time. For a five-week period—from December 11th to January 18th—I resided in the farming village of Shishipashi, located in the central district of Higashidorimura in northern Aomori Prefecture. During my stay there I also visited and documented three neighboring villages—Ōri, Iwaya, and Shiriya—in an attempt to identify the regional parameters of *nōmai*. I chose these villages based on the recommendation of Mr. Ōta, my main informant and a master *nōmai* singer and dancer. His criteria took into consideration both the mastery of a group and their retention of what he regards as the authentic *nōmai* style. Other considerations included the quality of the musicians and the schedule of performances.

Shishipashi was an ideal choice as the representative village because of its skillful musicians; the retention of what is held to be the authentic music, song, and dance style; and the opportunities I had to observe village life during my stay there. While living in Shishipashi I attended rehearsals of the young men's association (*seinenkai*) responsible for performing *nōmai*. My participation in the rehearsals included learning to play the bamboo transverse flute and small cymbals and observing the playing of rhythmic patterns on the double-headed barrel drum. These three instruments form the *nōmai* instrumental ensemble. At one of the rehearsals, Mr. Ōta taught me the folk dance, *oiwake*, which all neophyte performers learn. In addition to observing the Shishipashi group, I attended the rehearsals of two other *seinenkai* associations in the villages of Ōri and Shiriya.

Documenting *nōmai* in the four villages involved sound recording and videotaping or photographing performances and rehearsals. These materials made it possible for me to compare the music and dance of each village. I recorded six major performances: two in Shishipashi, one in each of the three other villages, and a joint performance of all thirteen *nōmai* troupes in the annual Higashidorimura Village Performing Arts Public Assembly.

Interviews with the leaders of the four *nōmai* groups took place in two stages: the first were exploratory and the second served to resolve questions raised in the informant's responses obtained in the first interview. These interviews informed me of the relationship of music to the dance, categories within the repertoire, training of the performer, stylistic interpretations and performance practices, and the function of *nōmai* within a community.

## ACKNOWLEDGMENTS

Special acknowledgment goes to Ōta Zennosuke who served as my main informant and mentor for this study. As the founder of the Kyōdō Geinō Hozon Rengokai (Federation of the Preservation of Village Performing Arts) on Shimokita Peninsula, Mr. Ōta serves as the primary carrier of the *nōmai* tradition. Special thanks also go to three professors at Hirosaki University, which served as my research base: Sasamori Takefusa, a musicologist and composer, and my academic advisor for this study, and Prof. Kiyoko Matsushita and Prof. Kiyomi Nishimura for their research assistance. I would also like to acknowledge the cooperation of my *nōmai* interviewees: Ageji Mitsuo of the village of Ōri, Masaya Tōitsu of Shiriya, and Ōtsuki Fumiaki of Iwaya. Final thanks go to Miyaji Yōko and Koshiyama Yasuko for their translation assistance, and to Elaine Yoneoka for layout.

## NOTES ON THE TEXT

The romanization used is that of the modified Hepburn system as found in Kenkyūsha's *New Japanese-English Dictionary* (1974 ed.). Macrons are used for long vowels instead of doubling the vowel (e.g., ō, instead of oo ).

The names of Japanese scholars, interviewees, and other Japanese people connected with this study appear with the surname first followed by their given name, as is customary in Japan.

## *NŌMAI* FIELD VIDEO RECORDING

A roughly edited video recording of the four types of *nōmai* dances documents *nōmai* performances attended during fieldwork conducted in 1983-1984. Accompanying notes will tell in which village the performance took place, a description of the features and type of dance, and an explanation of the music. The cost of the video recording is $30.00 (plus $5.00 shipping and handling charge). You can order a copy by writing to the author at: Music Department, 351 Ryder Hall, Northeastern University, 360 Huntington Ave., Boston, MA 02115.

# Introduction

In the northeastern portion of Shimokita Peninsula a piece of land juts out from the northernmost tip of the main island of Honshū. Thirteen villages in this geographically and culturally isolated district of Japan keep alive a rich artistic tradition: *nōmai* dance drama.

*Nōmai* opens a window onto the richness and complexity of Japan's folk performing arts. It is a medieval dance drama that blends music, dance, drama, literature, and ritual symbolism into a single tradition. Itinerant priests, known as *yamabushi* (ascetic mountain priests), introduced *nōmai* to villages on the peninsula about 370 years ago. *Yamabushi* performed *nōmai* as a vehicle in proselytizing to provincial audiences and eventually taught it to villagers to ensure its survival. Medieval religions—Buddhism, Shintoism, and Taoism—influenced *yamabushi* in creating a performing art that unified elements from a number of traditions. *Yamabushi* traveled extensively to sacred mountains throughout Japan to perform their austerities. Their trips brought them into direct contact with a variety of performances given at temples and shrines, which served as communal and commercial centers. As practitioners of Shugendō, an ascetic religious order, *yamabushi* synthesized Buddhist music elements and Shugendō beliefs with already existing folk Shinto performing traditions associated with agricultural rites and the appeasement of deities; this synthesis gives *nōmai* its unique character.

General features of *nōmai* include: (1) dance as storytelling, (2) an instrumental ensemble that plays a number of standard musical pieces, (3) singers who supply the narration for each piece, and (4) the use of masks and costumes borrowed from the performing genres *kagura* (Shinto music and dance), *bugaku* (court dance), and *sarugaku* (ancient theatrical). The sequence in which *nōmai* dance dramas are presented evokes a calculated dramatic effect and a structurally unified program.

The most important *nōmai* performances of the year take place over a one-month period, starting in mid-December and ending mid-January. Performances are evening events that start around 6:00 and end at 11:30 or 12:00. Such performances, similar to many throughout Asia, are informal affairs where people eat, drink, and talk while watching. The men's association in each village responsible for sustaining *nōmai* hold performances in a village's community assembly hall. The setup usually consists of a twelve by twelve foot *tatami* mat stage placed directly on the floor and a backdrop curtain, separating the stage and the backstage area. Important members of the community sit on the right side of the stage and are given a tray of food—most commonly sea-food— to eat and beer or *saké* to drink during the performance. The cymbal players sit to the left side of the stage, while the single drummer sits facing the stage from the front edge in the center, where he can closely follow the movements of the dancers.

The *gakuya*, or backstage area, is a busy place with performers dressing and singers, dancers, and men's association members sitting around a stove drinking, eating, and smoking. Another association member sits on the floor at a table, writing out *kojo*, which are lengthwise pieces of paper with donor's names written on them. *Kojo* are hung on a wall to show who monetarily supported the performance. The *gakuya* also houses an altar set up for the wooden lion's head, where the *gongen* (incarnation of Buddha) deity is believed to reside during performances. A burning candle, bottle of *saké*, *juzu* (Buddhist rosary), and sometimes *nōmai* paraphernalia adorn the altar. Protocol requires that anyone going backstage pay their respects to the *gongen* deity by kneeling in front of the altar, bowing their head, and clapping their hands twice in reverence. Finally, a single flutist and three or four singers perform from the *gakuya*, where amplification equipment is used to raise the volume of these musicians so they can be heard above the din of the percussionists onstage. Singing and flute playing from behind the backstage curtain creates the effect of music emanating from the backstage area. This effect corresponds to the belief promoted by *yamabushi* that the music emanates from the *gongen* deity placed in the *gakuya*. The stage is situated at one end of the hall, leaving the rest of the space for the audience. Audiences range from sixty to two hundred people, depending on the village. Children play noisily at the back of the assembly hall behind the audience when they get too restless to sit still. Audience participation consists of calls of encouragement or approval to dancers who exhibit great skill or to young dancers who need the support. The warrior dances and the *yamabushi* character in the prayer dance "Kanemaki" elicit the most enthusiasm from the audience. Audience members also participate by throwing money folded in a scarf (*furoshiki*) onto the stage when a dancer they admire performs. In these gatherings residents of a community strengthen their social ties and renew their commitment to preserve *nōmai*.

The instrumental ensemble of cymbalists, drummer, and flutist signals the commencement of a performance by playing an abridged version of a piece called *kiri*. Musicians rotate throughout the evening, since the instrumental accompaniment is continuous. In villages where there is a shortage of flute players, flutists play for longer periods, or sometimes all evening.

*Nōmai* pieces are primarily dances accompanied by singing and instrumental music, which narrate a myth, a famous episode of a medieval warrior epic, or a humorous story. Plays added to the repertoire later include dialogue, comedy, and a more theatrical sense borrowed from folk kabuki. In two of the four villages I documented, the opening piece is "Gongenmai," a prayer dance that is central to the *nōmai* tradition. "Gongenmai" is important because it is a ritual dance of exorcism, representing a *yamabushi*'s primary function as champion against evil influences plaguing the local people. In the other two communities, four ceremonial dances performed in succession open a *nōmai* presentation. These pieces are solemn but elegant dances intended to purify the stage area and invoke deities for the purpose of requesting favors for the coming year. Anywhere from one to five warrior pieces follow next to enliven audiences and create a sense of excitement. From this point on the program varies from one performance to the next and from one community to the next. Folk dances, called *te odori* (hand dances), if performed next provide a brief respite from the *nōmai* program in which association members exhibit delicate movements of the head and hands. In the village of Shishipashi, women from the *fujinkai*, or married women's association, also dance *te odori*. Dancing as part of the intermission is one of the few opportunities women have to participate in *nōmai* presentations. The instrumental accompaniment for these dances change to *shamisen* (3-string plucked lute), *shime daiko* (drum shaped similarly to a snare drum), and *fue* (bamboo flute). Contingent on an individual community's agenda, the prayer dance "Kanemaki" is performed either before or after *te odori*. This is one of the most dramatic *nōmai* pieces, requiring skillful dancers and musicians. It is a touchstone piece adapted by *yamabushi* that enacts an exorcism in didactically emphasizing the merits of Buddhism. Then one or two more warrior plays may follow and one or two comedy plays end the program. In some villages, a required adjunct is "Gongenmai," serving to ritually end the evening and bless the community. The progression from serious ritual to entertaining comedies and from sacred to secular illustrates the programmatic structure typical of medieval theater genres.

The use of costumes, masks, and dance movements visually enhances the drama in *nōmai* plays. Costumes and masks aid audiences in identifying the various characters and their social status. Dance movements vary between the ceremonial, prayer, warrior, and comedy dances. Dances of the ceremonial pieces point to the influence of choreographic symmetry and sleeve-waving seen in *bugaku*, while dance patterns of the warrior dances are carefully formulated and demonstrate a connection to *mie* (a frozen pose) featured in kabuki. The stamping choreography of the *yamabushi* character in "Kanemaki" associates it with that of *shushi* priests who performed exorcism ceremonies at temples at the New Year and other occasions, while the dances in the comedy plays are of local folk dance origin. The fusion of elements found in *nōmai* dance is indicative of the numerous performing arts from which *yamabushi* drew from in creating *nōmai*. It is also a result of the borrowing and exchange that took place between medieval performing genres, of both the lower and elite social classes.

# PART I

## HISTORICAL BACKGROUND

# 1

# Artistic Growth Fueled by the Emerging Warrior Culture and Popular Buddhism: Cultural Antecedents

Japan's medieval age began with the Kamakura era in 1185 and ended in the Muromachi period in 1573. During these four turbulent centuries great artistic growth accompanied political, social, and economic chaos and change. Feudalism provided the political and social framework with the provincial warrior aristocracy emerging as the civil and military leaders. The shift of political power from the civil aristocracy in the capital city of Kyoto to the military aristocracy in the provinces brought about a concomitant transformation of culture and learning. Art and religion were inextricably intertwined during this time, providing inspiration and creative energy toward the development of a native character and a new aesthetic. *Nō* drama, landscape gardening, tea ceremony, and flower arranging—art forms we associate with traditional Japan—all blossomed during the medieval age. This work brings together many aspects of the cultural milieu that fueled the creative surge of this time period.

## KAMAKURA PERIOD (1185-1333)

Two factors shaped Kamakura culture: one was the rise in power of the warrior aristocracy in the provinces, and the second was the influence of Buddhism. The preoccupation of court society with transforming culture borrowed from China led to their loss of political and economic power nationally. A shift took place in the 10th and 11th centuries when the provinces began to play a greater role politically and culturally. This growth continued in the Kamakura era buttressed by the rising power of provincial warriors who gained experience in managing their estates and building control.

The ascendance of Buddhism as a popular religion was the foremost influence in medieval Japanese culture, including the creation of *nōmai,* as we shall see later. Religion served to pacify the population during a chaotic period in Japanese history where suffering and hardship were commonplace. A Buddhist awakening occurred in the 12th and 13th centuries with the revival of two old Nara sects—Kegon and Ritsu—and the appearance of three new offshoot sects—Pure Land, Zen, and Nichiren.

The three new sects had the most impact in the provinces as a result of the increasing spread of cultural literacy among the rural population. The institution of a native written language and a simplification of doctrine and practices made Buddhism more accessible to the masses than the esoteric, highly intellectualized philosophy of the older Buddhist sects. The three founders of the new sects lessened the more austere concepts and a general reorientation of Buddhism converted it into a populist religion. Unorthodox doctrine promoting salvation of all classes through faith appealed to the majority of the population who belonged to the lower strata of Japanese society (Sansom 1978: 329, 332).

In contrast, the warrior class turned to Zen Buddhism for religious and intellectual expression. Japanese monks studying in China in the 12th and 13th centuries brought Zen Buddhism back to their homeland. The Zen ("meditation") sect was a religious tradition originating in India. As it made its way across China, Zen continued to develop, drawing from Taoism, a form of nature mysticism. The attraction of samurai to Zen was its emphasis on achieving unity with nature and the intense physical discipline and mental concentration needed to experience intuitive insight. These aspects resonated with an affinity to nature felt by Japanese and paralleled a warrior's training (Reischauer 1970: 61).

The advancement of the provincial warrior to a position of dominance in 12th century Japan resulted in a new culture in addition to a new political system. Kamakura culture shifted away from the graceful sensitivity of court culture toward a more realistic and unpretentious style (Tazawa, et al. 1973: 54, 59). The orientation toward realism was adopted in Buddhist art and the growing popularity of Buddhism widely dispersed the new aesthetic, which transformed literature, painting, sculpture, and the applied arts.

### Literature

Literature during this period developed a native character, parting from the dominance of the Chinese form in the Heian period (A.D. 794-1185). For the first time a national written language evolved, shaped by both foreign and native sources.

The warrior aristocracy left their stamp on the prose literature of the time, and realism took the form of narratives about warfare, usually between the Taira and Minamoto families, two powerful clans who vied for power during the beginning of the 12th century. These epic tales of heroism and loyalty contrasted greatly with the novels and diaries of court women, characterizing literature during the Fujiwara family's reign, lasting from A.D. 858-1160. Heroic narratives of this time became central themes in later Japanese literature.

The popularity of the Buddhist faith also left its mark on medieval literature. Buddhist terminology and phraseology filtered into the popular literature and is evident even today in everyday speech in Japan. Popular stories also featured events that were described in light of Buddhist conceptions.

### Performing Arts

Deterioration of the royal aristocracy's power base resulted in a decline in court music and dance and in the international character of court performing traditions prevalent in previous periods. Instead, the Kamakura era signals the incipient stage for the theatrical arts not only for the court and military but for provincial audiences as well. Traditions among the common people and from the provinces gained popularity, such as the comic dances of *dengaku* (rice-field entertainment). Buddhist chanting also grew in popularity as Buddhist beliefs dispersed and were so widespread that secular music of the time absorbed elements of this singing style. Epic ballads—*biwa* (4-5 stringed lute) accompanied stories of military conflicts and loyalty—are an example of Buddhist-influenced music that enjoyed growing audiences during this time. Itinerant storytellers practiced their art on street corners, making way for narrative styles used in theater. In general, vocal and more dramatic music rose in primacy, leading the performing arts into an active and creative period in the coming Muromachi age.

## MUROMACHI PERIOD (1338-1573)

The secularization of Zen Buddhism and the emergence of new artists from a variety of social backgrounds fueled increased artistic activity in the Muromachi period. Buddhist monasteries, similar to the Christian church in medieval Europe, were the centers for learning and the arts. Many of the great artists and men of letters of the period were either Buddhist monks or laypeople who took refuge in the monasteries to escape the treachery and misery of life outside its walls. The monasteries afforded a safe haven, as well as opportunities for artists to secure feudal lords as patrons. Zen Buddhist priests, in particular, secured such patronage because of their close ties to the warrior gentry. This period also delineates the end of court dominance of the arts and specialized artists came under the protection and patronage of the ruling warrior class.

An important social development was the growing delineation between two tiers of culture. Artists of both high and low status catered to two different audiences: the aristocracy and the upper echelons of the warrior classes and the masses, including the peasantry, merchants, and low-ranking samurai. Both literature and art were clearly divided although not mutually exclusive. The essence of the contrast was primarily that of style and subject matter. For example, the upper classes preferred the literary style, popular during the Heian period, employing many Chinese words and having a Chinese "tone" to it, while the literature of the lower classes more closely reflected the spoken language of the time and contained many idiomatic expressions. The aristocratic background of the Heian court was the most common subject and setting in literature of the gentry in contrast to themes depicting contemporary rural and popular life in lower class literature (Kato 1979: 275-276). This cultural divide mirrors feudal society, in which the warrior class politically replaced the court aristocracy and the common populace broadened the foundation for a new society.

Culturally, however, despite their ascetic life style and creed, the warrior aristocracy envied the refinement of court culture and in their new prosperity as landed proprietors desired aspects of the finer life. Moving the seat of government back to Kyoto from Kamakura bridged the evolving cultural activities of the warrior aristocracy with that of the court. The Ashikaga shoguns represent not only the most powerful of the warrior leaders, but primary arbiters of taste and culture from the 14th to the 16th centuries, eventually replacing the politically and economically eclipsed court aristocracy.

Popular Buddhism flourished with the decentralization of government and the mutable state of society. The Pure Land (Jōdo) sect and the Nichiren (Lotus) sect recruited many followers in the provinces, especially among the poorer classes. Zen monks devoted themselves to popular education and the Buddhist sects reached the peak of their influence.

The indigenous Shinto religion experienced a decline with the growing prevalence of Buddhism. Shinto's inherent adaptability, however, ensured its survival as priests combined the religion's tenets with that of Buddhism and created the hybrid religion called Ryōbu (Dual) Shinto—a term that came into existence in the 12th century. A syncretized Shinto theory reached its zenith in the hands of Yoshida Kanetomo (1434-1511), who classified all the elements of Shintoism—purification, ritual taboos, the various Shinto deities, and the like—into a system resembling that of esoteric Shingon Buddhism (Kato 1979: 273). Shinto shrines gained great influence in the middle ages by manifesting a Buddhist character and Buddhist temples became a standard feature within shrine compounds.

The provinces experienced continued growth with a substantial change in Japan's economy. The peasantry moved toward greater self-government as a result of the dispersal of private estates formerly owned by the aristocracy and the great Buddhist temples. There were also technological advances in agricultural production, improvements in merchandising agricultural products, and increased commerce in cities that sprouted up as trade with Ming China expanded (Kato 1979: 270).

### Literature

The literary trends of the Muromachi period reflect China's influence. Zen monks played a continuing role in enriching Japanese culture by reintroducing Chinese literature. The close contacts monks had with their Chinese religious leaders made them perfect vehicles for the dissemination of Chinese art. Chinese poetry and prose came into vogue again as important literary mediums, and Chinese poetry, in particular, was considered the best of the secular traditions. Chinese-language poetry and prose were written by Zen monks in the Gozan temples, which served as their power base with the Ashikaga shoguns. Confucianism was an important thematic thread running through the literature of the Gozan monks, following the trend of the "Three in One" (Confucianism, Buddhism, and Taoism) theory that was popular in Sung China. A renaissance in art and literature in China during this time strengthened its influence among the Muromachi intelligentsia.

From the 13th to the 14th centuries Japanese-language poetry also enjoyed widespread popularity. The most common form was the *renga*, a *waka* (31-syllable) poem in which different poets took turns composing the first and second halves. Over time a *renga* poem turned into a chain of verses with each succeeding poet completing his or her part. *Renga*, originally a court pastime, spread from the top to the bottom of the social hierarchy. *Renga* poets and *nō* and *kyōgen* actors and playwrights were instrumental in this social cross-fertilization of literature. Subject matter of this poetic form ranged from depictions of aristocratic life in the Heian court to the lives and emotions of the common populace. Thus, a former poetic form of the court became the poetry of all classes.

Two traditions of Japanese prose writing include epic narratives and long and short novels written in comparatively simple prose. Epic narratives continued to flourish, describing battles between warrior clans, while long novels dealt with classic revenge stories, such as *Soga monogatari*. The subjects in short novels, on the other hand, concerned love affairs of the aristocracy and the Buddhist priesthood, warriors' heroic acts, success stories of the common people, as well as novelty stories from China and Japanese folk tales (Kato 1979: 299).

### Performing Arts

The theatrical arts, for the first time, became a major form of artistic expression. Performing traditions of the common people borrowed from one another in creating more advanced forms. Artists of common origin promoted popular entertainment, bringing their art to the height of development and to the center stage of cultural life. Music, dancing, and literature were variously combined for dramatic effect.

The dramatic art known as *sarugaku* matured fully in the 14th and 15th centuries. Two types of *sarugaku* existed: *nō* (or *sarugaku no nō*), a didactic drama that featured singing, instrumental music, and dancing, and *kyōgen* (or *sarugaku no kyōgen*), a form of comic drama with some dancing and singing combined.

The Muromachi period marks the maturation of *sarugaku no nō* (from here referred to as *nō* drama), one of Japan's most distinct contributions to the performing arts. *Nō* drama is a synthesis of poetry, music, and dance borrowed from a number of secular and sacred performing traditions. It is important to note that *nō* drama is a blend of both Shinto and Buddhist influences that were absorbed into popular entertainment of the day. Kan'nami (1333-1384), the author of dramatic stylings of *nō* theater, was a low-ranking Shinto priest (*negi*) and actor whose son Zeami (1363-1444) gained the patronage of Shogun Ashikaga Yoshimitsu. This was an important development which raised the social standing of *sarugaku*. Chapter 2 describes in more detail the evolution of the dramatic arts in Japan through to the 16th century and provides a link between *nō* drama and *nōmai*.

As with the other arts of this time, Buddhist monks played an important role in the maturation of *nō* drama. This performing tradition served as a didactic entertainment that taught Buddhist concepts. The song texts contain ideas and language from popular Buddhism of the day. Zen Buddhism's hand is also seen in the highly developed aesthetic of a *nō* drama performance. A *nō* play's structure and presentational ambiance is recognizably Zen where "there is careful avoidance of the trite, the obvious, and the emphatic. The most powerful effects are those which are obtained by allusion, suggestion, and restraint, and in this respect the *nō* is a counterpart of the painting [of this period] which was governed by Zen principles" (Sansom 1978: 391).

The growing cultural literacy of the common people is seen in the fondness for *kouta*, short ballads having no particular form. The *kyōgen* stage was one venue for more than three hundred *kouta*. Most of the songs were love songs, some tinged with Buddhist overtones expressing the transience of life. Other song forms included epic ballads with *biwa* accompaniment which continued to be popular from the previous period.

Traditional music of the court continued its descent, hastened by the poverty of courtiers. The court, however, continued to hold regular Shinto music and dance performances, paving the way for increased public and private performances of dance dramas and variety acts.

### Aesthetic Code

The canons of taste that flowered from the 14th to the 16th centuries did not develop independently. Heian period aesthetics fostered the concept of beauty called *yūgen* (mystery, subtlety, abstruseness, the occult) in poetry. This idea, which appears in the poetry anthology *Kokinshū,* compiled in A.D. 905, is a concept freely adopted by Zeami in expressing the special quality of beauty cultivated in *nō* drama. Suggestion and allusion, prevalent in a *nō* performance, are aesthetic notions cultivated by Heian court culture.

Zen Buddhism added an ascetic and pure cast to the Heian artistic sensibility. Artist monks of this sect flourished because they enjoyed official patronage and they were the most closely connected group to China and the latest cultural trends on the Asian continent through their role as diplomats and traders. This branch of Buddhism appealed to the simple and ascetic ethos of the ruling samurai class and provided a new spiritual direction to accompany their political split from the Kyoto-based court aristocrats (Arai 1981: 61-62). The sect gained the favor of the Ashikaga shoguns and ruling class and established the Gozan Jissatsu system, which designated five temples of primary importance and ten temples of secondary importance. As a result of their growing web of influence, Zen monks became political advisors to the shoguns. Their role gradually expanded to include foreign affairs and trade, in addition to playing a dominant role in the areas of art and scholarship. During this period, the "religious" Zen of the Kamakura era closely aligned itself with the political source of power on the one hand, and spearheaded developments in art and literature on the other. The secularization of Zen occurred from the 13th century on due to its rise in prominence among the upper echelons of warrior society. This secularization revealed itself in artistic terms, involving a transformation from religious and philosophical Zen into cultural and artistic Zen (Kato 1979: 281).

During the Muromachi age a Zen idiom developed fully, as evidenced in minimalistic monochrome landscape painting, flower arranging, landscape gardening, and the tea ceremony. Zen aesthetics emphasized a closeness to nature in abandoning man-made artifice and uniformity, a reverence for simplicity, and the ability to capture the essence, or nature, of objects and beings. These preferences suited the austerity and self-cultivation of both Zen practitioners and samurai (Reischauer 1970: 72). The asceticism and discipline corresponded to the simplicity and hardship of medieval life in general.

## A HISTORICAL FRAMEWORK FOR *NŌMAI*

The growing importance of the provinces and the increasing involvement of artists from the common populace during medieval times paved the way for performing arts, such as *nōmai*, which combined elements from both court and folk traditions. Cultural life in the provinces began to blossom with the rising power of the provincial warrior class and more widespread education of the masses. During this point in history the source of artistic traditions was no longer restricted to that of the court. The provinces contributed in greater degree to a Japanese national culture, which was made possible for two reasons. First, advancements in agriculture and commerce raised the quality of life for the provincial population and opened the way for writers and artists to emerge; and second, unlike the court aristocracy who had themselves achieved certain artistic attainments, the newly emerging warrior ruling class in the provinces needed professional artists to provide them with entertainment (Kato 1979: 304). The medieval period experienced, for the first time in Japanese history, a certain social and cultural egalitarianism as lower class artists reached greater refinement in their art and upper-class audiences developed a taste for popular entertainment.

The exchange of repertoire and performing practices between court and local traditions resulted in new forms that exhibited a native character. China provided the models and impetus for court performing traditions throughout the Nara and Heian periods (A.D. 710-1185). The indigenous character of the folk performing arts played an important role in shaping a national culture. The blending of court traditions with folk traditions gave emerging genres a native Japanese cast. The strong influence of popular Buddhism and Zen Buddhism on the arts also contributed to an evolving Japanese character and an expanded and highly developed aesthetic.

The cultural milieu of medieval Japan provides a context for the emergence of *nōmai*. This chapter deals with certain aspects of court culture and the cultural attainments of Buddhist monks. This may seem remote to the development of *nōmai*, a folk performing tradition in an isolated district in northern Japan, but cultural contacts between the provinces and court culture of the capital city of Kyoto did take place, starting in the Heian period. Such contacts from the 10th century on gave rise to the transformation of a cultural base that blended the aesthetic tastes of both the provinces and the court.

Frequent pilgrimages of the imperial family to three important sacred shrines on Mt. Kumano (Wakayama Prefecture) resulted in cultural exchanges, particularly of the performing arts (Kageyama 1973: 118). These pilgrimages increased the interaction between courtiers and local people who lived along the route to the shrines or at way stations. Performances of both the court and the local areas were presented during stops on the round-trip pilgrimages to the Kumano shrines. This custom ultimately led to the adoption of new performing traditions in the local regions and at the shrines and temples at Mt. Kumano (Inoura 1963: 1099). Courtiers not only transmitted their performing arts, but also brought entertainment of the local regions back to Kyoto.

*Nōmai* is related to the performing arts that developed at the shrines and temples of Mt. Kumano. Rituals and entertainment at these sites grew into a cult that combined Buddhist ceremonies of the Tendai sect and later of the popular Buddhist sects with naturalistic folk cults of early Japan overlaid with influences from court traditions. *Yamabushi* played a considerable role in the shaping of this cult as a result of their ascetic practices in the mountains and their exposure to numerous performing traditions while on pilgrimages to Mt. Kumano and other temples and shrines on mountains throughout Japan. The eventual travels of *yamabushi* to the northern district where *nōmai* appeared points to the connection of this dramatic tradition to the Kumano cult and its combined features of both folk and court performing practices.

# 2

# Shamanic Beginnings: Dramatic Antecedents

Tracing *nōmai's* lineage sheds light on the formation of drama in Japan through to the medieval period. The history and background of *nōmai* links it to numerous dance and dramatic traditions of both the court and the lower classes. The merging of Shinto and Buddhist ritual elements together with dramatic aspects of secular performing arts illustrates the rich variety of entertainment genres that were drawn from in creating *nōmai.*

## THE BEGINNINGS OF DRAMA IN RITUAL

Ritual began as man expressed his wishes in supplications made to supernatural powers. Enactment of the "desired future event" through the use of sympathetic magic, referred to as *jujutsu* in Japanese, was believed to facilitate its occurrence. Seeking a bestowal of wishes by means of sympathetic magic is closely tied to the survival and cycle of labor in an agricultural society. Warding off of evil influences by such means is also associated with agricultural communities (Immoos 1969: 404, 412).

Japanese drama derived both its essence and form from ritual. An episode of the creation myth describes the beginnings of music, dance, and drama in Japan in which the goddess Ame no Uzume danced upon an overturned tub to coax the sun goddess, Amaterasu, from the cave where she was hiding. Ame no Uzume's dance is interpreted as a ritualistic one based in shamanism. Within this framework, the objects held by the goddess serve as *torimono*, offerings that serve to attract a deity to descend and dwell within the objects during a ritual dance, and the stamping dance is understood to be a form of trance inducement. Ritual offerings and stamping choreography are both features of a shaman's activities in communicating with deities on behalf of those making supplications.

After the 3rd century A.D., shamanism and religious rituals evolved in Japan as a reaction of settled groups of peoples to unknown powers of nature and death. Evidence of this coupling are writings in the *Kojiki* (A.D. 712), *Fudoki* (A.D. 713), *Wei Zhi* (Wei Dynasty Chronicles, 3rd century), as well as the existence of *haniwa* (clay figurines)[1] of women shamans found in burial tombs of Japan's Tumulus period (3rd - 6th centuries). The earliest forms of drama can be seen in such rituals, which were comprised of simple songs, dances, and imitative acts (Inoura and Kawatake 1981: 5).

Within settled agricultural communities many religious rituals centered on the natural environment and the production of rice. Religious beliefs formed based on a type of nature worship (later the Shinto religion) that ascribed divinity to phenomena that people considered powerful, or held in awe, such as the sun, moon, or objects in nature, including trees, rocks, streams, and flowers. This sensitivity toward nature created a religion of respect and appreciation rather than fear and apprehension; thus, religious rites served to praise and thank deities, as well as to appease them.

Shamanic practices of the indigenous cults of Japan were an important source for the techniques of possession found in performances by *yamabushi* and later preserved in *nōmai*. The anthropologist Yanagita Kunio paved the way for studies on Japanese shamanism with the information he presented on *miko*,[2] women who practiced techniques of possession. Other important connections made by Japanese scholars are the shamanic nature of the indigenous Shinto religion and the relationship between Japanese shamanic practitioners and the performing arts (Ortolani 1984: 174).

The musicologist Honda Yasuji researched elements of shamanism found in many varieties of folk *kagura* (Shinto music and dance). In his writings, he suggests the existence of old shamanic practices in early *kagura* and even proposed that some elements of *nō* drama originated in shamanic ritual (Ortolani 1984: 174). The correlation of shamanic practices to early *kagura* is of special interest here, since *nōmai* has retained many *kagura* elements.

## YAMATO PERIOD (3RD-6TH CENTURIES)

The Yamato period marks the establishment of early *kagura*. Rituals of this religious phenomenon included enacting the myths *Heavenly Cave Door* (*Ama no Iwato*) and *Luck of the Sea and Luck of the Mountains* (*Umi-sachi Yama-sachi*). The two oldest chronicles of Japan, the *Kojiki* (*Record of Ancient Matters* [712]) and *Nihon Shoki* (*Chronicles of Japan* [720]) recorded both myths. Many scholars describe the *Heavenly Cave Door* story as a mythical representation of ancient shamanic practices. The dance of Ame no Uzume, described earlier, is interpreted as a trance-possession, undertaken to establish contact with the sun goddess Amaterasu in order to restore light to the world. Uzume's trance-dance is a prototype for the *miko* trance performances in early *kagura*, which came to be known as Iwato *kagura* (*kagura* of the *Heavenly Cave Door*) or Jindai *kagura* (*kagura* of the age of the gods).

The myth *Heavenly Cave Door* serves as the basic structure of early *kagura*. As quoted in the *Kojiki*,[3] this myth is also the earliest existing record of a performing art in Japan. A later version of the myth that appears in the *Nihon Shoki* [4] is referred to as *wazaogi*, which is translated as "imitative gesture." This later account contains dialogue and a reference to the use of a mirror in producing a reflection of Amaterasu. Both suggest a hint of theater, and the myth becomes more than just a rite, incantation, or prayer. *Kagura* in the prehistoric period thus forms the foundation for drama by combining ritual elements with imitative gestures intended to portray characters in myths (Inoura and Kawatake 1981: 20).

The fact that *kagura* was originally a funeral rite, or *chinkon*, for the repose of souls of the dead reinforces the connection between shamanism and early *kagura*. Theater scholars Inoura and Kawatake assert that the *Heavenly Cave Door* myth reveals the concept of primitive death and the belief in resurrection (sun disappears and reappears) and that these concepts gave rise to the *chinkon* funeral rite (Inoura and Kawatake 1981: 19).

The dance or shamanic trance performed by Ame no Uzume is identified as *chinkon* in a document called *Kogoshūi* (A.D. 807). This source describes the performance of this goddess as a means of "revitalizing the withdrawn Amaterasu" (Hoff 1978: 161). The revitalization of the sun goddess exemplifies the nature of *kagura*, which presupposes that through the performance of song and dance, it is possible to "restrain or secure within the body" the life force of a person (*tama* or *tamashii*) that appears to be departing (Hoff 1978: 160). This characterization describes the belief and rituals associated with the *chinkon* funeral rite, also known as *tamashizume*.

One of the functions of *kagura*, as seen in the *chinkon* rite, is to pray for the prolongation of life. Prayers began with invoking deities, called *kami*, who were called upon to revitalize the life force of a particular individual; they ended by sending the *kami* back to their place of origin. The inclusion of dance and music in this prayer ceremony served to increase the effectiveness of the revitalization. The kinds of music and dance performed for this ceremony were not specifically prescribed, but it is believed they included shaman-related dances (Hoff 1978: 164.)

*Kagura*'s role as a rite for prolonging life is indicative of the growth of indigenous culture and religion in Japan during the Yamato period. Cultural influence from the Asian continent was minimal during this period and was reflected mostly in myths and folklore, although an influx of ideas concerning politics, economy, and culture began. Then, in the 6th century, between A.D. 538 and 552, Buddhism was introduced to Japan. This event changed the cultural fabric of Japan, and Buddhist thought permeated the indigenous religion of Shinto, as well as learning, aesthetics, and material culture. The end of the Yamato period began a new era for Japanese culture and the performing arts.

## ASUKA PERIOD (A.D. 578-710)

Imported to Japan along with the Buddhist faith and its allied arts was *gigaku*, an entertainment associated with the central Chinese state of Wu in the region now known as Suzhou. It is believed that Mimashi, a native of Kudara on the Korean peninsula, brought *gigaku* to Japan in the year 612. The *Kyōkunshō* (Selections for Instruction and Admonition), a record on music completed in 1233, states that *gigaku* consisted of a program of nine to ten dance pieces and pantomimes, in which performers wore large skull masks.[5] A transverse flute, drums worn hanging from the neck or attached to the hips (*koshitsuzumi*), and brass cymbals (*dōbyōshi*) provided musical accompaniment; it is an ensemble adopted by many later forms of Japanese drama, including *nōmai* (Araki 1978: 36).

Patronage of the performing arts by temples and shrines provided an impetus for the development of Japanese drama. *Gigaku* regularly provided entertainment following Buddhist ceremonies. As recorded in the *Kyōkunshō*, it was also performed at the great celebration held at the dedication of the large statue of Buddha at Todaiji temple in Nara in A.D. 752, and at similar spectacles at Kōfukuji temple, also located in Nara (Araki 1978: 37).

A program of *gigaku* began with a formal tuning, *netori*, and a prelude played by the instrumental ensemble. A procession of costumed performers followed. The first piece, "Gohō jishi" (Lions of the Five Directions), combined music and dance. Performed next were solo dances of various characters and pantomimic pieces of a didactic intent completed a program. Theater historians consider the pantomimic pieces to be one of the first dramatic forms in Japan (Araki 1978: 37).

*Gigaku* served as an important influence in the dramatic evolution of *nōmai.* The use of masks, the musical instrumentation, the lion dance, and the pantomimic numbers are all elements that emerge in later dramatic genres such as *sarugaku*, *dengaku*, and *nōmai.* The lion dance deserves particular attention as an element which flourished throughout Japan. It is still performed at shrine festivals as the basis for *shishi kagura* (lion *kagura*), and in *nō* drama and kabuki.

## NARA PERIOD (A.D. 710-794)

The performing arts were an integral part of court life in the 8th century. *Mikagura*, or *kagura* for court ceremonies, developed apart from earlier forms of *kagura*, which were performed in the provinces. Three occasions required a *mikagura* performance in the garden of a building in the imperial compound now known as Kashikodokoro Hall: at midnight on a day in December, for ancestral festivals, and for the enthronement ceremony of the emperor. A program of *mikagura* began with an opening song, called "Niwabi," followed by dances performed to the accompaniment of songs and instrumental music. A shamanistic ritual, possibly based on the legend of *Isora*,[6] was third on the program. Next was a section of imitative acts or parodies, and the program closed with songs that were also sung at religious events. This program tended to be lengthy, a performance lasting for two days (Inoura and Kawatake 1981: 21-22).

*Gigaku* prospered in the Nara period and continued to be performed in large temples in both the capital and the local provinces. Occasions for *gigaku* performances were on April 8 for the ceremony of Buddha's birthday, July 15 as entertainment following ceremonies performed for one's ancestors, and other special events during the year. The use of large masks persisted, as did a high degree of artistic quality in the making of the masks. A pair of small gongs was added to the musical ensemble of a flute, cymbals, and drum. Programs commenced with a procession followed by a sequence of dramatic numbers (Inoura and Kawatake 1981: 27). The artistic maturation achieved by *gigaku* in the 8th century lasted well into the 9th century.

In the 7th century the imperial court adopted *bugaku*, a classical dance form which emerged as an established tradition in the 8th century. Dances performed to classical court music (*gagaku*), much of *bugaku* originated either in China, the former state of Po-hai in southeastern Manchuria, Korea, or India. *Bugaku* enjoyed great appeal among the aristocracy, and performances became an adjunct to all formal ceremonies and gala events (Araki 1978: 43). Also, since large temples and shrines were under the protection of the court, both shared cultural activities with it, including *bugaku*. Within the sacred context, *bugaku* performances operated as prayer for rain during periods of drought; entertainment for Buddhist *ennen* (life-prolonging) ceremonies; and performances dedicated to the Buddha or to Shinto deities (Inoura and Kawatake 1981: 35). *Bugaku* spread to the provinces as a result of its function in ceremonies and as entertainment in temples and shrines.

Since its earliest stage, *bugaku* contains some dramatic elements. The theater scholar P.G. O'Neill notes that the dances are "generally symbolic representations of just one part, the most interesting part, of a whole story" (O'Neill 1958: 3-4). Chinese tales form the basis for the stories. Other sources are legends from India such as in "Genjōraku," which dramatizes a hero's victorious battle with a poisonous serpent. The following categories outline the *bugaku* repertoire: *bunnomai* or *hiramai* (civil dance), featuring graceful, elegant dances in which the performers wear civil-servant attire; *bunomai* (martial dance), consisting of heroic, virile dances, in which the dancer carries a sword or halberd; *hashirimono* or *hashirimai* (running dance), characterized by jumping motions within a brisk dance; *tobu*, which are children's dances; and *jogaku*, dances that are distinguished by the use of masks depicting women. Pieces within the *bunnomai*, *hashirimai*, and *bunomai* repertoire, in particular, contain dramatic elements. It is possible these pieces served as models for some of *nōmai*'s dances. The elegant, graceful *bunnomai* dances share similar movements with those in *nōmai* 's ceremonial dances borrowed from folk *kagura*. The brisk dance and jumping motions of *hashirimai* are a possible influence in the *nōmai* piece "Sanba." *Bugaku*'s martial dances probably played some role in the development of the warrior dances in *nōmai*. The *jogaku* category of pieces in *bugaku* are also of dramatic interest, since texts were originally recited in conjunction with dance to convey their meaning and content (Inoura and Kawatake 1981: 36-37).

The use of masks enhanced the primordial storytelling and drama of *bugaku*. Masks were carved from wood and colored with lacquer, displaying a more advanced mask-making technique than was found in *gigaku*. All but two of the masks portray facial expressions and shapes of male characters. The numerous masks are stylized rather than true-to-life representations of character. They are also lighter and slightly smaller than *gigaku* masks. Masks made from cloth or paper are even more stylized than those made of wood (Inoura and Kawatake 1981: 35). *Nōmai* masks emulate the smaller *bugaku* masks rather than the large skull masks used in *gigaku*.

*Sangaku*, originally from Central Asia, was another cultural form imported from T'ang China. The term *sangaku* is the Japanese pronunciation of the Chinese word *san-yüeh*, a term that referred to a type of sideshow consisting of a variety of entertaining acts. Presentations of *sangaku* included amusing songs and dances; acrobatics and tumbling; and juggling, conjuring, and magic. Indigenous Japanese songs and dances eventually became part of the repertoire. This performing tradition won the support of the court aristocracy, who organized the performers into a department of the Imperial Court called the Sangaku House. The Sangaku House was a training school for *sangaku* performers; its members provided additional entertainment for court festivities such as sumo wrestling matches and religious festivals. In 781, however, for reasons not clearly understood, the department was abolished and *sangaku* became a plebeian form of entertainment (Araki 1978: 51-52). Closure of the Sangaku House left *sangaku* performers without a means of making a living. Many of them continued to perform at major temples or shrines, where they functioned as lay priests. As a result, *sangaku* shifted from a court entertainment to one presented as entertainment following religious ceremonies and enjoyed by the common people (O'Neill 1958: 5).

Many performing arts survived outside the court under the auspices of temples and shrines, which provided regular places for performances. O'Neill mentions that one reason for such sponsorship is that temples and shrines were centers of activity not only for worship, but for routine commerce. This function of temples and shrines originated in their continual need for food, materials, and labor. Monasteries or temples in the provinces were also centers of culture and learning, where monks and priests offered material as well as spiritual benefits (1958: 59). Charitable institutions, infirmaries, and orphanages were, for the first time in Japan, established at temples (Sansom 1978: 35). Accordingly, temple and shrine grounds were filled with traders, travellers, itinerant musicians and preachers, as well as local residents. Such a confluence of people provided audiences for the performing arts and, from the Nara period on, Buddhist temples and Shinto shrines played a major role in the evolution of the dramatic arts in Japan.

The foregoing covers the incipient stage of performing traditions borrowed from the T'ang court in China. *Gigaku*, *bugaku*, and *sangaku* all received official recognition within the court in the form of special schools called *gaku-ko* (music houses), under the authority of the Imperial Department of Music. During the Nara period, the court, temples, and shrines shared cultural activities; this situation benefited performing traditions such as *sangaku*, which lost favor with courtiers but managed to endure at temples and shrines. With these institutions as strongholds for the performing arts, we shall see later how Buddhist philosophy and aesthetics in particular influenced music, dance, and dramatic forms in the medieval period.

## HEIAN PERIOD (A.D. 794-1192)

In the Heian period, two Buddhist sects shaped Japan's national character. Saichō (or Dengyō Daishi, 767-822) founded the Tendai sect, which combined tenets of the original Tendai teachings of the Chinese monk, Zhi-k'ai, with meditative, disciplinary, and esoteric elements. The monk Kūkai (better known as Kōbō Daishi, 774-835) brought Shingon beliefs to Japan from China.

The aim of Shingon ritual was to evoke the "three mysteries—one's own body, speech, and thought" (Anesaki 1963: 125). The accompanying arts and highly mystical aspect of Shingon Buddhism appealed to the emotional side of members of the nobility. These aspects complemented the more formal ethical teachings of Confucianism and its preoccupation with politics and civic affairs (Anesaki 1963: 135). In this way, Buddhism adapted itself further to Japanese culture. The Tendai and Shingon sects, despite their origins in India or China, also took on a distinctly Japanese character. Their doctrines and teachings were products of combined beliefs and precepts that the Japanese found attractive.

By the 12th century, Shingon Buddhism gave impetus to a syncretic religion called Ryōbu Shintō (Dual Shinto) which assimilated both Buddhist and Shinto forms of worship practiced within the same confines (Hall 1971: 74). It professed that Shinto deities were manifestations of Buddhist guardian deities (*bohisattvas*) in a Buddhist concept called *honji suijaku* (traces of descent from true home).

Ryōbu Shintō was the religious compromise reached between Buddhism and Shinto. It coincided with the administrative takeover of a large portion of local Shinto shrines by the Buddhist priesthood (Sansom 1978: 230). Syncretism led to combined presentations that featured performing traditions from both Buddhism and Shintoism, resulting in the exchange and borrowing of elements between the various performing arts. Out of this complex web of influences, hybrid genres such as *nōmai* emerged.

Temples and shrines also featured performing traditions from outside the court. A 10th century example was that of sorcerers, *shushi* or *jushi*,[7] who were esoteric Buddhist priests. To make their ceremonies more intelligible to devotees, they practiced magic, divination, and exorcism in official Buddhist rites (Ortolani 1984: 181). It is possible that the *shushi* tradition spread to the provinces via *yamabushi* who might have been *shushi* at one time, since both held esoteric Buddhist beliefs. There may be a connection between *shushi* performances and the beginnings of *shugen nō* later in the 13th century.

*Shushi* priests wore gorgeous costumes in performances, creating a certain drama. The Tsuina Festival, a New Year's ceremony of exorcism, as well as similar events presented in the second and fourth lunar months, were occasions for *shushi* performances. In the Tsuina Festival, a *shushi* acted out the role of a guardian deity of Buddhahood, who overpowered demons that were obstacles to enlightenment. Playing the parts of the demons were *sarugaku hōshi*, low-ranking sextons at Buddhist temples who were, as mentioned previously, former *sangaku* performers. Lighter entertainment such as acrobatics, which accompanied these dramatic presentations, also featured *sarugaku hōshi.*

As time passed, the *shushi* tradition gradually lost its serious religious significance. Beginning in the 12th century, the sorcerer *shushi* priest was often replaced by *sarugaku hōshi,* playing the role of the guardian deity. The repertoire of the *shushi* tradition varied greatly during this time, but it is known that the repertoire included dramatizations of Buddhist teachings, warrior pieces, and sword dances presented as parodies (Inoura and Kawatake 1981: 48). These pieces were all attempts to dramatize Buddhist magical rites practiced in temples.

*Sangaku* flourished as a popular variety show in the Heian period, from the 9th century on. After the middle of the 10th century, the term *sarugaku* was used interchangeably with *sangaku*. There is, however, disagreement among scholars concerning when the word *sarugaku* came into use and whether it was a tradition that differed from *sangaku*.

The literature scholar James T. Araki comments that the word *sarugaku* first appears in historical records to designate a later form of *sangaku*, which had acquired some characteristics of Japan's indigenous performing arts (1978: 199). It is also suggested that during the Heian period, *sangaku* began to include more and more elements of the rural dance called *dengaku* (Nakamura 1971: 59).

The theater scholar Gotō Hajime claims that the distinction between *sangaku* and *sarugaku* in the Heian period is based on a difference in function, *sangaku* referring to a plebeian form of entertainment and *sarugaku* to the ceremonial performances given within the court. Gotō asserts that the word *sangaku* was gradually replaced by *sarugaku*. He adds that *sarugaku* performers, in order to raise their status, etymologically ascribed the meaning of "divine" (*saru*) in the term *sarugaku*, rather than the original meaning of "monkey," which describes the imitative acts of the performing art. Gotō continues, saying that this conscious act of ascribing divinity to *sarugaku* took place during the Kamakura period, when low-ranking Buddhist temple officers, *hōshigen*, sought to raise their social status as performers (Gotō 1975: 572, 574).

The question of when the designation *sarugaku* replaced the older term *sangaku*—and whether there was a qualitative difference between the two genres—is still debatable, since Heian period records are not consistent in differentiating them. Here, the terms will be used as defined by Araki: *sangaku* as a variety of acts brought from China as early as the 7th century and *sarugaku* as the designation for the variety show performed for the general population beginning in the 10th century (Araki 1978:52).

The earliest regular performances of *sarugaku* took place at major temples and shrines for local audiences. These performances served as light entertainment following annual religious ceremonies. Some temples and shrines employed specific *sarugaku* troupes for their annual events. This custom provided continual patronage for the genre.

In the latter part of the 10th century, *sarugaku* shifted its emphasis from technical skills, such as acrobatics, to the art of *monomane* (imitation of things). *Monomane* is a Japanese form of mimesis that evolved from the earlier *wazaogi* mimetic tradition mentioned in the *Nihon Shoki* (Ortolani 1984: 171). This innovation had far-reaching effects in the history of Japanese drama and laid the groundwork for *sarugaku nō*, one of the early predecessors of *nō* drama. In the 11th century when the *Shin sarugaku ki* was written, *sarugaku* featured experienced players, who created different varieties of the tradition according to their own ideas and tastes. This was a period of growth during which urbanity and an emphasis on *monomane* characterized the transformation of *sarugaku* into a form historically referred to as *sarugaku nō*. Historically, the appellation *nō* is added to performing genres that featured *monomane*. These genres were viewed as more realistic styles of drama.

The *Shin sarugaku ki* describes the 28 pieces of the *sarugaku nō* repertoire in four categories. The first category was an eclectic combination of pieces borrowed from other popular performing arts of the time. These included "Noronji," a performance of sorcery; "Hikihito no mai," a dance of a dwarf; "Dengaku," a dance and song derived from rice-planting rites; and "Kugutsu" (Puppeteer), performed by dancers or puppets (Inoura and Kawatake 1981: 43). The second category consisted of typical acts of *sangaku*, such as dextrous tricks, juggling, acrobatics, and conjuring arts. A third set of pieces featured solo mimicry performance and two lion dances, "Mukotsu" and "Ukotsu." The fourth group, which formed the main body of pieces in the repertoire, consisted of 16 dramatic sketches. The sketches were clever parodies and satires of monks, politicians, old men and women, and various other characters. Musical accompaniment enhanced the drama or provided continuity between acts. For the first time, consideration of the program as a whole determined which pieces were to be performed (Inoura and Kawatake 1981: 43-45).

The evolution of *sarugaku* in the Heian period was a creative extension of the imported traditions of *sangaku* and *gigaku*. *Sarugaku* featured the combination of both sacred and secular elements. The sacred aspects were cultivated through *sarugaku*'s affiliation with major temples and shrines, where elements of ceremonial dances and sorcerer's rituals were absorbed. *Gigaku*'s lion dance endured in modified form and the use of masks, as well as a varied repertoire, were contributions of both *gigaku* and *bugaku*. Japanese drama continued its genesis as performing traditions borrowed and adapted elements from one another, forming genres that matured during the next period.

## MEDIEVAL PERIOD (A.D. 1185-1573)

Medieval drama developed during the Kamakura period (1185-1333), a time when concepts in structure and production made great advances. During this time, *ennen nō* emerged as a new dramatic genre developed from *ennen*, a Buddhist ceremony of prayer for the prolongation of a high-ranking person's life (Keene 1966: 30). As early as 1100, *ennen* featured songs, dances, and imitative acts as entertainment following the ceremony. Then, in the early 13th century, a recitative prologue called *kaikō* was added to the program of songs and dances. *Ennen* continued to evolve in the latter half of the 13th century, when it shifted to the more dramatic *ennen nō* in which presentations of dramatized legends blended elements of *shirabyōshi* (female temple and palace dance), *bugaku*, and plays that emphasized singing (Inoura and Kawatake 1981: 52-53).

In the first half of the Kamakura period, shrines and temples maintained *kagura* and *bugaku* while *gigaku* declined. Mythology became the basis of many *kagura* plays, which enacted portions of the creation myth. The interchange between performing genres at this time was significant. Dramatic arts such as *sarugaku nō* combined with *kagura*, while *kagura* in turn absorbed fragments of other traditions.

In the latter half of the Kamakura period the growth of performing traditions persisted. *Dengaku* became *dengaku nō* in expanding from a variety show of folk dances, juggling, and acrobatics to include humorous skits and imitative acts. The more sophisticated *sarugaku nō* influenced *dengaku*'s transition toward becoming more of a drama.

Also noteworthy is the emergence of *enkyoku* (or *sōga*) and *kusemai*, two song forms that figured prominently in the development of *nō* drama (Inoura and Kawatake l981:12).

Medieval drama reached its apex in the Muromachi period (1338-1573) when many dramatic arts matured to an unprecedented level of elegance. Temples and shrines in the provinces continued to provide a context for *ennen nō*, *kagura*, *dengaku nō*, and *sarugaku nō* performances. Within this context, these genres influenced one another to varying degrees. One result is that the repertoire, dramatic form, and style of both *dengaku nō* and *sarugaku nō* became less distinguishable from one another.

The Muromachi period is also when *sarugaku nō* [8] matured into the present *nō* drama. *Sarugaku nō* reached a higher level of artistry than other genres due to the innovation of two great masters. The first is Kan'ami (1334-1384), a Shinto priest at the Kasuga Shrine in Nara whose high sense of drama refined *sarugaku nō*. Kan'nami's son Zeami (1363-1444), a gifted producer and author of *nō* plays, further developed this performing art as he incorporated transcendental concepts of Buddhism and wrote many treatises on the art of *nō*.

An urbane quality that developed in response to changes in society, culture, and military court patronage characterizes the formation of *nō* theater from *sarugaku nō*. *Nō* drama, nonetheless, maintained its appeal to provincial audiences. Advances in *sarugaku nō* embraced ideals of beauty cultivated by the court and aristocracy. The ruling military government upheld these ideals, and theories of aesthetics particular to *nō* emerged. The sponsorship and support of the shogun Ashikaga Yoshimitsu, and others of the samurai class, also changed the course of *sarugaku nō* and brought to it a refined level characteristic of aristocratic culture.

The evolution of *nō* drama illustrates the complex web of relationships between performing traditions and performers. Theater scholars Thomas Immoos (l969), Ernest Kirby (l973), and Benito Ortolani (1984) all hold that *nō* theater originated in the shamanistic music and dance of Shinto. Ortolani points out that "only the primitive rituals of ancient *kagura* and the entertainment for the gods need to be considered as possible antecedents to and origins of essential *nō* elements" (Ortolani l984: 175). He supports this assertion by relating Zeami's claim, which connects the origin of *sarugaku* to the "Age of the Gods," and "mythical *kagura* " (Zeami as cited in Ortolani l984: 175). As an indigenous form, *kagura*'s influence permeates most performing arts that developed during this period, including the dramatic form introduced a little later that served as the prototype for *nōmai*.

The connection between Shinto and Buddhist religious practices is a strong one. The shamanistic practices of early *kagura* overlap with mystical elements that permeated both medieval Tendai and Shingon Buddhism. The *ennen* Buddhist ceremony shares the same intent as the *chinkon kagura* rite, described earlier: to prolong life by attempting to secure the life force of a person through the performance of music and dance. The ceremonies of magic, divination, and exorcism practiced by *shushi* priests at Buddhist temples coincide with the Shinto practice of *kamigakari*, in which a shaman-medium serves as a vessel for a spirit to communicate directly with the faithful.

Companies attached to Buddhist temples and monasteries connect *sarugaku nō* to *shushi* priests. Nose Asaji (1953) theorizes that *sarugaku nō* performers who lived in villages close to temples where they performed served as substitutes for *shushi*, resulting in an added dimension to *sarugaku nō* which incorporated elements of divination, exorcism, and magic.

*Sarugaku nō* actors as *shushi* priests provide insight on the gradual transposition of ritual into dramatic presentations. Esoteric rituals became more accessible to the common people through drama and didactic plays. Kirby hypothesizes that the transposition of "an actualizing, effective ritual into representation and mimetic enactment" is manifested in *sarugaku nō* (1973: 283). He believes that the official decrees of 780 and 807, which prohibited shamanic ecstasy outside shrines and temples in an attempt to stem the spread of Buddhism, necessitated this transposition. These decrees, he asserts, were responsible for the formation of an outcast class of trance practitioners, who veiled their songs and dances by adding dramatic elements and presenting them as entertainment.

Kirby proposes two related reasons to account for the transposition of ritual into drama. First, although functional aspects of rituals, such as curing and divination, were minimized, their representational and dramatic aspects in plays served as a form of proselytizing outside the confines of shrines and temples. Such proselytizing by various groups was common, including among *yamabushi*.

Kirby's second reason is secular in nature, citing the practical alternative taken by unemployed shamans. These individuals presented rituals as entertainment for a living, since the proscription against trance negated their practices. Many chose this alternative as a logical response to the prohibitive decrees (1973: 283).

In the transposition of ritual into drama, Kirby continues, heroes or well-known figures in classical literature and historical epics functioned as logical substitutions for souls or spirits invoked in a ritual. Texts from literary sources were necessary for the verbal refinement required by ritual movement and form (1973: 284). Music was retained, although in modified form, adding to the ritual refinement of gesture and speech.

*Shugen nō*, a hybrid tradition that emerged in the 13th century and became fully developed in the 15th, is also a genre of the medieval period that exemplifies the transformation of ritual into drama. *Shugen nō* is a masked dance drama used by Shugendō (esoteric Buddhist sect) priests, also known as *yamabushi*, to propagate their esoteric Buddhist beliefs, and it is one of the prototypes of *nōmai*.

*Yamabushi* probably pieced together this dramatic tradition from *sarugaku* and *dengaku* performances they had seen at local temples and shrines. The term *shugen nō* gives recognition to its Buddhist elements, while the musicologist Honda Yasuji (1976), emphasizes the *kagura* elements of the same tradition by referring to it as *yamabushi kagura*. In either case, the established repertoires of *sarugaku*, *dengaku*, *ennen*, and *kagura* benefitted *yamabushi* in crafting this folk dance drama.

Gotō maintains that the spectacular development of *sarugaku* into a masked dance drama in the 13th and 14th centuries took place in the hands of lower-class performers in the provinces. He describes the transformation of *sarugaku* into *nō* as the result of a "complex pattern of social climbing" by outcast *sarugaku* performers, who were motivated by their desire to improve their social position (Gotō 1975: 574). In expanding their art, these performers found that maintaining popular religious beliefs assured the patronage of provincial audiences. So they augmented the entertainment and ceremonies characteristically performed at shrines and temples with dramatic enactments of myths celebrated in religious services. According to Gotō, such enactments made it possible for *sarugaku* actors to develop their imitative acting skills. In addition, masks were adopted to tangibly represent gods and various spirits.

*Sarugaku* performers became more highly regarded because of their superior acting abilities. They also began to refer to their occupation as a divine service and to consider themselves as priests (Gotō 1975: 574). This development paved the way for the acceptance of figures such as *yamabushi*, who through their performances raised their social standing and gained the trust of villagers. The acceptance of *yamabushi* as religious leaders was essential to their evangelizing efforts in the provinces.

The point of departure for *sarugaku nō* and *yamabushi kagura* took place during the Muromachi period, when *sarugaku nō* was further transformed to include secular and more urbane elements drawn from other performing genres. Two influential genres were *kusemai*, a dance that was extremely popular in cities performed by singing girls, and *imayō*, popular song that had flourished since the late Heian period.

*Yamabushi kagura*, on the other hand, continued to emphasize its ritualistic aspects and remained a plebeian performing genre, functioning primarily as an evangelistic vehicle for mountain priests. *Nōmai*, as a variant of *yamabushi kagura*, is thus derived from the same parentage as *nō* drama, but its performance today distinguishes it as a tradition more representative of the plebeian and ritual character of earlier *sarugaku* performed by *shushi*.

## SUMMARY

Central to the historical development of *nōmai*, as derived from *shugen nō*, are ritual elements incorporated into the ceremonial and prayer dances that form the core of its repertoire. *Kagura* is one major ritual source. Ceremonial songs and dances of *mikagura* and *bugaku* served as a basis for *nōmai*'s ceremonial pieces. Early *kagura* based in shamanic practices played an important role, providing a ritual framework for *nōmai*'s programming and presentation as a whole. Buddhist temple rituals performed by *shushi* monks and *ennen* dance also operated as major ritual sources that contributed to *nōmai*'s evolution. *Sarugaku nō* performed by *shushi* stands out as a salient antecedent of *nōmai*. *Sarugaku nō* performances took on a ritualistic intent in the hands of *shushi* who dramatized

**Figure 2.1 Diverse Influences in the Development of *Nōmai***

***nōmai*** ← ***yamabushi kagura***

***kagura*** (ceremonial Shinto music and dance intended as a form of prayer to prolong life)

***ennen* dance** (sixth discipline in Shugendō training)

***bugaku*** (stylized court dance)

***shushi*** performance of exorcism and magic

**sacred *sarugaku*** (sacred enact ments of myths)

**secular *sarugaku*** (mimed plays that drew on medieval legends of heroes)

***gigaku*** (masked dances and pantomimic pieces imported from China and Korea)

***dengaku*** (dramatized rice-planting ceremonies)

***dōkemai*** (comic dances)

***nō*** (classical masked dance drama)

***kōwakamai*** (narrative art with a limited element of dance)

***kōjakumai*** (style of acrobatic dancing)

their magic and exorcism to make it more palatable and entertaining to provincial audiences. This coincided with and reinforced *nōmai*'s shamanistic origins in early *kagura*.

Other major influences were *gigaku* and *dengaku*, which furnished elements of mimicry, magic, dancing, and singing. Later on, in the 13th century, the drama of *sarugaku*, *dengaku*, and *ennen* heightened and matured into *sarugaku nō*, *dengaku nō*, and *ennen nō*. These developments led to the heightening of drama in *nōmai* (see Figure 2.1).

A striking feature in tracing the lineage of the dramatic arts in Japan is the significant role temples and shrines played in providing audiences for the performing arts. As centers for religious, social, and communal life they created fertile ground for the syntheses that took place between performing traditions, resulting in the emergence of new forms and the falling away of old forms. The historical lineage of *nō* theater, included in this chapter, served to trace the evolution of *nōmai*, since *nō* drama and *nōmai* share many of the same influences. Correlations between these two genres exist, since the time frame in which both evolved coincides to a large degree, and the artists of both came from the same social and cultural milieu, that of the Buddhist clergy and the lower classes.

## NOTES

1. *Haniwa* are burial mound figures. There are two types: cylindrical, in the simple shape of a receptacle, and figurative, in the shape of humans, houses, or animals. These clay images were found in tumulus burial mounds as funerary objects that are believed to be substitutes for the actual person or object represented in clay.

2. *Miko* dances (*mikomai*) are still performed at shrines in Kyoto, Nara, and Ise as one of the two main styles of female Shinto dances. The dancers wear women's red and white Shinto robes. Their faces are powdered white and their hair is worn in a Heian period style. An important element of the dance is a bell tree rattle, *suzu*, which each dancer holds while dancing (Malm 1974: 46).

3. See Basil Hall Chamberlain's 1919/1920 translation of the *Kojiki* published in 1982 by Charles E. Tuttle Co.

4. See Robert Aston's 1915 translation of the *Nihon Shoki* published by Cambridge University Press.

5. More than 220 *gigaku* masks made of lacquered wood are preserved in the Imperial Storehouse (Shōsōin) and Tōdaiji temple in Nara and the National Museum in Tokyo (Araki 1978: 36).

6. *Isora* was a legend about a servant of the sea god, who danced while holding two magic balls that assisted Empress Jingu and her expedition while enroute to Korea.

7. Other pronunciations of the two Chinese characters for this term that appear in Heian period documents include *sushi*, *zushi*, and *noronji* (Blau 1966: 427 as cited in Ortolani 1984).

8. By the 15th century, *sarugaku nō* was referred to as just *nō* following further developments of the art that took place in the hands of Zeami.

# 3

# Shugendō Religion and Folk Dance Drama: Religious Antecedents

The Shugendō religion was an unwitting agent in the dissemination of folk dance drama in Japan. Practitioners of this religion played an important role in synthesizing and creating anew a performing tradition used to proselytize to the masses. Inoura's in-depth history of drama (1963) relates the evolution of *nōmai* from *shugen nō*, a dramatic genre associated with Shugendō. This religion serves as a framework for identifying elements and traditions that coalesced to form *shugen nō*.

An understanding of the religious orientation of Shugendō practitioners and their use of the performing arts helps clarify the nature and intent of *nōmai*. The gradual addition of entertainment elements to ritualistic performances made this genre more palatable to provincial audiences. *Nōmai*'s appeal lay in its function as both a form of worship and a means of entertainment for the local people.

## RELIGIOUS BACKGROUND OF SHUGENDŌ

A complex religious order, Shugendō began in the 9th century, combining diverse belief systems and philosophies, and became highly organized by the 12th century. This religious movement acquired the appellation Shugendō during the Heian and Kamakura periods and it combined (1) shamanistic practices and *kannabi shinkō* (belief in the sacredness of mountains where the dead and agricultural spirits reside) included in primordial folk Shinto beliefs; (2) "Tantric Buddhism, including spells and rituals, and some aspects of Buddhist ethics and cosmology; and (3) Ying-yang and Taoistic magic" (Swanson 1981: 56). The tripartite fusion was very much a product of medieval religious inclinations. Through *kannabi shinkō*, Shugendō became associated with agricultural religious ceremonies performed at the foot of sacred mountains in prehistoric times.

The sacred mountains serve as a natural environment for activities and not as an object of worship. In ancient mythology, sacred mountains functioned as a place where *kami* (deities) could descend and dwell. In the earliest written records of Japan, mountains play a role in the cosmogony and theogony of the established mythology by providing burial sites, sacred places of great beauty, and dwelling places for deities. The prominence of sacred mountains also lies in the belief that they serve as a place where the living, the souls of the dead, and the *kami* all converge. *Kannabi shinkō* comprehensively encompasses mythology, folk beliefs, festivals, rituals, and asceticism, all united in their relation to the mountain as a religious site.

Buddhist and religious Taoist symbolism and beliefs permeated *kannabi shinkō* in the 6th and 7th centuries, shortly after these religions made their way to Japan. Buddhist asceticism and Taoist mysticism influenced the Shugendō belief that mystical power could be attained through ascetic training and retreat in the mountains. Shugendō adopted doctrine and rituals from the Shingon and Tendai esoteric Buddhist sects; the mysticism and ritualism of the Shingon sect, prominent among the aristocracy during the Heian period, in particular, reinforced the ascetic and mystical elements in Shugendō.

Shugendō continued to develop through the 12th century, when esoteric Buddhism prevailed and all religious elements in Japan converged to form a complex religious milieu. As a highly organized sect of that milieu, Shugendō became firmly established on chosen mountains all over Japan.

In the 16th century, the common people, reacting to the overly formalized religions of Shinto and Buddhism, depended increasingly on popular practitioners for their spiritual needs. Shugendō priests fulfilled this role since they lived among the people and were familiar with their life and religious beliefs.

Shugendō flourished from the 17th to the 19th centuries, with *yamabushi* ministering directly to the people by reciting prayers and conducting exorcisms. It was at this time that many *yamabushi* formed marital unions with *miko* (*itako*)[1] —women who were shamanic mediums. Each couple travelled and worked together, with the *miko* functioning as a medium in diagnosing sickness and the *yamabushi* serving as the exorcist who cured it.

Then, during the Meiji period (1868-1912), along with the dismantling of the feudal shogunate and the restoration to power of the imperial line, an official decree prohibited the practice of Shugendō. Shinto and Buddhism were then separated, with Shinto established as the national religion. Consequently, Shugendō centers splintered into separate Buddhist and Shintoist institutions—an artifice to some degree, since Shugendō was a combination of both. Although officially terminated, the religious phenomenon survived in ritual traditions of Shinto shrines maintained by Shugendō priests, who had assumed the role of Shinto priests. At the end of World War II, Shinto was disestablished and religious freedom restored. Shugendō sects since this time have reemerged as independent groups (Earhart 1970: 6, 35).

## ORGANIZATION OF SHUGENDŌ

The *Nihon Ryōiki* (9th century) associates the sacred mountain Kimpu, Yoshino, and Kumano, located on Kii Peninsula in Nara and Wakayama Prefectures, with the legendary founder of Shugendō, En no Ozunu (En no Gyōja). Religious emphasis eventually shifted from Mounts Kimpu and Yoshino to Kumano, which became Shugendō's central headquarters around the 10th century. Kumano was soon the major destination of religious pilgrimages for people practicing *tōso* (pilgrimage and asceticism). The Shugendō center at Kumano established offices to serve the influx of people making pilgrimages. The offices made arrangements for pilgrims to be led through various rituals in the mountains by ascetics, called *hijiri, ubasoku, genja,* or *yamabushi*, who served as pilgrimage guides. Kumano headquarters served as a prototype for the internal organization of Shugendō bases in the local provinces.

## SHUGENDŌ DOCTRINE AND PRACTICE

Esoteric Buddhism (*mikkyō*), which was systematized into both the Shingon and Tendai sects, was superimposed onto *sangaku shinkō*[2] beliefs in the formalization of Shugendō doctrine. The use of the mandala, an iconographic representation of the universe found in every aspect of Shugendō, is a manifestation of esoteric Buddhist beliefs. An iconographic representation of the three sacred mountains of Kumano, Yoshino, and Kimpu best illustrates the Shugendō use of the mandala. The conceptualization of the mountains as a natural mandala reflects the coupling of the indigenous notion of sacred mountains and the attainment of Buddhahood or enlightenment in these mountains.

Shugendō and Shingon Buddhist doctrines share many aspects, especially with regard to the main Shingon divinity, *Dainichi nyorai* (Sun Buddha), considered the source of the universe. Another shared element is the idea that all persons possess a Buddha nature or Buddhahood. For instance, Shugendō teaches that ascetic practices conducted in sacred mountains are the way to accomplish the Shingon concept of *sokushin jōbutsu* (becoming a Buddha in this body). Shugendō's formal doctrines fixes its belief on becoming a Buddha through mountain ascetic practices combined with rituals (Murakami 1943: 190).

The method of attaining this state of enlightenment involves magicoreligious powers. Shugendō doctrine does not specify any pantheon or theology, although deities of esoteric Buddhism are revered, including *Fudō myō ō*, one of the Five Great Bright Kings (*Godai myō ō*) who act as agents or messengers of the Buddha (Blacker 1975: 175). Others include the local mountain deity, who is treated as the manifestation of a Buddhist deity called *gongen.*

Shugendō's emphasis on pilgrimages to sacred mountains, as well as retreats in the mountains, fosters distinct ascetic training and practices. Mastering magicoascetic powers is central to the difficult training. Specific techniques for attaining such powers distinguished Shugendō practices. The magicoascetic techniques, adapted mainly from the Chinese influences of Shingon Buddhism and religious Taoism, took on a Japanese character when carried out on sacred peaks in Japan.

The Shugendō custom of entering sacred mountains to attain enlightenment consists of ascetic practices built on a ranking system of ten worlds, called *jukkai shugyō* (Miyake 1978: 19). The Tendai Buddhist concept of *jukkai shugyō* is a hierarchy of ten stages divided into six preliminary stages (*rokudō*) and four enlightened states. Each stage symbolizes a progression from hell to enlightenment or Buddhahood. The practices of the ten Buddhist stages (Miyake 1978:141) are:

1. *Jigoku,* the practice of hell
2. *Gaki,* the practice of hunger
3. *Chikushō,* the practice of animality
4. *Shura,* the practice of anger
5. *Ningen,* the practice of humanity or tranquility
6. *Tenjō,* the practice of heaven or rapture
7. *Shōmon,* the practice of disciples
8. *Engaku,* the practice of a self-enlightened being or saint
9. *Bōsatsu,* the practice of an altruistic enlightened being
10. *Butsu,* the practice of a Buddha

The first six stages are especially important in Shugendō, as recorded in the writings *Shugen sanjūsan tsuki* and *Shugenshuyō hiketsushū* of the Muromachi period (1338-1573), perhaps because they were the most difficult. Six training steps are specified for each of the stages:

1. *Go-hakari* or *Gōyō*—weighing one's karma or evil conduct
2. *Koku-dachi*—fasting, which theoretically involved abstaining from the five cereals (rice, wheat, millet, barley, and beans)[3]
3. *Mizu-dachi*—abstaining from water
4. *Sumō*—Japanese wrestling
5. *Sange*—repentance
6. *Ennen*—dance of long life

Practice of the ten stages, with the six training steps prescribed for each of the first six stages, formed the ascetic regime performed on sacred mountains.

*Ennen,* the sixth training step, is pertinent to studying the role of the performing arts within Shugendō. *Ennen*, as described earlier, is a *gigaku* dance (the widely performed "Okina" dance) performed ritually for the purpose of prolonging life. Considered a kind of entertainment, this dance is customarily presented after the first night of training newcomers. Neophytes learn to dance to the accompaniment of a sistrum while holding a flaming fan in each hand and chanting the word *misosai*, meaning "to increase your age." The performance concludes with the reading of a simple prayer (Miyake 1978: 138).

The inclusion of *ennen* as part of Shugendō training reflects the importance of music and dance in Shingon Buddhism. Along with music and dance, painting, sculpture, and other allied arts are also considered as necessary aspects of Shingon mysteries. This emphasis on artistic display in Buddhism provided the impetus for the growth of the performing arts in the Kamakura period.

## PRACTITIONERS OF SHUGENDŌ

Ascetics known as *hijiri* or *ubasoku* first appeared in Japan in the late Nara or early Heian periods (8th-9th centuries). In Buddhism, such men took vows and preferred to live in certain mountains instead of a temple or monastery.

Many of the *hijiri* were indirect descendants of members of the government bureau, *Onmyō ryō* (Bureau of *Yin-Yang*), modelled after a Chinese tradition of religious Taoism. Appointed members of this bureau conducted divinations and duties relating to astronomy and the calendar. The increased importance of Buddhist magic and rituals, however, brought about the closure of the bureau. Many yin-yang practitioners and their descendants subsequently resorted to travelling throughout the provinces. In their travels, they disseminated the beliefs, customs, charms, and formulas of religious Taoism, while making a living as fortune-tellers and exorcists.

*Hijiri* synthesized ideas from religious Taoism that included mountain retreats and a special diet to promote their becoming sacred wizards (*shinsen*). As ascetics, their proclivity for practicing religious austerities on sacred mountains to acquire magicoreligious power distinguished them. Within the mountains, these ascetics followed a regime of austerities that included periodic abstention from food,[4] standing under a waterfall or pouring cold water over the head and body a prescribed number of times (*suigyō*), and the recitation of mystic words or syllables of power.

The first two austerities provided an efficacious means of cleansing the mind and body and developing mental clarity and concentration. The third ascetic practice, recitation, was strongly rooted in the magic of esoteric Buddhism. They believed that repeated phrases from sutras and magical formulas imparted a magical power to spells that could cure illness, overpower demons, defeat enemies, create rainfall, and induce childbirth. Certain sounds were believed to imbue power to those who recited them. Recitations derived power either from the meaning of words contained in the text, the uttering of a certain succession of syllables from Shingon Buddhism called *shingon* (Skt. *mantra*), or mentioning the names of divinities (Blacker 1975: 93-95). Observance of these ascetic practices served as a basis for Shugendō.

*Yamabushi* ("those who lie down in the mountain") or *shugenja* ("those who accumulate power or experience [through ascetic practices in the mountains]") are the terms used to refer to ascetics of the Shugendō order. *Yamabushi* are the most direct lineal descendants of the itinerant *hijiri* and *ubasoku* of the 8th and 9th centuries, who formally organized their most effective power-inducing mountain austerities into the Shugendō religious movement. These ascetics, of various priestly and semipriestly ranks, acquire their *yamabushi* status from one of many Shugendō headquarters, located on or near sacred mountains. To gain this status, the ascetics have to fulfill specific requirements involving mountain retreats and training. In the initial stages of Shugendō's development, *yamabushi* were primarily unmarried mendicants, who travelled extensively practicing austerities in mountains. As this religious phenomenon evolved, most *yamabushi* married and resided either at temples located at the foot of sacred mountains or in villages in close contact with the common people. If they chose to live in a village, they had to make periodic religious pilgrimages and go on retreats to mountains where the spirits of En no Ozunu or other leaders were believed to reside.

In ministering to the needs of the local people, *yamabushi* healed, taught, and preached. Ceremonies related to life, death, and reincarnation, in particular, required their involvement. Among the most important of these ceremonies were mystical rites performed to preserve the lives of old people and the sick. Two such rites were "pure birth," which involved the sprinkling of water, and "passing through the womb," in which a deity spirit would pass between large rocks or underneath a lion dancer in a performance of "Gongenmai." The religious duties of these Shugendō priests also included conducting funerals and memorials, purifying homes at New Year, and blessing the planting of rice during religious celebrations of the agricultural year. As practitioners of Shugendō, they were also responsible for leading male adolescents to sacred mountains and initiating them into the mysteries associated with their religion (Anesaki 1980).

A *yamabushi*'s religious duties involved serving people mainly by performing exorcisms and similar occult practices to induce healing. Many illnesses were attributed to *rokusan,* a demon or evil spirit whose origins and essence remain largely unclear. *Rokusan* caused sickness in one part of the body and required a divination necessary to ascertain which part of the body was affected so that the infected part could be exorcised. Exorcisms were referred to as *kitō,* literally meaning "prayer." It is part of the Buddhist term *kaji kitō,* which denotes prayer by drawing on the strength of Buddha. As Shugendō practitioners, *yamabushi* performed *kitō* to cure by means of driving out the demon or spirit causing the sickness. Women desiring safe pregnancies, as well as people seeking employment, deciding to be engaged or married, or about to receive medical treatment, also consulted with *yamabushi*. Shugendō adopted the use of amulets for the *yamabushi*'s occult practices, while the mystic incantations and formulas of the various rituals arose from Shingon Buddhist mysteries.

Shugendō standardized the practices and ranks of wandering ascetics, linking them to specific headquarters. Around three thousand Shugendō bases of operation existed all over Japan, many of them in the northern half of the main island of Honshū. This reflects the increased activity and influence of *yamabushi* in this region of Japan. Sacred mountains in the north, such as Haguro, Hayachine, and Chōkai, served as powerful bases. *Yamabushi* settling in local villages was widespread after 1331 when local communities functioned as smaller bases for Shugendō activity, bringing *yamabushi* close to the people they served. The later development of ascetics living in villages rather than in the mountains accompanied their use of the folk performing arts in their mission to preach, teach, and heal. Offering services to heal illness was a means for *yamabushi* to make a living.

Emphasizing the role of *yamabushi* as cultural agents in the medieval period provides a new perspective on the history of Japanese drama. This perspective supports recent studies of these priests as carriers of traditions. *Yamabushi* are credited for bringing the performing arts of outlying rural areas to the capital of Kyoto and its environs and, conversely, with dispersing the performing arts of the capital to the provincial regions. Local festivals and rituals led by *yamabushi* featured elements of local performing traditions, which they merged with *ennen* dance and other rituals required of them in their training.

The integration of regional performing traditions, *ennen* dance, and performances from the capital, such as *bugaku*, can be tenuously assumed. It is important to consider the cultural exchanges that took place between court nobility in their pilgrimages to Mt. Kumano and Shugendō practitioners at their Kumano headquarters. It is probable that the exposure of *yamabushi* to performing traditions brought to the Kumano shrine from the capital by courtiers influenced their *ennen* performances. With the Kumano shrine as a center for such exchanges, it is likely that the priests in turn transmitted performing arts from the capital to provincial areas of Japan.

## *SHUGEN NŌ*

As *yamabushi* dispersed to local villages throughout Japan, the performing arts became an important medium in teaching Shugendō beliefs to the common people. Religious and semi-religious ballads and plays were among the arts used for didactic purposes. Artful dances were also widely used by *yamabushi* in their priestly functions. Honda describes the dances as a medium for performing exorcisms. Dances were also performed by these mountain priests on special occasions such as New Years, marriages, and dedications of new homes. This repertoire of ceremonial dances came to be known as *shugen nō*. *Shugen*, mountain-based asceticism, was used to refer to the ascetic practices of *yamabushi*, while *nō* describes the ceremonial dances of these priests that developed into a dramatic form. *Shugen nō* developed a dramatic character, resulting from the inclusion of *modoki* (mimicry or a simplified explanation of a ritual).[5]

The 10th century marks the incipient stage of *shugen nō*. Early *shugen nō* grew out of the ascetic practices of Shugendō. These practices include incantations spoken as part of the rituals *yudate*[6] and *hibuse*.[7] The knowledge and training *yamabushi* acquired in music and *ennen* dance influenced the formation of *shugen nō*'s performance style. "Okina" (Old Man) is an *ennen* dance which prays for longevity and abundant harvests. Other more theatrical dances were intended to stimulate interest and teach villagers about the history of mountain gods and Buddhist deities, as well as to promote understanding of the spiritual powers of Shugendō priests (Inoura and Kawatake 1981: 75-76).

One of the original pieces of the *shugen nō* repertoire is "Gongenmai" (Dance of the Gongen), a dance of exorcism categorized as *kitōmai* or prayer dance. As described earlier, *kitō* were exorcisms carried out by *yamabushi* to drive out the demon or spirit causing illness. "Gongenmai" is performed with a lion's head mask, symbolizing the presence of Buddha, whose strength is needed to successfully carry out an exorcism. This dance is supposedly connected to the lion dance of *gigaku,* which later became a ritual of *shushi* priests.

The ceremonial beginnings of *shugen nō* highlight its emphasis on the prayer and profound thought characteristic of esoteric Buddhism. By the 14th century, however, comic dances known as *dōkemai* were incorporated. The addition of *dōkemai* reflects the fusion of comic and serious elements common in performing traditions of the time. The inclusion of more entertaining dances made *shugen nō* performances more accessible, conforming to a standard pattern found in all Japanese festivals of serious ritual combined with comic amusement (Blau 1966: 326). The added element of comic parody to the repertoire is indicative of the coupling of entertainment and religion in medieval Japanese culture.

In the 15th century, a further development occurred. *Bushimai* (warrior dances), depicting heroes in battle, became part of the *shugen nō* repertoire. At least three genres contributed to *bushimai*: (1) *kōwakamai,* a narrative art with a limited element of dance popular during this time, influenced *shugen nō* to heighten the heroism of its warrior dances; (2) *kōjakumai*, a style of acrobatic dancing; and (3) plays adapted from *nō* drama (Inoura and Kawatake 1981: 77). As a popular addition to the repertoire, warrior dances catered to the romantic tastes of the provincial population. The dances were an artistic response to the prevailing feuds and battles between powerful clans during the 15th century.

General characteristics of *shugen nō* included the use of masks and costumes borrowed from *gigaku, kagura, dengaku,* and *kyōgen.* Singers provided the narration for each dance, with an ensemble of flute, cymbals, and a large drum to accompany the dancing and singing. A simple stage of two to three meters was used and props were minimal. A typical *shugen nō* program featured four types of dances. The first category was *gireimai*, or ceremonial dances, followed by *kitōmai*, or prayer dances. Performed next were *bushimai*, or warrior dances, and the program ended with comic dances, or *dōkemai.*

*Shugen nō*'s eclectic combination informs us of the variety of performing arts that flourished during the medieval period. Shugendō embraced a wide-ranging dogma, so it was easy to combine not only performing traditions associated with mountain beliefs, but also those of the surrounding villages. This confluence of performing traditions occurred because centers of Shugendō activities were established in local villages, as well as in the mountains (Inoura 1963: 1103-1104). As a result, each Shugendō headquarters took on a local color from the traditions and folk customs of the surrounding area.

*Dengaku* was one of the traditions embraced by Shugendō. Originally consisting of rice-planting dances in villages where people believed that the mountain deity descended to the fields for spring and summer and ascended to the mountain for fall and winter, *dengaku* first appeared in Kyoto as early as 671 and later was refined (Inoura 1963: 1102). Acrobatic elements in *dengaku* performance added to *shugen nō* were comparable to elements found in the *yamabushi*'s training. In catering to the provincial population, *yamabushi* wove Shugendō beliefs into the fabric of folk beliefs and traditions.

Several types of *sarugaku* also exerted their influence. One was *senmin* (low-class) *sarugaku*,[8] a performing art of the lower classes presented at local temples and shrines by *hōshigen*, low-class performers who served as Buddhist temple officials. Their status was lower in the hierarchy than that of *shushi* or the Buddhist clergy called *hōshi*. *Senmin sarugaku* served as entertainment at popular religious services and festivals throughout Japan, with *hōshigen* specializing in tricks, acrobatics, magic, and comic imitations of characters and situations (Ortolani 1984: 172).

Secular *sarugaku* troupes, which performed mainly in the provinces, composed pieces that used various tales of the medieval period, such as *The Tale of the Soga Brothers* and legends of the warrior hero Yoshitsune, as themes. Their plays were mainly combinations of characters, situations, and mime, embellished with song and dance. *Gōmin* (village folk) *sarugaku*, an art performed by villagers at temple and shrine festivals, included plays featuring familiar aspects of daily life. These plays acted as a stimulus for the further development of *shugen nō* (Nakamura 1971: 77).

Besides provincial *dengaku* and *sarugaku*, *shugen nō* borrowed from sacred *kagura*, adding Shintoistic aspects found in this tradition. *Kagura* performed for ceremonies at the imperial palace served as a model; *shugen nō* borrowed elements of pantomime, accompanied by music or song, that characterize this genre. *Shugen nō* also borrowed from *kagura* ceremonial song texts for its songs (Inoura and Kawatake 1981: 18).

Aspects of *bugaku* also appear in the ceremonial dances of *shugen nō*. A story exists about a *yamabushi* named Nichizō, who reportedly dedicated himself to severe asceticism at the sacred Mount Kimpu and learned the *bugaku* dance "Banshūraku" while in the "realm of the departed." It is also said that a mountain deity performed the *bugaku* dance "Somakusha" when En no Gyōja played a tune as he wandered through the mountains of the Ōmine mountain range. Details of costuming and dance movement also reflected the influence of *bugaku*, particularly in the ceremonial piece "Torimai."

As a distinct performing art of the medieval period, the well-structured *shugen nō* included an increased amount of mimicry. The shift in emphasis from ritual to mimicry in *shugen nō*, owing to the absorption of many secular elements, resulted in a dilution of the *yamabushi*'s preachings and an increased secularism of the form.

### *YAMABUSHI KAGURA*

In an area of northern Honshū located between the central mountain range and the Pacific Ocean, *shugen nō* is referred to as *yamabushi kagura*. This area, historically known as Rikuchū, is comprised of eleven districts in Iwate Prefecture and one district in Akita Prefecture. The designation *kagura* is thought to have come into use because *yamabushi* in this area embraced many elements of folk *kagura*. Another suggestion for the use of the word *kagura* is given by Gorai Shigeru, who recounts that toward the end of the Heian period, court *kagura* filtered into *ennen* dances, which Buddhist monks performed during temple services. *Yamabushi* learned these dances and dispersed the *kagura*-influenced *ennen* dances to the provinces (1972a: 4).

*Yamabushi kagura* is associated with the villages of Take and Ōtsugunai in Iwate Prefecture. Both villages rest at the foot of Mount Hayachine, the central peak of the Kitakami mountain range. Mount Hayachine has long served as a center for worshiping mountain spirits. From the medieval period until modern times, the mountain was the site of ascetic practices by *yamabushi* who inhabited the Hayachine foothills. *Yamabushi kagura* is closely connected to the time when Mount Hayachine was opened for spiritual practices, and it has been retained by certain families in the villages of Take and Ōtsugunai (Honda 1976: 3).

Folk *kagura* strongly influenced the development of *yamabushi kagura*. The essence of the older, more ritualistic folk forms of *kagura* was rooted in a less elaborate concept of deities, the repose of souls, and performances dedicated to deities in order to appease them. Music and dance functioned to provide repose to souls; performances calmed *aramitama*, or haunting spirits of the dead which were likely to bring evil or misfortune to people (Gorai 1972b: 4). In order to avoid crises such as poor harvests and epidemics, rituals were performed to calm these spirits. Commoners believed that only *yamabushi*, who were considered spirit manipulators, could perform the appropriate religious acts. This belief stems from the spiritual powers *yamabushi* obtained in their ascetic practices.

The *yamabushi*'s function as an exorcist and spirit manipulator found form in *shishi* (lion) *kagura*. This folk genre is one of the three basic types of *kagura* defined by Honda. The way in which a deity is conjured distinguishes the three types. The central characteristic of the first type, Ise *kagura* (also called *yudate kagura*), is purification through dance, in which boiling water is offered to deities as a means of invocation. The second form, Izumo *kagura*, is based on performances at Sada Shrine in Izumo of Shimane Prefecture. A set of seven dances that feature symbolic offerings (*torimono*) held by the performers, as well as other masked dances characterize this form. *Shishi kagura* is the third type, and it is differentiated by the practice of using a wooden lion's mask in which the *gongen* deity, a manifestation of Buddha, is believed to reside. In Ise and Izumo *kagura*, the deity is present only during a performance, while in *shishi kagura*, the deity resides in the lion's head during the entire New Year's season (Hoff 1978: 155-156).

In ancient times, Japanese people believed the *shishi* was a sacred animal with great power. In *shishi kagura*, a wooden lion's head (*shishigashira*) is manipulated in a dance called *shishimai* (lion's dance). The central purpose of *shishimai* is to offer prayers to dispel all evil spirits present in a certain area. Together with singing and instrumental accompaniment, the dance functions to ward off evil (*akuma barai*) or prevent destruction by fire (*hifuse* or *hibuse*) (Misumi 1967: 212). Instrumental accompaniment is provided by flutes, drum, and cymbals.

Traditionally, *shishi kagura* troupes performed their dance rituals while travelling from house to house in specific areas at the end of the year. During the day, *shishimai* was performed at each house in a village. At night, villagers enjoyed dance performances given for them in a room of the farmhouse where the performers lodged (Honda/Hoff 1974: 193). *Yamabushi* combined *hibuse*, the Shugendō exorcism ritual, with the *shishi kagura* practice of performing dance rituals from house to house in a village as a means of bestowing good health and safety for the coming year. Combining these activities facilitated acceptance of *yamabushi* by villagers and provided them a source of income.

*Yamabushi kagura* is a subgenre of *shishi kagura*. As in *shishi kagura*, the principal religious practice of *yamabushi kagura* lies in the practice of revering a wooden lion's mask and dancing with it in the prayer piece "Gongenmai." This piece derives its name from the belief that the lion's head houses an embodiment of the *gongen* deity, an incarnation of Buddha associated with Kishū-Kumano Shugendō headquarters in Wakayama Prefecture. "Gongenmai" is the *yamabushi*'s Buddhist version of the *shishimai* lion's dance.

Elements of Izumo *kagura* are also evident. Most notable is the bipartite distinction between the offering dances (*torimono no mai*) and masked dances, which serve as a basis for the general structure of *yamabushi kagura*.

As mentioned above, *yamabushi* appropriated the *shishi kagura* custom of travelling from village to village, performing the lion's dance of exorcism at individual homes. Also, in keeping with established custom, performances of ten or more dances were presented in the evening at a designated house in a village. *Shishi kagura* thus served not only as a vehicle for spreading Shugendō doctrine, but as entertainment. This practice was most prevalent in the northeastern prefectures of Iwate, Aomori, Akita, and Yamagata (Honda 1976: 4).

The repertoire of *yamabushi kagura* also includes early dances of *shushi* Buddhist priests. Their dances contained even earlier magical stamping and other rites to drive off evil, such as symbolic hand gestures (Jap. *hōin*; Skt. *mudra*); repeated choreographic movement that involved the interlacing or crisscrossing of dancers; and aspects of costuming featuring paper rings on the fingers, swords, bells, an offering wand, and a branch of the sacred *sakaki* (Lat. *Cleyera ochnacea*) tree, along with sticks that were struck together. These features are all magical techniques used by *shushi* to repel evil (Hoff 1978: 168-169). The repertoire categorizes these dances as prayer dances (*kitōmai*), which are presumed to have grown out of ascetic practices (Honda 1976: 3).

Today, *yamabushi kagura* is known for its emphasis on sacred aspects of *shugen nō* and the retention of many of the genre's original ceremonial elements. This emphasis contrasts with the greater secularization of *shugen nō* before its demise in the Meiji period (1868-1912).

## *NŌMAI*

Shugendō also spread to Shimokita Peninsula, the northernmost geographical point on the main island of Honshū. The original intention of *yamabushi* in travelling this far north was to make pilgrimages to Osorezan (Osore Mountain), a mountain centrally situated in Shimokita Peninsula. Osorezan has long been associated with the world of the dead. Its surrealist landscape, created in part by hot springs, represents the various realms to which the dead are destined to go, according to Shinto and Buddhist beliefs. *Yamabushi* performed their ascetic practices on Osorezan, communing with blind women mediums (*itako* or *ichiko*) in summoning the spirits of the dead. Pilgrimages of ascetic priests to Osorezan soon led to the establishment of Shugendō temples and training centers in this northern peninsula.

It is believed *yamabushi kagura* was first brought to Shimokita Peninsula around 1630. Two Buddhist temples, Daikakuin and Sankōin, served as bases for *yamabushi* on the peninsula. Daikakuin, a temple of the Gokain complex in Tanabu, was established in 1524. Sankōin temple in the village of Mena was also built around this time. The Sankōin temple is cited as one of the first places for *nōmai* performances. The village of Shishipashi learned this dance drama from *yamabushi* at Sankōin temple. Sankōin's *nōmai* masks are now part of the village of Shishipashi's paraphernalia. At Daikakuin, *nōmai* masks have disappeared, but the dance "Gongenmai" is still performed. The documents *Daikakuin bunsho* and *Sankōin bunsho* provide information on these two temples (Inoura 1963: 1126, 1128).

Daikakuin and Sankōin are located in the district of Higashidorimura in the northeastern portion of Shimokita Peninsula. In this region *nōmai* is the appellation applied to *yamabushi kagura*, which was transmitted from Iwate Prefecture to Higashidorimura in Aomori Prefecture approximately 360 years ago. The term *nōmai* apparently existed toward the beginning of the 19th century, because it is described in the book *Hina no asobi*, written by a traveller named Sugae Masumi in 1809.

The word *nōmai* appeared to be in general use in the Nukabe district, directly south of Higashidorimura, toward the close of the Tokugawa period (1600-1868). The date of *nōmai*'s beginnings in Shimokita, however, is not known, but from around the year 1500, Shugendō practitioners travelled back and forth between Iwate Prefecture and Shimokita Peninsula before becoming established at temples and training centers in Shimokita. With the eventual settling of Shugendō practitioners, *yamabushi kagura* came to Higashidorimura, where it became known as *nōmai*. The intrinsic characteristics of *nōmai* are clearly those of *yamabushi kagura*. Its enhanced elements of entertainment and comic parody, however, differentiate it slightly from the more ritually oriented *yamabushi kagura* of Iwate Prefecture.

The term *shishimai* (pronounced *shishime* in the local Zuzu dialect) is used interchangeably with *nōmai*. The synonymous usage of the two terms connects *nōmai* to *shishi kagura*. In addition to the terms *nōmai* and *shishimai*, the name *Kumanomai* (not in current use) is found in a libretto of a *nōmai* group in

Higashidorimura. *Kumanomai* suggests *nōmai*'s lineage to performing traditions at Shugendō headquarters in Kumano, Wakayama Prefecture (Inoura 1963: 1111). After the Meiji period (1868-1912), *nōmai* was the favored designation and it became the official name for this performing art. Some villages in Higashidorimura, however, still refer to this dance drama as *shishimai* (Koida 1981: 25).

## THE DISTRIBUTION AND LINEAGE OF *NŌMAI*

*Yamabushi* disseminated *nōmai* while travelling from village to village to collect donations from individual households in exchange for performances of the exorcism dance "Gongenmai." Each *yamabushi* sect had its own districts throughout Japan to which they could go in collecting donations. *Nōmai* performances for villagers provided programming that sometimes lasted two consecutive days. These performances both entertained the local people and educated them about Shugendō. Geographic areas in which we find *nōmai* range from the district of Higashidorimura, west to Mutsu City and the town of Tanabu, and as far south as the Kamikita district. In 1984 thirteen out of twenty *nōmai* groups were still performing.

The primary informant for this study, Mr. Ōta cited local history about three *yamabushi* who arrived in Higashidorimura around 1630 to evangelize about Shugendō. One went to the village of Ōri, another to Shishipashi, and a third to Kamitaya. Each performed *nōmai* not only as a means of evangelism, but as entertainment, affording them the opportunity to collect contributions from audiences. The local people attribute the slight differences in *nōmai* music and dance of these three villages to the individual taste and talent of each *yamabushi*. From the individual styles of these villages, three lineages of the tradition emerged. Male leaders in each of these villages learned *nōmai* from the visiting ascetic priests. In turn, the three villages trained men in other villages, often ones in fairly close proximity. It is not clear whether the three lineages outlined in the story of the three *yamabushi* are historically correct, but the villages of Ōri and Shishipashi are definitely leaders in maintaining what they consider the authentic *nōmai* style. There appear to be no written records of *nōmai*'s beginnings in Shimokita that could substantiate the existence of the lineages, and today they are no longer clearly defined, with some villages having developed slightly varying styles of their own. The differentiation of the lineages, however, is significant as part of the oral history surrounding *nōmai*.

*Nōmai*'s transmission on Shimokita Peninsula is evident in a listing of thirty-two towns and cities where it was or is at present practiced. This compilation appears in the book *Higashidorimura no nōmai* (*Nōmai* of Higashidorimura), published in 1984 by the Higashidorimura Board of Education. The thirty-two places where *nōmai* was dispersed include:

District of Higashidorimura:

1. Ōri
2. Ishimochi
3. Shishipashi
4. Gamanosawa
5. Horobe
6. Iwaya
7. Iriguchi
8. Shiriya
9. Shikkari
10. Kamitaya
11. Sunakomata
12. Shimotashiro
13. Sarugamori
14. Shiranuka

Mutsu City:

1. Kawadai
2. Onnadate
3. Nakanosawa
4. Shinmachi
5. Sekine
6. Yanagimachi
7. Kogawamachi
8. Myojinmachi
9. Yokomukaemachi

Kawauchi Township (southwest of Mutsu City):

1. Yunokawa

Yokohama Township (northern Kamikita district):

1. Yokohama
2. Arito
3. Fukkoshi

Noheiji Township (southern Kamikita district):

1. Makado
2. Karibasawa

Rokkashomura (western Kamikita district):

1. Obuchi
2. Futamata
3. Togusari

In 1947, Mr. Teizo Imamura and Mr. Kiyoshi Okukawa wrote and published the seminal source on *nōmai.* In their book, *Nōmai,* they classified twenty-three communities into four groups of three straightforward lineages and one mixed lineage:

Ōri Lineage

a. District of Higashidorimura
    1. Ōri
    2. Sunakomata
    3. Iwaya
    4. Shiriya
    5. Noushi
b. Town of Tanabu
    1. Onnadate
    2. Kogawa
    3. Yachi
    4. Sekine

5. Kawadai
c. District of Kamikita
1. Makado

<u>Shishipashi Lineage</u>
a. District of Higashidorimura
1. Shishipashi
2. Ishimochi
b. Town of Tanabu
1. Karasuzawa
c. District of Kamikita
1. Futamata

<u>Kamitaya Lineage</u>
a. District of Higashidorimura
1. Kamitaya
2. Gamanosawa
3. Shikkari
4. Shiranuka
b. Town of Tanabu
1. Hamaokunai

<u>Mixed Lineage</u>
a. District of Higashidorimura
1. Odazawa
2. Shimotashiro
b. District of Kamikita
1. Yokohama

A majority of the villages are small. Ōri, Sunakomata, and Shishipashi each have only about forty homes (Inoura 1963: 1112).

There is a thirty-eight-year lapse of time between the two preceding listings. In comparing them one sees which villages continue to perform *nōmai* and which have discontinued the tradition. It is also apparent that *nōmai* continued to spread to communities that did not initially perform it.

The inhabitants of Higashidorimura distinguish two types of *nōmai: gobyōshi* and *sanbyōshi.* Thirteen villages originally learned *gobyōshi nōmai,* considered the standard, and the two villages of Horobe and Iriguchi learned *sanbyōshi nōmai,* a later manifestation. *Gobyōshi* literally means "five beats" and *sanbyōshi* "three beats"; the two terms are ambiguous and the several explanations offered by both *nōmai* performers and scholars appear in Chapter 5 on performance practices.

*Sanbyōshi nōmai* is also referred to as *okajishimai* or sometimes simply *shishimai.* In the designation *okajishiimai, oka* refers to a northern locale in Iwate Prefecture called Oka. Since someone from Oka taught *shishimai* to villagers in Iriguchi, the term *okajishimai* came to be used. Iriguchi and Horobe are relatively new communities established just prior to the Meiji period (1868-1912). Oral history explains how these two villages learned *okajishimai*. According to Mr. Ōdate Kanetaro of Iriguchi, a seed-seller who lived in Mutsu City stayed at the Ōdate home every December distributiing seeds for *daikon* (white radish), *nanban* (cayenne pepper), *saibaru* (green leafy vegetable), and red peppers. The seed-seller was originally from the town of Ichinohe in Ninohe County in northern Iwate Prefecture. During his stay in Iriguchi, he directed training sessions of *shishimai* (*okajishimai*), starting on December 19 and sometimes staying well after the New Year. The seed-seller is evidently responsible for transmitting this Iwate Prefecture form of *shishimai*, which only recently came to be referred to as *sanbyōshi nōmai*. Not understood is whether the seed-seller transmitted all the pieces in the *okajishimai* repertoire, or whether some pieces were added later. It is also unclear whether Iriguchi passed *okajishimai* on to Horobe, but it seems likely since the designation for this art is the same in both villages. A study of the repertoire of each would substantiate their shared lineage. Its connection to *nōmai*, at any rate, is based on the fact that the Kumano *gongen* deity is central to the tradition, pointing to the influence of *yamabushi*.

A comparative study of the musical style, dance, and repertoire of *nōmai* and *okajishimai* would demonstrate *nōmai*'s variety and the greater secularization and theatricalism of the latter. The focus of the present study, however, is *gobyōshi nōmai* as it is practiced in the village of Shishipashi and twelve other villages in Higashidorimura.

## SUMMARY

The study of Shugendō points to the importance of music and dance in medieval religious practices. Many Buddhist temples utilized the drawing power of performing traditions in which music and dance of a less serious nature followed ceremonies. The popularity and appeal of performances, coupled with training in *ennen* dance, inspired *yamabushi* to institute a dance drama that absorbed aspects of folk performances and beliefs from areas where they travelled and eventually settled. During their extensive journeys, they came into contact with regional performing traditions; they then proceeded to combine elements from these various traditions in forming *shugen nō*, the prototype of *nōmai*. The peripatetic *yamabushi* are the key to understanding the efficacious means in which performing traditions and rituals merged to form a unique repertoire so dynamic that it survives today.

## NOTES

1. *Itako* is the term used to refer to women shamanic mediums in northeast Honshū. These mediums tend to follow folk art traditions rather than fulfill pure shamanic functions, since their training involves learned techniques in ecstasy and possession. Also, *itako* do not exhibit any physical illness or neuroses before their initiation, as do shamans of the arctic hysteria type (Hori 1968: 7). *Itako* is one of the various names found in the Kuchiyose-*miko* system, i.e., shamans of Japanese rural communities.

2. *Sangaku shinkō* refers to an indigenous Japanese religion whose beliefs and activities are associated with mountains considered sacred.

3. The "Five Cereals" were avoided according to the Taoist idea that human life was shortened by parasitic worms that fed on these cereals within the body. Abstinence from these cereals would thus force the worms to exit from the body and thus prolong life (Blacker 1975: 86).

4. Certain foods were believed to be averse to the acquisition of power. The abstention from meat, salt, the "Five Cereals," and cooked foods are all described as a potent austerity in the legends and biographies of ascetics in the early part of the medieval period (Blacker 1975: 86).

5. The verb form *modoki* means '"to imitate" or "to modify" some action. *Modoki* became a kind of comic parody, performed after more serious pieces. *Sambasō* after *Okina* in *nō* and *Ninomai* after *Ama* in *bugaku* are examples (Inoura and Kawatake 1981: 28). It is not clear how *modoki* and *wazaogi* differ. The term *wazaogi*, meaning "imitative gesture," appears in the *Nihon Shoki* and may be an older and more general term for mimicry. I believe the term *modoki* has a more specific meaning in referring to modifying rituals through the technique of mimicry.

6. *Yudate* (water boiling) is a ritual in which large cauldrons of boiling water are literally the center of certain festival events. The boiling water is first purified, often by means of dance, then offered to the gods of various important shrines throughout Japan, who are believed to be invoked in this way (Hoff 1978: 151).

7. *Hibuse* (fire prevention) is a type of ritualistic exorcism performed these days at dedication ceremonies of newly built homes. In Iwate Prefecture, *hibuse* is done once a year by villagers at all homes in a village. Food and drink are offered in return for this service. Within the ritual, a bundle of reeds tied together forming a torch is lit. The *gongen* deity, represented by the wooden lion's head which is manipulated by a dancer, carries the lit bundle in its mouth as a sign that the house will be protected from fire.

8. I believe the terms *senmin* and *gōmin sarugaku* are used by scholars from the 1930s on when Japanese scholars began researching the importance and impact of the lower classes and outcasts in the development of dramatic genres.

# PART II

## *NŌMAI* THEATER

# 4

# Keepers of a Tradition: Performers and Cultural Setting

This chapter places *nōmai* within the life and culture of four communities documented for this study: Shishipashi, Ōri, Shiriya, and Iwaya (see Figure 4.1). The four villages provide a representative sampling of *nōmai* as it is practiced in the district of Higashidorimura, the seat of this tradition. *Nōmai* is significant not only as an art form, but as a cultural, economic, social, and spiritual communal activity performed by the local people.

## KEEPERS OF THE *NŌMAI* TRADITION

The young men's associations in thirteen villages throughout the district of Higashidorimura supervise the retention and annual presentations of *nōmai.* Leaders of these associations assume full responsibility for maintaining the dance drama and its performance standards. Various designations of these groups include *seinenkai* (young men's association), *keishindan* (reverence society), and *san'yokai* (public participation society). Use of these terms is relatively recent, replacing the traditional designations *wakamonorenchu* or *wakamonogumi*, both meaning "young men's group."

In earlier times, all men in a village were required to join the associations and within three years learn the entire *nōmai* repertoire. Those who could not perform at all were responsible for building fires for warmth and taking care of any details or duties related to performances. Instruction in *nōmai* in those days was strict and the in-house training included teaching of the regulations and manners of the association. Attendance was mandatory, and violators were severely disciplined.

Admission into an association requires members to be *ujiko* (shrine parishioners)—born to a family living in the village. Adopted sons from other villages cannot join unless their parents request so and the association grants permission. Families without sons often adopt ones from families, mostly relatives, who have more than one. This practice stems from the rule of primogeniture. Association membership was once compulsory, but with the recent flight of young

Figure 4.1 Japan; Shimokita Peninsula: Four Villages Documented

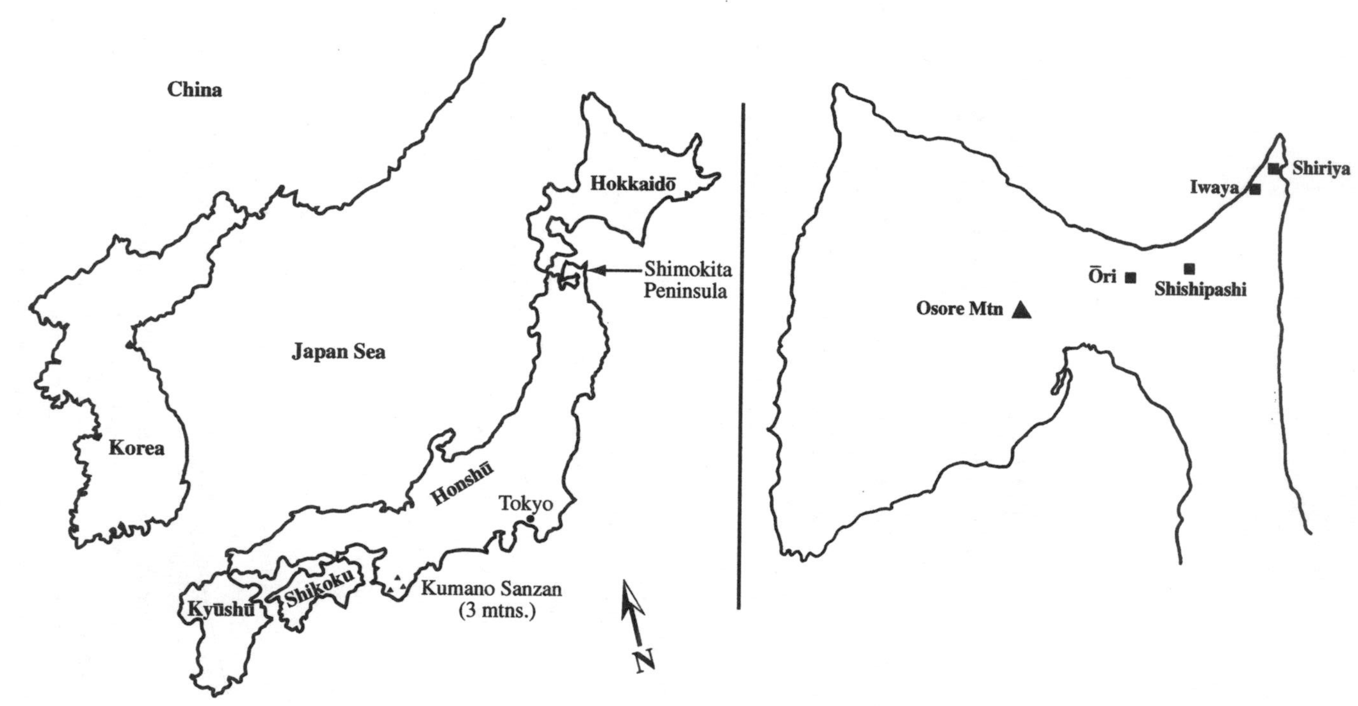

job-seekers from the villages to urban centers, affiliation has become optional in most villages. The result has been a drop in the number of members, creating a problem for the transmittance of *nōmai* in some places.

The social hierarchy of the *seinenkai* is based on seniority. Members past the age of forty-two are respected as *senpai* (seniors or elders), while those who have mastered dance, playing an instrument, or singing are called *shishō* (masters). Both the *senpai* and *shishō* are responsible for teaching the younger members.

## HIGASHIDORIMURA DISTRICT

Shimokita Peninsula is an isolated part of Japan where the folk performing arts and traditional customs remain an important part of people's lives. Its isolation rests partly in the fact that the bullet train, bringing tourists and rapid change, does not reach here yet, leaving this part of the country relatively untouched. The district of Higashidorimura, located in the northeastern portion of the peninsula, is lovely with rolling hills, pine trees, and pastures. This district has a population of 10,000 people living in twenty-nine communities. Except for nine communities, which were settled in the late 1920s, the other twenty communities have a very old legacy of performing arts that include *nōmai*, *kagura*, *shishimai* (lion dance), and *odori* (dance). Higashidorimura is the center for *nōmai* activities and thirteen out of twenty villages actively perform. An article in the local newspaper, *Tōnippō*, reported that *nōmai* came to Higashidorimura around 1630 when it is believed that the towns of Kamitaya and Mena served as bases for *yamabushi*.[1]

## SHISHIPASHI

I based my choice to live in the village of Shishipashi because of its strong musicians and the leadership of Mr. Zennosuke Ōta, my main informant who is a master *nōmai* dancer and musician. Mr. Ōta is also the founder and president of the Higashidorimura Rural Performing Arts Preservation Alliance, an organization whose members include all the villages that perform both *nōmai* and *kagura*. He is a respectable source who has taken an active role in preserving *nōmai*, including having written a small book explaining the background story of each drama.

Shishipashi is located inland and is typical of the small communities that dot the Higashidorimura district landscape. Driving through Shishipashi one sees a mixture of traditional farmhouses with thatched roofs, later-built wooden structures with many windows, and modern homes with ceramic tile roofs. A hill, rice paddies, and fields encircle homes nestled together. Fifty-three families comprise the village, forming a population of approximately 250. Shishipashi's main industries are farming, lumber, and animal husbandry, while other occupations include being a taxicab driver and a motel owner.

Villagers assert that Shishipashi was established more than 800 years ago at one-third the size of its present population. They claim this date according to the age of the *sennen katsura* (1000-year-old Judas tree), which is centrally located at the site of the original village shrine. The lineal descent of the families in this community has created strong kinship bonds among its members. This proved to be true as I met many of the residents and all seemed to be related to one another in some way. The level of community involvement in *nōmai* performances reflects this bonding.

Mr. Ōta revealed to me that Shishipashi's *seinenkai* fills a major role in community life in addition to being responsible for the transmission and retention of *nōmai*. Its members regulate the village's social activities and provide various services such as street cleaning, cutting timber for firewood, and cleaning the grounds of the village shrine and repairing its structure in preparation for festivals. For young men in Shishipashi, the *seinenkai* provides an important context for education and socialization, combining entertainment and instruction. They learn to give assistance to one another when needed and to respect their elders. The respect and deference shown to older members models the social behavior within the community and Japan in general.

Members of the Shishipashi association range in age from sixteen to fifty (traditionally forty-two) and number twenty. Men past the set age limit often participate in the training sessions as valuable instructors. In a substantial number of cases, these men remain not only members, but leaders as well. The official hierarchy of the Shishipashi *seinenkai* includes the *kaichō* (president); the *fukukaichō* (vice-president), who acts in the absence of the *kaichō; kaikei*(treasurer); the *gorakubuchō* (entertainment director), whose duties are to plan performances and rehearsal schedules; the *riji* (counselor), who assists all of the above officers except the treasurer; and the *kanji* (auditor), who assists the treasurer.

In its obligation to preserve *nōmai*, the young men's association functions as a support group, in which every member has an opportunity (no longer obligatory) to participate as a dancer, musician, or singer. Everyone has a chance to establish his skills, whether as a performer or as someone who manages details of meetings, training sessions, and performances to build their self-esteem. The *seinenkai* fosters respect and mutual support important to the village's system of cooperation.

A second social group affiliated with *nōmai* performances is the *fujinkai*, or married women's association, who are not allowed to perform *nōmai*. Their minimal role is a custodial one, involving the mending and cleaning of costumes and occasionally providing food during the two-week training sessions in December. They do participate in the evening *nōmai* performance on January 16 by performing local folk dances and music during the intermission, but this is purely extracurricular. Their peripheral role reflects the gender restrictions of the *nōmai* tradition as long as it continues to be the domain of the *seinenkai*.

## ŌRI

Ōri is the second community I documented. It is a small village of forty-four homes with a population of 200, situated a little over three miles northeast of the city of Mutsu, the largest city in Higashidorimura. Industries in Ōri are farming, forestry, stock breeding of horses and cows, and hemp-growing and weaving into cloth. Contrasting occupations in Ōri include elementary and middle school teaching.

*Nōmai* in Ōri is passed on by the *keishindan*. As spokesman for the men's association, Mr. Mitsuo Ageji provided many details about the *keishindan* and the transmission of *nōmai*. This is a communal men's group which is composed of the *kowakamono*, a group of young bachelor men from age sixteen to twenty-two; the *kowakarenchū*, bachelor men between the ages of twenty-three and twenty-seven; and men up to the age of fifty-five years and sometimes older. Similar to Shishipashi, membership in the *keishindan* used to be mandatory and there were many restrictions. Today membership is voluntary, because many men have to leave the village to find work, and a loosening of restrictions is meant as a means to attract young men. Members in general are decreasing; in 1984 there were only fifteen.

Mr. Ageji also outlined the social/moral code of Ōri and its relationship to *nōmai*. The author's diagram (Figure 4.2) graphically represents the relationship of these aspects which are connected through the *ujigami* (tutelary god of Ōri) and *gongensama* (incarnation of Buddha, central deity of Shugendō).

**Figure 4.2 Social/Moral Code of the Village of Ōri**

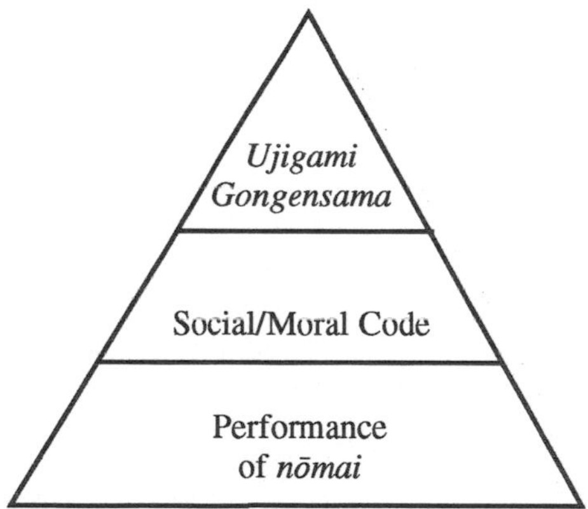


Mr. Ageji remarked that the social/moral code associated with the two deities asserts "(1) the superiority of men [over women]; (2) one must respect elders; and (3) one should not gamble and should prevent doing evil." *Nōmai* performances serve to mediate the relationship between Ōri villagers and their tutelary god and the *gongen* deity, as well as operating to teach and reinforce the code and its principles.

A feature of Ōri's *nōmai* is the music, which Mr. Ageji said is "more calmly and quietly performed, especially compared to the village of Kamitaya, whose music is more rough and vigorous."

The married women's group is not involved in maintaining *nōmai* in Ōri. The *keishindan* does, however, request assistance from the mothers of new members and officers in mending and making *nōmai* costumes. Prior practice required *keishindan* members to make and mend costumes themselves, but this is more difficult as the membership dwindles.

## SHIRIYA

The third village documented for this study is Shiriya, which is built on a promontory on the northernmost coast of Shimokita Peninsula and seems particularly subject to wind and weather. The community consists of forty-five homes, although today Shiriya includes company housing for a nearby cement factory. The population of 250 increases to 800 if one includes those living in the company housing. Shiriya's main industries are fishing, farming, mining, and cement manufacturing. Stock breeding of cows and wood-cutting are secondary occupations.

*San'yokai* is the name of the young men's association in Shiriya. Mr. Tōitsu Masaya, president of the *san'yokai,* stated "membership is mandatory for all young *ujiko* men in the village, even those who are not interested in joining. Since the transmittance of *nōmai* is inherited by young men from their fathers, they are obligated to participate in some way in *nōmai* performances, even if they are not talented. All members are required to dance and young members must carry out duties assigned to them by their seniors. They must be obedient, even gang leaders among the young people. Everything is based on seniority." In contrast to equivalent groups in Shishpashi and Ōri, Shiriya's actual compulsory participation ensures *nōmai*'s survival. The association made a conscious decision to continue mandatory membership; Mr. Masaya confirmed this by saying "the *san'yokai*'s philosophy is that for *nōmai* to be retained, all men must join; if they relied on only those who are interested, *nōmai* would die out." He also mentioned that strict rules of the association still hold, including punishment for missing a rehearsal, and "if a member violates any of the rules, he is required to make a public apology to all members. In olden days, if a member continued his misconduct, he would be beaten and his parents would have to apologize for their son's negligence."

The Shiriya *san'yokai* is a relative newcomer to maintaining and transmitting *nōmai*. Mr. Masaya narrated how during World War II *nōmai* masters from Ōri came to Shiriya to teach this dance drama to the young men's association. He continued "our dances were the same as Ōri's back then, but thirty years ago Shiriya's style began to diverge, being influenced by various other villages. The *san'yokai* still compares their performances to those of Ōri even though at this point their dances are slightly different."

The *fujinkai* in Shiriya also has no role in helping the *san'yokai* prepare for *nōmai* performances. In fact, there are strict rules in the association that disallow women to even touch costumes or go backstage. In comparison to the other three villages, this association is more strict in its regulations.

## IWAYA

Iwaya is the largest of the four communities studied and it is located on the northernmost coast of Shimokita Peninsula, just west of Shiriya. This village consists of ninety homes with a population of 500. Fishing and farming were traditionally Iwaya's main occupations, but today 90 percent of the younger generation works for Nitetsu, the nearby cement factory, while older men continue agriculture and fishing. Fishing today only serves as supplementary income for some households, although Mr. Ōtsuki, the leader of the seinenkai, mentioned "if the factory nearby closes, then many people will go back to fishing for a living." Mr. Ōtsuki also made a point of saying that "there is no sign of dance movements being affected by the fact that many men work for the factory." This comment implied that the *nōmai* tradition was not stylistically affected by the change in the occupation of its members. Yet he said that "long ago, as fishermen and farmers, members had time to train longer, but now since men work all day they only have a limited time to rehearse at night. Also there are fewer members because of these kind of jobs." So changes in the village's main industry perhaps does affect the quality of *nōmai* performances.

The *seinenkai* are the designated keepers of Iwaya's *nōmai.* Mr. Ōtsuki related that the *seinenkai* "had a lot of authority and in olden days, men who didn't join were denied fishing rights in the village. Long ago, it was mandatory for all men in the village to join the *seinenkai,* which had a large membership." He also talked about the role of the *seinenkai*, remarking that "the association is responsible not only for *nōmai,* but for other community business, such as cultivating seaweed which they fish and sell. Each family in the village financially supports the *seinenkai* in the form of *kitōryō* ("money for purification") which is given to the *gongen* deity and which the association is in charge of." Surprisingly, new members were not currently being recruited to add to the membership of twenty-five. Mr. Ōtsuki said "there are enough members and the association doesn't want to recruit men who are not really interested, since they would not attend rehearsals regularly. If people want to join, they request so and are welcomed by the members." Perhaps voluntary membership is due to Iwaya's larger size and the modern occupation of many of its inhabitants, resulting in the *seinenkai*'s loss of authority and a less traditional lifestyle.

Iwaya faces the same difficulties of retention experienced in other *nōmai* communities. Mr. Ōtsuki recalled: "When I was twelve or thirteen years old (around 1951), some community members were very enthusiastic at *nōmai* performances, but when I became eighteen, fewer people were interested. Nowadays the audience has increased." A growing interest from outsiders in *nōmai* performances is perhaps the reason for its local revival. I believe my presence and research on *nōmai* helped to raise the local population's awareness of its value. Also, during my five-week stay in Higashidorimura I was a witness to the attendance of scholars, photographers, and television camera crews at *nōmai* performances that I myself was documenting.

The Iwaya *seinenkai* promotes relationships with other associations in Iwaya, such as the *fujinkai.* Similar to Shishipashi and Ōri, Iwaya relies on assistance from the *fujinkai* to make and mend costumes and lend a hand in cleaning and straightening up after association activities. Mr. Ōtsuki mentioned the services offered by the *seinenkai*, saying "other associations in the village do ask the *seinenkai* for various kinds of assistance in affairs other than having them perform *nōmai.*" Evidently, *nōmai* performances are one of the services requested by community organizations for a variety of festivals and occasions.

## TRAINING

The training sessions held for young members are called *uchi narai*, or in-house training. The term implies an exclusivity of each association in teaching only young men who are members. Villages override this exclusivity as they lend assistance to one another in sharing techniques of performance and repertoire. Master performers, sent from villages where *nōmai* is well established, provide such assistance. The borrowing of dancers and musicians is also commonplace. Many groups ask players from neighboring villages to play in their major performances because they lack competent flutists (for the instrumental ensemble) or sometimes dancers. The sharing of techniques and repertoire among villages has blurred earlier stylistic distinctions among the three *nōmai* lineages described by performers. This practice will eventually lead toward a more unified *nōmai* style within Higashidorimura.

Shishipashi is the model for looking more closely at how young men learn *nōmai*, since this village was my research base for studying *nōmai* in Higashidorimura. Before the period of training in Shishipashi begins, a meeting is held on December 11 to discuss a plan for the in-house training. Then, every evening from December 12 to December 30 rehearsals are held. The Shishipashi *seinenkai*, said to have been established in the middle of the Meiji period (l868-1912), has twenty members. Training sessions require the attendance of all members, and according to Mr. Ōta, former president of the *seinenkai*, if a member violates this regulation he is summoned to a village meeting where he is given a warning. Often in the past, the relatives and parents of such a member brought *saké* and formally apologized to members of the *seinenkai*. When I observed rehearsals, however, this strict treatment had apparently been relaxed, with some of the younger members attending only on evenings when dances they were learning were rehearsed. There were only three or four young men who came faithfully and practiced diligently. Mr. Ōta also remarked that rehearsals are fewer in comparison to former times, when the training period was longer and also served as a time for teaching regulations of the association, as well as courteous manners in general.

The method used to teach *nōmai* dances in Shishipashi follows a certain progression. First, the younger members learn to dance. The first pieces they learn are simpler folk dances that employ arm and hand movements, an important feature in many of the *nōmai* dances; such pieces include *te odori* (hand dances) called "Jonkara" and "Shiogama," followed by "Tsukiage" and "Oiwake." After beginners memorize the movements of these four pieces, they learn dances of the *nōmai* repertoire proper. Ceremonial dances are the first dances taught, as they are considered to be central to the repertoire; they are also pedagogical, involving many of the basic dance movements used in all *nōmai* dances.

The young men find learning dance movements challenging. Visual aids called *aruku junjo* (walking sequence) assist trainees. *Aruku junjo*[2] are drawings that graphically depict the sequence and direction of foot movements. These drawings aid novices in visualizing a dance and reinforce their memory of the sequence of movements. The drawings specify floor patterns for particular dances or characters portrayed in *nōmai* pieces. With the advent of tape recorders, trainees often record the music in rehearsals and practice dances at home. A traditional aid to learning dances is memorizing lyrics to *nōmai* songs. This facilitates keeping track of the sequence of movements and their synchronization to the appropriate text.

*Nōmai* music is learned conjunctively with dance. Trainees learn by participating; masters and senior members who accompany those learning to dance encourage young members to play and sing along. Mr. Ōta mentioned that everyone is expected to play *taiko* drum and the small hand cymbals called *tebiragane*, since sounds from these instruments can be produced easily. Young men learn to play both instruments as soon as they become members, but, Mr. Ōta believes, only when they know how to dance and sing will they be able to play rhythms accurately. Prior dance training, therefore, is desirable, and a drummer should know dances well in order to accompany the movements of a dancer.

Trainees learn *taiko* drumming by playing along with master performers. They imitate and eventually memorize rhythmic sequences and patterns that begin and end specific pieces. Before reaching this level of proficiency, basic drum rhythms are learned through the use of onomatopoetic syllables such as *dan*, *don*, *kon*, and *tan*. These syllables describe the sound created when striking the drumhead a certain way, representing the most basic drum strokes. Taught next are combinations of these syllables with other syllables depicting a variety of drum strokes that form standard rhythmic patterns. Drum patterns such as *sutaraku dan* and *dakasuku* are strung together to form rhythmic phrases. Damping strokes learned next use the syllables *zuki* and *tsuku*, which are onomatopoetic equivalents of two techniques used to damp a drum sound. Additionally, there are rhythms which incorporate sharp-sounding strokes on the rim of the drum, described by the words *sucharaka* and *chakachaka*. The process of learning *taiko* drum is an aural/oral one that uses syllables called *kuchi jamisen*. *Kuchi jamisen* are important in learning any aurally transmitted music in Japan, and they are the primary means used to teach most Japanese instruments.

The hand-held cymbals, *tebiragane* (referred to as *kane*), are the least difficult of the musical instruments to learn. Rhythms of the *kane* are not as varied as those of the *taiko*. The two basic strokes are referred to in terms of dynamics—strong and weak—as is evident in the use of the term *kyōjaku* in which *kyō* means "strong" and *jaku* means "weak." All members are required to play *kane*; everyone rotates playing this instrument during performances. Hand motions are first taught without holding the *kane*; then, when the motion is learned, the instrument is held. Combinations of strong and weak strokes form rhythmic patterns used for various dances. There are only a few *kane* rhythmic patterns that change according to the dance. Members learn these rhythms before improving the resonance and sound quality of their strokes. Timbre is determined by how a player holds the cymbals: a good clear sound is created if handles are held lightly, and a poor sound is produced if the handles are held too tightly. The difficulty in playing *kane* lies not in creating a certain resonance, but in synchronizing the rhythms with the *taiko* and the flute.

The flute, called *fue* (pronounced "fwee" in the local Zuzu dialect), is also aurally learned. The syllables specifically created and employed in teaching flute are *tere*, *toro*, *torira,* and *tororirori.* These words indicate to the learner the contour and direction of consecutive pitches and serve as small units that are combined to play entire melodic patterns and sequences. It is not compulsory for all members to learn flute, since many people have difficulty in even producing a sound on the instrument. At the present time, no one is learning flute in the Shishipashi group owing to its difficulty, but there are already two flute masters.

Learning to dance, sing, and play an instrument are integrated activities, since the synchronization and progression of these elements must be coordinated. In this way, trainees acquire a sense of the relationship of the music to dance and vice-versa.

In some *nōmai* groups, playing an instrument or dancing is handed down lineally—that is, a performer would be an instrumentalist if his father were an instrumentalist, or a dancer if his father were a dancer. In Shishipashi today, this custom is not strictly adhered to, owing to the shortage of performers. This shortage has placed more demand on members, who must learn to be competent both in music and dance. Still retained, however, is the practice of individuals specializing in male and female dance characters. The training system is self-contained and reflects a flexible tradition that involves interaction between master and student, establishing patterns of learning that have made the continuation of *nōmai* possible.

The social aspect of the training is important. The hierarchy of age within the associations is representative of the traditional concept of seniority in Japan. Young men are taught to show deference toward older members, who are respected for their skill and experience. The relationship between a master and his student reflects the social hierarchy of the community, in which young people learn to obey and respect their elders. This kind of behavior is essential to the student-master relationship central to *nōmai* training.

Also of social significance is the rapport promoted by the interaction among members during rehearsals. The rapport-building activity of eating and drinking that takes place at the beginning of rehearsals, during breaks, and at the end of the sessions helps to bond members as a group. All matters of interest are discussed during these breaks, including issues concerning the association or comments about some aspect of training. The younger members make tea and serve food. The training sessions serve not only as a time for serious training, but as activities in which men of a village have the chance to socialize and relax, forming a camaraderie important for the survival of *nōmai.*

The training methods of most *nōmai* groups are similar. "The concept and approach to *nōmai* is universal among all the villages," Mr. Ōta states, "even though characteristics of performing style, organization, and customs surrounding the art slightly differ." The transmission of *nōmai* through the generations has always been and remains primarily an aural one, although performers use song texts and graphically drawn choreographic patterns as memory aids. Also, videotaped recordings of performances are a modern-day analytical tool for learning *nōmai.* The variations seen in dance movements and the slight differences heard in the melody of the flute and rhythms of the drum and cymbals are a result of this method of transmission.

## STATUS OF THE PERFORMERS

The status that performers enjoy stems from their social and spiritual role as members of the young men's association responsible for organizing and enacting important ceremonies in the community. Their role also includes being caretakers of the village tutelary shrine; they provide labor for shrine repairs and preparation of the shrine grounds for festivals. Traditionally, the *seinenkai* is also obligated to lend a hand to any member of the cooperative group (*kōjū*) in a village who is shorthanded or ill during a busy season working in the fields.

In Shishipashi, the ritual and symbolic value attached to *nōmai* performances upholds the status of members of the *seinenkai.* As *nōmai* performers, they act as leaders in many of the events and ceremonies associated with New Year's celebrations, serving as guardians of the *gongen* deity, who is invoked and enshrined during this season; actors of ceremonies of renewal for the coming year; and solicitors of prayers for the health and welfare of everyone in the village.

Their function as caretakers of the village tutelary shrine supports the sacred beliefs and activities of Shishipashi inhabitants. The village shrine offers protection to the community by serving as the abode of the village tutelary deity. Customarily, villagers rely on this deity for general health, the prevention and cure of sickness, and protection from supernatural forces that cause misfortune within a family. The deity is also depended upon for good harvests, adequate rain, and the dispelling of crop diseases. Careful maintenance of a village shrine thus requires constant vigilance.

Socially, the young men's association serves to strengthen bonds within the community, not only in ceremonial life, but through the provision of entertainment that can be shared and enjoyed by all. Social cohesiveness in a village is maintained not only by the strong kinship ties among extended families, but in kinship attitudes toward non-kin through formal ceremonial events and, in the case of Shishipashi, through *nōmai* performances. The intimacy between *nōmai* actors and their audiences forms a ritual kinship. Within the bounds of ritual kinship, performers receive moral support and encouragement for their presentations, and the audience is brought together to enjoy evenings not only of formal ceremony, but of informal socialized eating, drinking, and fun. The coupling of ritual and entertainment in *nōmai* reinforces kinship and non-kinship ties in Shishipashi. This important function of *nōmai* grants *seinenkai* members status as spiritual and social leaders.

Outside the realms of the sacred and the social is the status afforded performers for their artistic talents in music, dance, and drama. Artistic status, among peers and within the community, is established when a member's command and refinement of either dance, playing a musical instrument, or singing bring him recognition. For younger members, their esteem as artists is initiated following their debut in formal *nōmai* presentations. The aesthetic appreciation of talent is one motivating factor for many young men who strive to achieve the artistic status enjoyed by master performers.

## ECONOMIC COOPERATION

In general, the community involvement in *nōmai* performances reinforces the social solidarity necessary for the economic survival of the village. In Shishipashi, the hill, fields, rice paddies, and residential areas are all cooperatively owned by families, or by a collective of community members, according to the policy of land distribution dictated by the local government. Each family is assigned a plot of land, which they divide among their branch families (*bunke*). The main industry is farming: rice is grown in addition to potatoes, soy and azuki beans, millet, white radish, carrots, and burdock.

In villages like Shishipashi, agricultural cooperatives play an important role in rice cultivation and farming. Rice cultivation in particular requires a great deal of community effort due to the extensive irrigation and the lack of land and technology needed for high productivity. Cooperatives serve to effectively organize the manpower needed. Like traditional associations, agricultural cooperatives are organized on the basis of virtually mandatory membership. Legally, however, they are a voluntary association presumably organized by individual farmers, who receive initiatives from the national and local governments. The cooperative is a principal agency through which members sell their products and also buy both capital equipment and consumer goods. It also provides the community with a number of services by functioning as a bank both for savings and loans; issuing insurance policies both for business and personal property; providing guidance and educational services; and organizing auxiliary groups for youth and women. In fact, the cooperative offers services in more spheres of life than any other group outside the family (Befu 1971: 90-91).

For the lumber industry in Shishipashi, wood is cut for use by local carpenters. This industry also requires cooperation among its workers. These days, many of the younger village men are white-collar workers, either in companies or with the government in nearby Mutsu City. Most, however, still farm or cut wood on the side and therefore participate to some extent in the village's economic cooperatives.

Within Shishipashi, an important cooperative activity is the community meeting (*buraku sōkai*). The meeting serves as a forum to discuss financial matters and decide on how half of the tax money and half of the community funds should be spent for repairs and maintenance needed in the village. Women, who do 50 percent of the village's agricultural labor, are active participants in the community meetings.

## RITUAL FUNCTION

The need for a *kami*'s blessing and protection in farming was the basis for the development of the folk performing arts. Festivals in honor of various deities and aspects of the environment traditionally filled the farmer's year. *Nōmai*, like many other performing traditions, is rooted in agricultural festivals, which consist of stages of expecting, welcoming (*kami mukae*), and sending off deities (*kami okuri*) associated with farming and the natural environment. At the New Year, prayers for good crops are a central element in annual agricultural rituals. Early on, these rituals—particularly those concerned with rice—involved magical incantations accompanied by semidramatic and (later) dramatic pieces. These pieces represent the villagers' livelihoods of sowing and harvesting, and they depict the *kami* overcoming the evil spirits of the field (Raz 1983: 17,18).

The New Year (January 1) marks the beginning of the agricultural year, so it is an important occasion for enacting prayers for abundant crops before cultivation is begun in the spring. *Nōmai* is an integral component of the ritual events at the New Year in Shishipashi. The oldest and most central pieces in the *nōmai* repertoire are the ceremonial and prayer dances. These dances express the desire not only for economic renewal, but for spiritual renewal and the general health and welfare of the entire community. Performances are part of a larger schedule of ritual activities associated with the New Year. The following are traditional activities associated with this holiday:

**December 19**: Designated as *Kumanosama no toshikoshi* (Kumano *gongen* deity's New Year's Eve). On this day, the *gongen* deity is moved from the village shrine to the house of the *ujikosōdai* (assistant or caretaker of the village shrine). Inhabitants of Shishipashi go to the house of the *ujikosōdai* to worship the deity and give offerings of *saké* and money.

**December 20**: Two-week *nōmai* training period begins.

**December 22**: *Shōtokutaishi*—A festival celebrated by people in the lumber business.

**December 26**: *Ubusunagami no tsuya* (mourning of the god Ubusunagami)—Mourners gather at night and cut pounded rice cakes into diamond-shaped pieces.

**December 27**: *Susuhaki*—Everyone cleans their Shinto deity shelf, Buddhist altar, and entire house for the New Year.

**December 28**: *Mochi*-pounding—Rice is pounded into a dense, sticky substance and made into rice cakes for offerings and eating.

**December 31**: *Toshikoshi* (New Year's Eve)

**January 1**: *Wakamizukumi* ritual—In formal kimono attire, heads of households go to nearby wells or brooks to fetch fresh water with a ladle and bucket, carrying with them rice cake offerings, starch grains from a sago palm (*osago*), and a torch. The water brought home is placed on the Shinto deity shelf and the household guardian deity is worshipped. Just after dawn, people go to the village shrine to pay their first visit of the year (*hatsumōde*).

**January 1**: *Gongensama no kadouchi*—Members of the *seinenkai* enact the annual *kadouchi* ritual. This involves taking the *gongen* deity, residing in the wooden lion's head, from the home of the *ujikosōdai*, and bringing it first to the village shrine of the Ishigami deity (the village tutelary god), where the prayer dance of exorcism, "Gongenmai," is performed. From there, the musicians and dancers move on to each house in the community, presenting "Gongenmai" at the front entrance to exorcise all evil influences that may plague the household in the coming year.

**January 1**: *Saisen hiroi* (picking up money)—Families go to the village shrine to make their first visit of the year. While at the shrine, parents scatter money, then have their children pick it up. Only boys are allowed to pick up the money.

**January 2**: *Maikomi* (refers to opening presentation) performance of *nōmai*—Prayer dances and other selected dances are presented.

**January 6**: Second *maikomi* performance of *nōmai*—This performance prefaces the curtain opening on the following day.

**January 7**: *Makubiraki* (curtain opening) performance of *nōmai*—"Gongenmai" and other dances are presented. In past times, the performances continued every day until all the pieces in the repertoire were presented; today it lasts only one evening. Traditionally, the younger generation of males in the community were trained to perform *nōmai* music and dance for this event.

**January 11**: Storage house opening—This is an event in which people visit their storage houses and worship the god of storage. For the visit, people take *zōkagami* (round, flattened ceremonial rice cakes), *osago* (starch grains from a sago palm), *saké*, fish, money, and a torch. The storage god is the god of wealth, called Daikokusama. When a storage house is constructed, a pillar in the center—called the *daikoku* pillar—is built to reinforce the structure. A *kamidana*, or Shinto deity shelf, is made near the pillar and offertory objects placed on it.

**January 12**: *Kirisome*, which refers to the initiatory use of carpentry tools for the new year, falls on this day. Saws and broadaxes can be used from this day on. People go out and bring back branches of a willow tree after placing rope, rice cakes, and *saké* as offerings underneath it.

**January 13**: Rice pounding is followed by attaching small globs of *mochi* (pounded rice), to willow branches that have just been cut; such *mochi* is called *awabo*. Next, silkworm cocoons and *mochi* made from wheat are attached to a dogwood tree.

**January 14:** *Niwa taue* (rice-planting in the garden)--When the sun is about to set, rice-planting is imitated near the house gate. A miniature seedbed is made from snow (in this northern area there is always snow by this time of year) and bundles of straw are placed in it to represent rice plants. Two cogon grass stems are bundled together, from which a *shimenawa* (New Year's decoration lanyard) and *gohei* (paper pendant offerings) are hung, and pine branches attached. A candle, special New Year's food, and *saké* are placed on a tray and put on the seedbed. Next, prayers are said by clapping the hands twice and bowing the head in wishing for a good harvest in the coming year.

- ***Toshitori* of *koshōgatsu***: After performing the *niwa taue* ritual, people symbolically become a year older.
- ***Tomado fusagi***: After *toshitori* of *koshōgatsu* occurs, shaved cedar tree branches are put in the windows and doors of houses together with small sardines. This is to protect the house from demons.

**January 15**: *Wakamizukumi* ritual (the fetching of fresh water described above) and *hatsumōde* (first visit to the shrine) are enacted again. *Saisen hiroi*—the custom of boys picking up money at the shrine—is also repeated.

- ***Naetori*:** On the morning of the fifteenth, boys go to each door in the village saying "I came to pick up a rice seedling." They receive money upon saying this, since a rice seedling symbolizes money.
- ***Seijin no hi:*** Special occasion when ceremonies are held for young people turning twenty years old in the coming year.
- ***Taue*:** After the boys finish the *naetori* custom, girls go to each house to say "I came to plant rice," and they dance the rice-pounding dance, called *mochitsuki odori.* After the girls leave, older girls circulate the village, receive money, and perform *mochitsuki odori*, as well as other dances (*tsukiage*, *oiwake*, and *jonkara*). In addition to money, people give the girls rice cakes and uncooked rice. Members of the married women's association also circulate the village performing the *mochitsuki* dance, separately from the first two groups; this is a recent development, since it was customary for only unmarried women to perform this dance.
- ***Shūtorei*:** Either on the fifteenth or sixteenth day of this month, the head of a household visits the father of his daughter-in-law or son-in-law.

**January 16**: *Maikomi* performance of *nōmai*—At night, *seinenkai* members perform *nōmai* and members of the married women's association perform a genre of dance called *te odori.*

**January 17**: General meeting of the *seinenkai.*

**January 18**: *Taue burumai*—Event in which young girls of the village gather to cook, using the money they received for *taue* (circulation of the village performing *mochitsuki odori* described above).

**January 20**: The deity *Sōzensama* is enshrined in Mr. Ōta's house as one of the village guardian deities. People bring *saké* and uncooked rice to the house for a celebration.

**January 23**: *Sanyasama*—If the moon is out, young members of the *seinenkai* circulate the village blowing a conch shell (*horagai*). At the sound of the *horagai*, villagers go to Mr.Ōta's house, drink *saké*, and worship the moon.

**January 27**: *Makuosame* (curtain closing) performance—Final New Year's presentation of *nōmai.* After the presentation ends, a custom of toasting, called *omikiage*, is done, and the *gongen* deity residing in the wooden lion's head is placed back in the shrine until the next year.

These New Year's customs form a complex of rituals and activities grounded in folk beliefs and agricultural rites. Together, they compose segments of the larger New Year's ritual of renewal, in which people welcome the new year, renew community bonds, pray to guardian deities for health and safety (Shinto), and venerate ancestors (Buddhist) (Beardsley 1959: 188). An outstanding aspect of this larger New Year's ritual is that many of the events are carried out communally. Such events at this time of year serve to strengthen the social ties among relatives and neighbors. In turn, this strengthening reinforces the cooperation necessary for the economic productivity of the village.

It must be noted, however, that some of these customs are no longer observed in Shishipashi with the prevalence of mass media, the modernization of rural life, and the slight shift away from farming as the dominant economy. Still maintained are all of the rituals and performances associated with *nōmai*, but the activities and rituals observed on an individual family level may fall by the wayside, depending on a particular household. As a result, the social and economic organization of the community has loosened, but the essence of renewal at the New Year is still an important occasion celebrated by the village.

## EXPRESSION OF THE SACRED

A *nōmai* event is an act of communication between deities and the community, made possible through the medium of the performing arts—music, dance, mimicry, and disguise (mask and costumes).

The retention of *nōmai* performances within the New Year's schedule of events is linked to its ritual origins and close connection to agricultural life. This is indicated by the central importance of ceremonial and prayer pieces in the *nōmai* repertoire. These dances function as communal rites that induce a desirable, collective consciousness on the part of both performers and audience. The ceremonial dance "Torimai" is a reenactment of an auspicious portion of the *Heavenly Cave Door* myth, which conveys spiritual renewal. The pieces "Henzai" and "Okina" are intended to manifest the spirit of Okina and to listen to its utterance of blessings for longevity and prosperity. Belief in the power and presence of the Kumano *gongen* deity is expressed in the prayer dance "Gongenmai." In this dance, the *gongen* deity is symbolically conjured to exorcize the community from malevolent spirits and to ensure the welfare of villagers. Thus, the ceremonial and prayer dances express what villagers consider sacred within the context of their social and natural worldview.

The ritual nature of *nōmai* is further substantiated by the existence of the protocol and preparation surrounding performances. Within the *nōmai* tradition, the backstage area, where the *gongen* deity is enshrined, the dance space, and the audience area serve as one unit, unifying the villagers with the *gongen* deity. The auspicious occasion of the New Year is the designated ritual time for *nōmai* presentations. The use of ritual objects held by dancers in the ceremonial and prayer dances include a Buddhist sistrum (*shakujō*), a Buddhist rosary (*juzu*), pendant paper strip offerings (*gohei*), a paper- festooned offering wand (*bonden*), ceremonial trays (*obon*), and a white fan. Mudra-like hand gestures (*hōin*) of esoteric Buddhism, introduced into *nōmai* by *yamabushi*, are a ritual form of expression. Ritual behavior is also manifested in a custom called *naorai* in the postperformance banquets held by *seinenkai* members. Eating and drinking is a Shinto concept that symbolizes everyone sharing the protection and blessings of a deity.

Preparations for *nōmai* performances also involve ritualistic activities centered around revering and enshrining the Kumano *gongen* deity, who is believed to reside in the wooden lion's head called the *gongengashira* (head of the *gongen).* The enshrinement of the *gongengashira* is central to *nōmai* performances. The protocol required to display respect toward the Kumano *gongen* entails placing the lion's head in a designated sacred place, such as a *tokonoma* (alcove) or *kamidana* (Shinto deity shelf), together with symbolic paraphernalia. A candle, customarily set in front of the *gongengashira,* is lit during performances to symbolize a constant vigil toward the Kumano *gongen.* Offerings presented to the deity include salt, uncooked rice (both placed on a wooden ceremonial offering tray (*sanbō*), and a bottle of *saké.* On New Year's eve, *mochi* (pounded rice cakes) are also offered to the *gongen* deity as *osonae* (rice cake offerings). Other paraphernalia kept near the wooden lion's head include props used by the dancers, such as a white folding fan and a Buddhist sistrum. Reverential behavior toward the *gongengashira* requires placing any food about to be eaten by the *nōmai* group during rehearsals or performances on the offering tray before the *gongengashira.* Everyone then claps their hands twice and bows their head. The deferential treatment and behavior is evidence of the importance of the Kumano *gongen* as the main *nōmai* deity.

A final preparatory ritual act is *sangu* (also *uchimaki* or *sanmai*). This Shinto custom involves throwing uncooked grains of rice onto the dance area to purify it. This action is believed to exorcise the dance area. Once this is done, the stage is ready for the sacred ceremonial and prayer dances presented first in a *nōmai* program.

## MUSIC AND RITUAL

We now turn to the relationship between music and ritual. In order to understand this relationship we must regard music as a symbol, "an essential component of ritual action, a multivalent means by which ritual transforms those experiences that no other medium can adequately express" (Foley 1984: 20). Music, since ancient times, has been closely associated with the sacred and with ritual, and it has been regarded as a powerful medium in making contact with the divine (Danielou 1980: 4). The divine symbolism attached to *nōmai* music lies in the belief that it originally emanated from the *gongen* deity. This belief within the *nōmai* tradition dictates the placement of the flutist and singers in the backstage area behind the curtain, where the *gongen* deity is enshrined. The *kai no kudari* instrumental piece, in particular, is associated with the *gongen*; its performance is intended to invoke the deity. The instrumental piece accompanies the prayer dance, "Gongenmai," which enacts a symbolic possession of the dancer by the conjured deity.[3]

The divine symbolism attached to *nōmai* music is also confirmed by sacred aspects of the musical instruments. The sound of the *taiko* arouses special, sacred associations for both believers and nonbelievers among the Japanese (perhaps the heartbeat of the universe). Also, drums in Japan, as in many other cultures, are traditionally considered trance-inducing instruments. The flute is an important instrument in Japan for summoning spirits in the Shinto *kami oroshi* (descent of the gods) ceremony. The use of cymbals is ritually less specific, however. The music created by the flute and drum, the combination of rhythmic repetition and prescribed melodies serves as a "purely connotational semantic," a symbol that expresses a specific level of reality created by these dances (Langer 1976: 215 as cited in Foley 1984: 20).

The ceremonial and prayer dances achieve a ritual effect not only through music. As a presentational form of communication ritual, *nōmai* employs dance, symbolizing "man acting out with his body what he thinks with his brain in using the language of demonstration" and the visual aspect of dance being able to bring people together in sharing "emotions, thought, attitudes, the experience of life itself" (Grainger 1974: ix).

The choreography of certain *nōmai* pieces that incorporate a number of elements derived from Buddhist rituals[4] affirms the link between dance and ritual. The following choreographic elements found in *nōmai* are all remnants of ritual magic that were used at one time to ward off evil: stamping, mudra-like hand gestures, repeated patterns involving the interlacing and crisscrossing of dancers,[5] and use of ritual objects, such as a Buddhist sistrum, rosary, or sword.

Stamping, symbolic hand gestures, and the use of a sistrum and rosary are all featured in the prayer dance "Gongenmai." Interlacing and crisscrossing choreography, along with the use of the sistrum as a hand bell, characterize "Torimai." Next, a dancer holding a sistrum is also included in the ceremonial piece "Sanba" and the prayer piece "Kanemaki." The *yamabushi* character in "Kanemaki" performs wearing a sword for the first portion of his dance. Finally, the vigorous manipulation to and fro of the back curtain—by *yamabushi* characters and warriors before they enter the stage—is also characteristic of dances derived from ritual (Hoff 1978: 169, 171).

Music and dance function as both symbolic and presentational expressions of the rituals dramatized in the ceremonial and prayer pieces. The medium of sound and the visual impact of dance are both effective in uniting performers and audience in a collective display of their sacred beliefs.

## COMMUNAL ENTERTAINMENT

The entertainment portion of a *nōmai* program features warrior dances and comic dances. The warrior dances are dramatizations of famous episodes of medieval epics; the comic dances are satires of rural life. Much socializing takes place among audience members during the informal setting of these dances. Well-known historical characters and plots featured in the warrior pieces serve to reinforce cultural ties among members of the audience. Enjoying the humor portrayed in the comic pieces strengthens social bonds among relatives and neighbors. Kinship unity is created when three generations simultaneously belong to the *seinenkai* and collectively perform. Participating together either as performers or as viewers creates harmony between the young and old.

Intermission is a social occasion: people share food that they have brought and all enjoy the company of those around them in the festival atmosphere. As communal entertainment, *nōmai* performances promote conviviality and social unity.

## AESTHETIC VALUES

*Nōmai* dance drama is an expression of medieval folk performing traditions and the initial combining of ritual and entertainment in a single presentation. This aesthetic has its basis in Shinto ceremonies, featuring music and dance as entertainment to deities that are invoked with the intent of appeasing them and receiving their favor. The ceremonial and prayer pieces form the solemn and sacred portion of a *nōmai* program, while the warrior and comic pieces provide humor and entertainment. Evangelizing *yamabushi* cultivated this aesthetic. They turned toward existing folk performing arts, both sacred and secular, as a means of capturing the attention of the provincial population, devising repertoires that were both didactic and entertaining.

Shintoism and Buddhism are both sources for the sacred symbolism and aesthetic value found in folk performing arts of the medieval period. In *nōmai* these two aspects occur particularly in the ceremonial and prayer dances which feature: (1) choreography linked to ancient ritual practices, including sacred objects held in the hands of dancers; (2) the use of folk Shinto instrumental music and the Buddhist vocal style to accompany and enhance the ritual aspects of the dance; (3) the employment of symbolic hand gestures associated with Shugendō and ritual magic; and (4) song texts borrowed from both Shinto and Buddhist sources.

Aesthetic parameters include the mode of presentation, which for *nōmai* is derived from music and dance forms of Shintoism, Buddhism, and the secular *sarugaku* tradition. Elements of folk Shinto music include the musical accompaniment provided by flute, drum, and cymbals and the melody of the *hairi no uta* song, which is reminiscent of *kami uta* or deity songs. Folk Shinto dance emerges in the reenactment of a portion of the *Heavenly Cave Door* myth in "Torimai," and the appropriation of dance movements from the *shishi kagura* tradition in "Gongenmai." Buddhist influence is evident in the singing style and melodies employed in *nōmai* songs and the ritual stamping in "Gongenmai" and "Kanemaki."

The mode of expression is also an important aesthetic aspect. The emphasis on subtlety, obliqueness, and implicitness of the classical performing arts in Japan is absent in *nōmai*; instead a certain spontaneity, exuberance, boldness, and directness is characteristic (Befu 1971: 177). The aesthetic of classical theater is the result of the refined sense of the Ashikaga shoguns who served as primary patrons of *sarugaku nō*. The Japanese aesthetic of melancholy, sadness, and suffering, however, is present in *nōmai*. Examples of this aesthetic are evident in the parting scene of the warrior Suzuki and his mother in "Suzuki," and the portion of "Kanemaki" that depicts a young woman slowly losing her sanity as she attempts to complete the 1000-day austerity required in order for her to become a nun at Kanemaki temple. The Japanese term *mono no aware,* which is best defined as feelings of melancholy mixed with some sadness, more accurately describes this aesthetic, and it reflects the theory of fatalism among Japanese and their attitudes toward a harsh natural environment. It must be understood that the psychological state of unhappiness is not the issue in *mono no aware*, but the aesthetic appreciation of this mood.

The aesthetic value of the musical accompaniment to the ceremonial and prayer dances lies in its connection to dance and drama and to the sacred ideas of the local people. Within the context of the *nōmai* tradition, the sound of the flute, drum, and cymbals embodies the belief that music is sound that originally emanated from the *gongen* deity. The aesthetic perception and appreciation of this music is a remnant of medieval culture when the nexus of music, dance, and drama served to express the provincial population's sacred beliefs.

In contrast, music accompanying the warrior dances is based on a different aesthetic related more to the appreciation of dance as storytelling rather than the dramatization of ritual. Japan's rich historical accounts of famous warrior heroes were popular sources for entertainment in the medieval period. The audience's familiarity with these historically based narratives shaped its appreciation of the accompanying music. The music helps to create excitement in the warrior dance dramas by being played in a faster tempo than in the ceremonial and prayer pieces, giving the music a more spirited feel.

The aesthetic value of the comic pieces, which have minimal music, is predicated on its recreational function and the humor featured in the satirical vignettes of rural life. Coupling of the entertaining warrior and comic pieces with the sacred, symbolic nature of the ceremonial and prayer dances reflects the aesthetic paradigm, mentioned earlier, of combining the sacred and the profane in a single program.

## NOTES

1. "The Big Problem of Training Flute Players," *Tōnippō*, article 33157, no. 2 (April 2, 1984), p. 10.

2. *Aruku junjo* for specific dances will be presented in more detail in Chapter 5.

3. Possession does not actually occur in "Gongenmai." Instead, this dance is a symbolic, presentational enactment of possession that represents the invocation and descendance of the *gongen* deity.

4. Specifically, Buddhist rituals that were performed by special groups of monks, introduced in Chapter 2, called *hozushi*.

5. The interlacing and crisscrossing choreography is equated with the movement leading toward possession (Hoff 1978: 70).

# 5

# A View From Within: Performance Practices

Describing the setting and practices of a *nōmai* performance brings this tradition to life and gives us a closer view of the performing art itself. The preceding chapters described the historical background and function of *nōmai* within communities. This chapter presents information on where performances take place, descriptions of what elements compose a *nōmai* dance drama, the organization of music and dance within the structure of pieces, and details about when performances are given. One section introduces *nōmai* dance, since the study of the dance and its relationship to *nōmai* music is essential in creating drama. Most of the information focuses on the village of Shishipashi, although the practices of other villages are sometimes cited to complete or enhance details of a performance.

## PERFORMANCE SITE

The location of a *nōmai* performance varies according to the event and the space available in each community. Full-length performances during New Year's celebrations are invariably held at community assembly halls.[1] Performances in most villages used to be held at the home of the caretaker (*betto*) of the village shrine. An inner room, sharing a wall with a larger room, served as the backstage area, while the larger room provided the dance area and audience space. With the advent of community assembly halls after the Meiji period (1868-1912), these halls accommodated growing audiences for performances as the villages grew in population.

The performance site for the spring and fall festivals continues to be the village shrine. The worship hall of a shrine or shrine grounds outside serve as the dance site for these festivals. The relationship of Shinto shrines and *nōmai* melded considerably after the Meiji Restoration. This relationship resulted because of the anti-Buddhist policies of the Meiji government, which forced the closure of Buddhist temples and the shift by *yamabushi* from Shugendō to Shinto. Many *yamabushi* became Shinto priests and lived at shrines.

The shorter ritual *nōmai* performance, called *buchi komi,* is still held at the *betto*'s house. This occasion is not public and is attended only by members of the *nōmai* association. The final New Year's performance (*makuosame*) in Shishipashi is also held at the village shrine as a closed affair attended by *seinenkai* members.

## STAGE LAYOUT

The traditional stage layout includes a dance area and a separate backstage area called *gakuya* (see Figure 5.1). A curtain serves as a backdrop to the dance area, separating it from the backstage area. The traditional size of the dance area is three *tatami* [2] mats, a rectangular area approximately six feet wide and nine feet long. With the development of dances that incorporated more vigorous movements, however, a larger dance area of four and a half to six *tatami* is now necessary.

Within the backstage area, the *seinenkai* enshrines two wooden lion's heads, called *gongengashira*. One is the younger manifestation of the Kumano *gongen* deity, or *gongensama* (honorific term for *Gongen*) and the other is the old Kumano *gongen,* or *inkyōsama* (retired master). Both sit in a recessed alcove (*tokonoma*) or a shelf, traditionally called a *shinza*, a divine place or a place where a deity may reside. In Shishipashi the recessed alcove located in the backstage area serves as the shinza.[3] Placement of the wooden lion's masks in the area where dancers don their costumes and prepare to perform corresponds to the sacred belief that a *nōmai* dancer who emerges from the backstage area is an incarnation of the Kumano *gongen* (Inoura 1963: 1117).

The backstage area marks a sacred space. The curtain separating the dance area from the backstage is called *shikimaku* (ceremonial curtain). Shishipashi beliefs affirm the sacred character of the curtain. Inhabitants believe that the curtain is a manifestation of the Kumano *gongen* deity and the *makuosame* performance is a ceremony thanking the curtain deity for the care and protection of the villagers.

As in many dramatic traditions, the backstage area, or *gakuya*, is where the performers put on costumes and masks and prepare for their entrance onto the dance area. It is also where the flute player and singers position themselves. As discussed in chapter 4, the reason the flutist and singers assume this location is that, in olden times, their music was perceived as the voice of the Kumano *gongen* deity. In dramatic forms prior to *sarugaku nō,*[4] singers and flutists performed from the dance area. In the case of *nōmai,* the musicians play from behind the curtain to create the effect of the music emanating from the dancers, who are, according to sacred beliefs, possessed by the Kumano *gongen* before entering onto the dance area. Their possession symbolizes the presence of the deity itself (Inoura 1963:1117). From behind the curtain, the musicians view the dancers through open slits (*nozoki ana*) in the horizontal seams of the curtain. This allows them to follow the movements of the dancers and perform the music accordingly.

The other musicians—at least three *tebiragane* (cymbals) players and one *taiko* drummer—sit in front of the curtain around the perimeter of the dance area. The *tebiragane* players place themselves at stage right facing into the dance area, while the *taiko* drummer performs at stage front center facing the curtain. This positioning allows the musicians to rhythmically synchronize the music with the dance. Because both the *taiko* and *tebiragane* players provide the rhythmic foundation of the music, it is important for them to fully view the dancers and for the dancers to receive cues from them in successfully syncronizing the dance and music. As the rhythmic leader, the *taiko* drummer also accentuates dance movements. The positioning of the *taiko* drummer in stage front is also important in the comic pieces, in which there is dialogue between this musician and the main

**Figure 5.1 *Nōmai* Stage Layout**

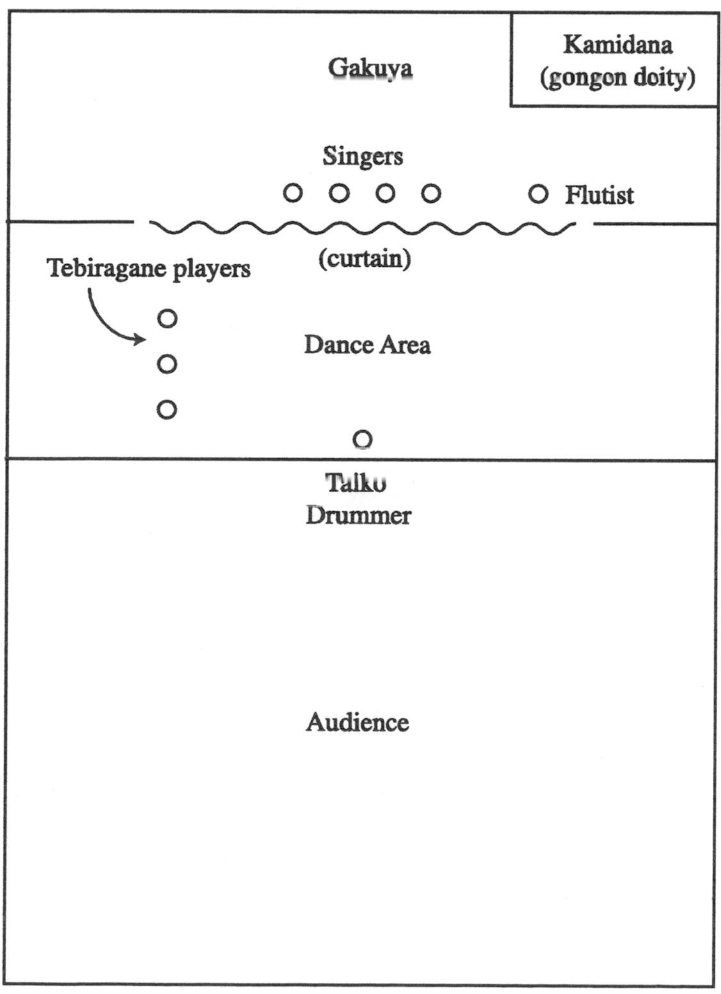


Source: *Higashidorimura no nōmai* 1984 : 8

comic character. Because the percussionists in front of the curtain would drown out the sound of the backstage musicians, microphones, placed behind the curtain, amplify the singing and flute playing.

The audience sits primarily in front of the dance area. Important people in the community, special guests such as officials from the government district office, and contributors or benefactors of the *nōmai* association are usually seated to the side on stage left.

The following description of the connection between the dance area, audience, and backstage area represents practices formed in Japanese drama during the medieval period. These practices became standardized in drama of the latter part of the Tokugawa period (A.D. 1600-1868). Inoura proposes that the dance area, the audience, and the backstage area, with the *shinza* as its center, form one unit (see Figure 5.1). Accordingly, since the backstage area can be viewed as the *shinza* itself, the integration of the three areas establishes a relationship between the audience, the dancers, and the Kumano *gongen*. It can be speculated that the audience comes in contact with the deity through the mediation of the artists. The presence of dancers from among people of the community was also the pretext to combine dance and audience areas. The tripartite relationship of the three areas, however, gradually became obscured by the increased emphasis on *modoki* (comic parody), which was incorporated into many folk performing arts after 1600. The element of parody diminished the seriousness of the sacred connection between the audience, dancers, and deity.

## DANCE

Dance is the most central element of a *nōmai* performance. For the audience it is visually the most entertaining component. The fact that titles of *nōmai* pieces often add the word *mai* ("Torimai," "Okinamai," "Sanbamai"), meaning "dance," substantiates *nōmai*'s roots in dance.

### Origin of Japanese Dance

Japanese dance traces its origins to ritual. As described in the myth of the *Heavenly Cave Door*, the goddess Ame no Uzume danced upon an overturned tub in her efforts to entice the sun goddess, Amaterasu, from her hiding place in a cave. The fact that this myth traditionally serves also to explain the origin of music (the rhythm of Ame no Uzume's dance steps) points to the inseparable relationship of music and dance in Japan. The *Heavenly Cave Door* myth is an interpretation of *tamafuri* and later *tamashizume* (spirit quelling) rituals of ancient *kagura*, which expressed the ancient concept of death and the belief in resurrection and healing through magic and trance. Through the magicoritual of dance, man was believed to have the power to summon, subdue, or drive away the spirit of a human being called *tamashii*. Ikeda Yasaburō implies that the two basic forms of Japanese dance—*mai* and *odori*—are ritualistic embodiments of the *tamafuri* and *tamashizume* funeral rites. He describes the horizontal, quiet, dignified, circling *mai* as originating in the *tamafuri* rite, which later became the basic element of *nō* dance; and the vertical, jumpy, and rather violent *odori* as originating in *tamashizume*, which became a central element in numerous performing arts, including kabuki dance. Ikeda, and Ueda Masāki contend that rituals introduced into Japan by Taoist priests led to the development of *henbai*, a rather violent stamping intended to drive away evil spirits or *kami* (Ikeda 1970: 26, 29, as cited in Raz 1983: 12). The pacification of souls of the dead in the *tamashizume* ritual later incorporated *henbai* (Honda 1974: 195).

A ritual of divine possession called *kami gakari* also includes *mai* and *odori*. Honda describes *mai* as the circular motion undertaken to lead a performer into trance or possession by a deity, and *odori* as an expression of the ecstasy of possession, in which the performer jumps, leaps, and dances using vertical movements (Honda 1983: 100).

Until the 17th century, these two basic Japanese dance forms remained distinctly different. At present, the distinguishing features of *odori* include a dancer who often simultaneously plays a musical instrument or sings, and a dancer whose movements synchronize with the rhythm he himself provides if he is playing an instrument or with some pulse that seems to arise spontaneously from within him. In contrast, the basic source of energy in *mai* lies not within the performer himself, but comes from music or storytelling by other participants nearby. Musically, the difference between *mai* and *odori* is that rhythmic pulsation is central to *odori*, while melody or the flow of sound is the impetus for *mai*. *Odori* is also a group activity in which anyone can participate. It is a dance that has long been a plebian dance form, requiring no special performance place or stage. *Mai*, however, requires a specially qualified performer or small group, and the dances are performed in a restricted place for the enjoyment of an audience (Yamaji 1983: 106).

The dramas enacted in *nōmai* use both *mai* and *odori*, although elements of the former are predominant, as inferred by *mai* in *nōmai*. The basic *mai* posture for *nōmai* dance is similar to that of *nō* dance, in which correct posture comes from the proper placement of the pelvis. This placement involves holding the stomach and buttock muscles inward, slightly bending the knees, and directing the whole pelvis forward and down while holding the spinal line of the torso straight. The *nō* and *kyōgen* actor Nomura Shirō has described this as a counter-balancing relation between the front of the pelvis, which is pulled down, and the back, which is pulled up. The head and neck should also be held straight as a natural extension of the torso (Berberich 1984: 207-208).

Dance sequences are quite complex and can be divided into smaller individual patterns, such as rice-scattering (to purify) or manipulation of a kimono sleeve, fan, sword, or other object held in the hand. Fluid movements and gestures of the head and arms lead to postures and poses, called *kata*, that are held momentarily before continuing. Accents in movements of the feet are created by first placing the edge of the heel on the floor forming a forty-five degree angle, and then stepping. The following sections describe dance movements characterizing various dance types.

### Ceremonial Dances (*Gireimai*)

Dancing in the pieces "Torimai," "Henzai," and "Okina" all exhibit elements of *mai*. The quiet and dignified movements of *mai* suit the sacred and solemn character of these dances. The influence of *mai* is most obvious in "Torimai." Symbolically, the dancers, portrayed as birds, function as mediums, and the dance depicts spirit possession. The idea of "Torimai" as a kind of ritual possession is supported by Hoff, who proposes that the circular movements of the dancers in patterns arranged along coordinates in the four directions may be a form of worship in the four directions associated with the shamanic-derived dance of priestesses (see Figure 5.2). He admits that there is a paucity of evidence supporting his proposition, but he contends that circular patterns may be characteristic of movements that occur prior to possession (1978: 170). This idea coincides with the associations of *mai* to the *kami gakari* ritual of spirit possession.

In his analysis of traditional Japanese dance, Honda states that *mai*, originally intended to lead one into trance, was later refined and fixed into the dance now known as *mikomai* (shrine maiden dance). He also points out that the original purpose of leading one into trance has changed into one of dance as prayer. Such dances are at present performed by *miko* (shrine maidens) at Shinto shrine festivals as a means of increasing the religious content of the festivals (1977: 269-281).

The influence of *bugaku*, a type of *mai*, is apparent in *nōmai*. Features of this dance form elucidate the style of the three ceremonial dances mentioned above. As in *bugaku*, symmetry is a dominant feature of "Torimai." The two dancers mirror one another's movements; if a movement is done to one side, it is often repeated to the opposite side. The position of the dancers, and the choreographic formations in these ceremonial pieces, achieve a geometric effect even in "Okina" and "Henzai," which are performed by one person (see Figure 5.3). Ceremonial dance movements are symbolic and interpretive. They involve manipulations of a kimono sleeve or prop held in the hands of the dancer. The abstract and formalized movements of these dances most likely had some meaning and expressed a particular idea or quality, but the original meanings have been lost and movements are now modified and stylized. As in *bugaku*, the portion of dances performed to the slow musical accompaniment of the *hayashi* consists of slow stamping steps. The adhesive quality of the sliding steps emphasizes the force of gravity and gives the dance a sense of weight and solemnity (Wolz 1965: 91).

Enactment of a portion of the *Heavenly Cave Door* myth in "Torimai" is an example of dance as an expression of myth. The mythological characters featured in this dance are two birds whose calls were heard just before the sun goddess emerged from the cave. By imitating this auspicious event—alleviation of the eclipse of the sun caused by the hiding sun goddess—in the *Heavenly Cave Door* myth, "Torimai" is intended to ensure a favorable year ahead for the village. The efficacy of "Torimai" is rooted in the belief that dance in imitation of myth aids the divine powers in the battle between death and regeneration (Immoos 1977: 36).

**Figure 5.2 "Torimai" Choreographic Pattern**

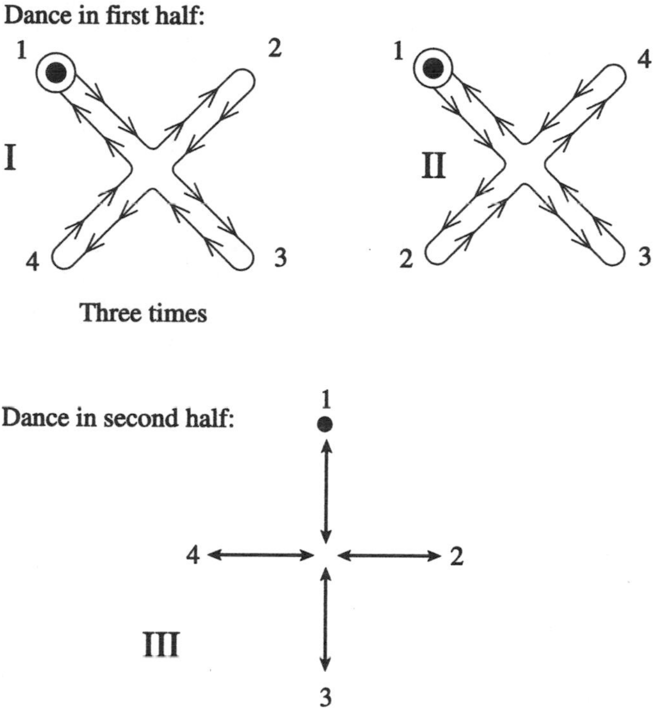


**Figure 5.3 "Okina" and "Henzai" Choreographic Pattern**

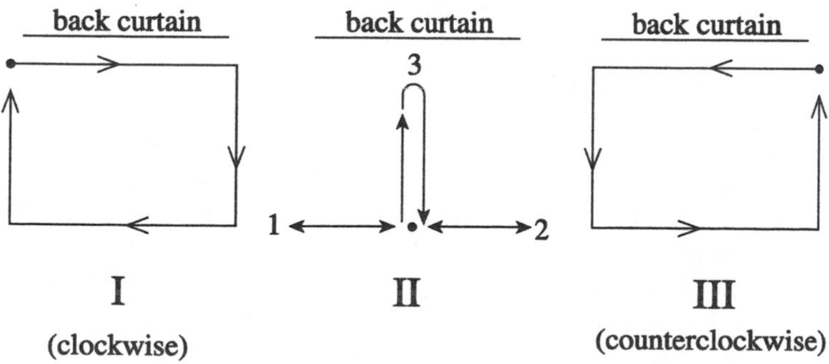

The ceremonial piece called "Sanba" contrasts with the above dances by being based not on *mai*, but on the *odori* form of Japanese dance. The dancer performs running, frog-like leaps, back-bending and other acrobatic movements in a geometric pattern in which he alternates moving toward the four directions from a central point on the dance floor (See Figure 5.4). The active movements operate to portray the main character, Sanba, as a young boy, and the choreographic pattern fulfills some sacred meaning associated with shamanism. The dance ends with Sanba sitting on his knees in front of the curtain at the back of the dance area, facing the audience. He directs symbolic hand gestures, called *mushofushi in* [5] (see Figure 5.5), toward the audience, while moving his arms from left to right in a semicircular motion. Next, he clasps both hands with the index and third fingers pointing toward one another in a gesture called *kuji* [6] or "nine realms." With his hands in this mudra-like position, the dancer makes criss-cross motions in midair, creating invisible lines in a grid-like pattern representing an esoteric Buddhist gesture of magic known as *kuji o kiru.*[7] These ritualistic hand gestures are remnants of *yamabushi* beliefs and magical practices in esoteric Buddhism which were incorporated into *nōmai*. They add sacred meaning to "Sanba" and can be interpreted symbolically as displays of spiritual power or energy. *Yamabushi* were known for their spiritual powers to heal and exorcize, and the display of these powers in "Sanba" can perhaps be tied to the intent of this dance as one of regeneration and renewal, an extension of the "Okina" dance of renewal and blessing.

The ceremonial dances are structurally binary. The choreography is the same for both halves, but the tempo of the *Sagari ha* accompanimental piece played by the instrumental ensemble in the first half is slow, while the *Kiri* accompaniment in the second half doubles in tempo. This creates a change in mood: the *Sagari ha* music in the first half is a slow, solemn flow of sound for the elegant and graceful dance, while the fast tempo and bright sound of the *Kiri* accompaniment energizes the dance and brings the piece to an exciting climax. The use of masks in "Okina" and "Sanba" emphasizes the binary structure of these dances. In the first half the dancers do not wear masks; for the second half, however, masks delineate the main characters of the two pieces: the old man, Okina, and his son, Sanba.

The use of masks may be attributed to the close association between masking and shamanism, where the mask becomes a means for attracting to the performer the god it invokes (Honda 1974: 195). In "Okina," the old man's white mask is considered the abode of the divine form of Okina. In the first half of the dance, the performer appears unmasked and still fully mortal. At the very moment the mask is put on, however, he becomes the divine Okina: an act of primeval transformational magic. The old man as a divinity identifies the dance as a ceremonial benediction calling down peace and prosperity for the entire village. The intent of this dance derives its meaning from blessing ceremonies that have been performed at the Wakamiya shrine in Nara for 1,300 years (Immoos 1977: 37, 39). Use of the black mask in the second half of "Sanba" dramatizes the story of the death and rebirth of Okina's son. Masks are not worn by dancers in either "Torimai" or "Henzai." Both pieces are examples of early *kagura* dances in which masks were not worn.

**Figure 5.4 "Sanba" Choreographic Pattern**

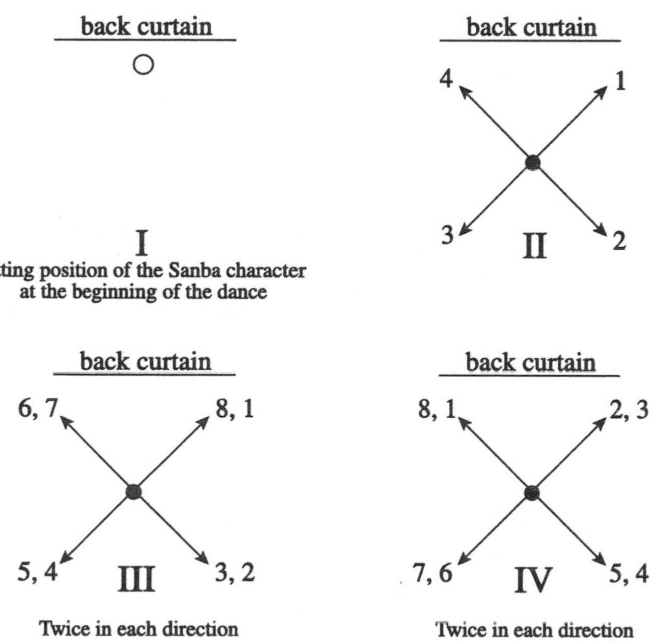


**Figure 5.5 *Mushofushi in* Symbolic Hand Gesture**

The sacred intent of the ceremonial dances involves the use of certain properties, which assist in the method used to invoke the gods. An object held in the hand of the dancer serves as a temporary place for the invoked god to alight (Honda 1983: 99). In "Torimai" each dancer holds a black, lacquered tray filled with uncooked rice grains, which they sprinkle on the dance area as a symbolic act of purification. As a dance of purification, "Torimai" establishes favorable conditions for calling down the gods, and *nōmai* performances invariably begin with this piece. The Buddhist sistrum (*shakujō*), held in the left hand of each dancer, is symbolically shaken to attract the attention of the deity being summoned.

"Henzai" is also a dance of purification intended to rid the Okina mask from any impurity before it is donned by a performer in "Okina," performed next. The mask is placed on a black, lacquered tray held in both hands by the dancer. Another prop ubiquitously used in all the ceremonial dances is a white fan, which symbolically represents the seat or abode of the gods. All of these props identify the ceremonial dances as a method of praying for the descent of gods. Within the choreography of each dance, objects held in the hands of the dancer act to embellish hand and arm movements.

**Prayer Dances (*Kitōmai*)**

These dances contain elements of the prayer dances that were once performed as purely ritual events by *shushi* priests. These rituals, recorded in documents dating back to the Heian period in the 11th century, featured *henbai* or ritual stamping. Records reveal that the dances were especially associated with several large-scale ceremonies held annually in Buddhist temples. In the repertories of *yamabushi kagura* and *bangaku*, *henbai* was refined and choreographed into staged performances. In *nōmai,* manifestations of this restrained form of stamping are seen in the dance "Gongenmai," which *yamabushi* performed to exorcize malevolent spirits (Honda 1974: 195).

Like other dances, "Gongenmai" has a binary structure. The first half features a solemn dance referred to as *shitamai*, or "Bangaku." "Bangaku" is one of the most basic dances in *nōmai*. Its stately choreography is modelled after the two ceremonial dances "Okina" and "Henzai" and is similar to the dances by women and priestly characters. The second half features a symbolic possession of the dancer by the *gongen* deity. The possession takes place while the dancer manipulates a wooden lion's head mask, the temporary abode of the deity. "Gongenmai" is stylistically freer and more theatrical than other *nōmai* dances in its use of the lion's head. The choreographic pattern is the same as the first half, but the dance is performed by two dancers. The first manipulates the wooden lion's head with both hands and performs a series of turns that are punctuated by a snapping movement of the lion's jaw. This snapping motion symbolizes the removal of evil from the community. The second dancer, called *otori* (tail), assists by holding the lion's body, a long cloth attached to the wooden head, and twisting the cloth to prevent it from getting tangled as the first dancer performs his movements.

Several choreographic turns, alternated with ritual stamping, compose a portion of the dance where the main dancer and his assistant synchronize their movements as they proceed in the choreographic pattern provided in Figure 5.3. Each stamping step is accentuated by a rhythmic snapping of the lion's jaw in the following rhythm:

The dance reaches a climax when the dancer manipulating the lion's head enacts being possessed by the *gongen* deity. In becoming the *gongen*, the performer raises the lion's head above his own and lets the attached cloth body fall around him, covering him completely.

Next, the figure of the lion sits in front of a small table set up as an altar and performs a series of symbolic acts of exorcism. First, he alternates taking a Buddhist sistrum and rosary in his mouth. He then enacts the *yamabushi*'s magical gestures of *kuji o kiru*. Completion of the divine purification occurs when the lion removes the sistrum from its mouth and uncooked grains of rice are thrown at the lion as a gesture of purification. "Gongenmai" ends with the two dancers and the leader from the young men's association facing each of the four directions together. The leader holds a symbolic offering tree, called *bonden*, which he shakes in each of the four directions. This finalizes the symbolic purification of the village and everyone bows their heads in reverence to the *gongen* residing in the lion's head.

The other prayer piece, "Kanemaki," features four different dances. The first is a stately dance of the steward of Kanemaki temple. This dance is identical to the choreography of "Henzai" and "Okina." The main character in "Kanemaki" is a young woman who performs a slow dance referred to as *onnamai* (women's dance). The choreography of this dance is based on the first and third sequences of the dance pattern in Figure 5.3, in which the dancer first forms a square in a clockwise direction and then double tracks in a counter clockwise direction. *Onnamai* falls under the *mai* form of dance. It involves taking a step forward, pausing for one beat, taking a step with the opposite foot, and pausing for another beat. The sequence of this stylized walk is repeated until the rectangular outline of the dance is completed twice. A second sequence of movements involves the dancer taking steps, in the same style, while moving from the center of the stage to the stage left corner, where an assistant winds a piece of cloth (symbolizing an offering) onto a wood spindle (see Figure 5.6). This sequence is followed by the dancer taking backward steps, in the same stylized manner, away from the stage left corner as the cloth is unwound. The dancer performs this sequence of winding and unwinding the cloth ten times. The slow tempo of this dance makes it difficult to perform the above movements smoothly and gracefully.

The next two dances feature the *yamabushi* character. His special stage entrance and first dance belong to the warrior dance category discussed in the next section. In this dance, like that of "Sanba," the *yamabushi* starts out in a central spot and dances outward in the four directions (see Figure 5.7). The *yamabushi* performs this portion of the dance kneeling on one leg. The sequence is repeated four times.

**Figure 5.6 "Kanemaki" Choreographic Pattern**

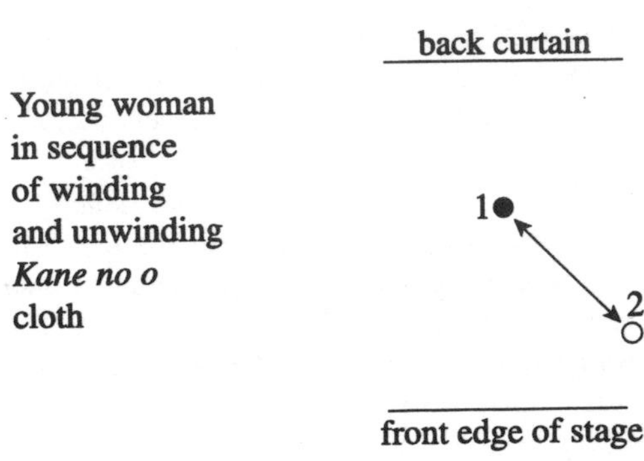


**Figure 5.7 Dance of *Yamabushi* Character**

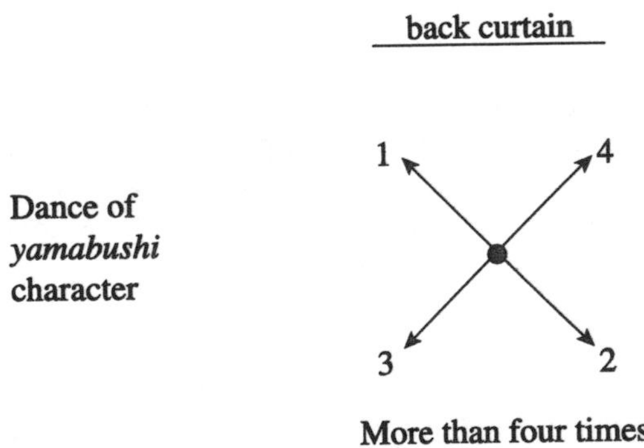


The fourth dance in "Kanemaki" is a duet dance of exorcism between the *yamabushi* character and the young woman, who now appears as a demoness, resulting from the severity of the 1000 days of ascetic training required to become a nun at Kanemaki temple. The choreographic pattern is the same as that of the *yamabushi*'s dance in Figure 5.7, but with the addition of a second dancer who mirrors his dance movements. Symmetry is maintained throughout by the two dancers. For example, there is a sequence in which the demoness hovers over the *yamabushi*, followed by the priest hovering over the demoness. The final portion of the dance features the *yamabushi* standing over the demoness, exorcising her with the *mushofushi in* hand gesture and the rubbing of Buddhist rosary beads.

### Warrior Dances (*Bushimai*)

Sources of dance movement in the warrior dances include *kōjakumai* (a type of acrobatic dancing), *nō* dances based on stories of warriors, and folk kabuki of the local region in which *nōmai* developed. Folk kabuki, in particular, had a great influence on these dances and many postures, poses, and gestures were adopted from this genre.

The predominant structure of warrior dances is binary. The dancer performs without a mask in the first half of a piece, called *hirumae* (morning or forenoon), depicting the warrior in his youth. Performance of the second half, or *hirukara* (afternoon), requires the dancer to don a mask, and is a danced version of the battle scene in which the warrior hero displays his valor. In contrast with the unmasked performance in the first half, the use of a mask in the second half dramatically enhances the action being narrated. Dancers manipulate a white fan and sword in the fighting sequences and stances. When the sword is not in use, it is worn on the left side of the dancer's body, held in place by a sash worn around the waist, and the dancer positions his left hand on the top of the sword handle as he dances. The accompaniment of both singers and the *hayashi* in a section called *utagakari* creates drama at the end of the second half. This thickening of the texture builds tension and brings the piece to a climax. The *bushimai* pieces "Shinobu," "Yashima," "Soga," "Kiso," "Watanabe," and "Jūbangiri" are all based on the binary format. Two pieces that do not follow this format are "Suzuki" and "Kurama," which are one-act pieces without the second *hirukara* portion.

The choreography consists of a series of movements that lead into poses or stances, called *kata*, which the dancer momentarily holds before the next dance movement. There are eight *katas*, named according to the position in which the white fan is held in the hand of the dancer: *kake ogi, tate ogi, sashi ogi,* two types of *haji no byōshi, mukai sashi, okuri sashi,* and *kakomi*. These poses are equivalent to *mie* in kabuki dance. Other stances, such as the *ejiki* and *niodachi* gestures seen in "Suzuki," are also incorporated into the dances.

Combinations of dance movements leading into the *katas* form three different sequences. Two are danced during the *makudashi* sections of the piece, accompanied by the *hayashi* or the singers, while a third is performed for the *makuzuki* section, accompanied by only the *hayashi* (see Figure 5.8). The fast tempo of the *kiri* instrumental accompaniment creates excitement and momentum in the *makuzuki* section.

"Kurama" is atypical for a warrior dance in that its choreographic sequence depicts a battle between two well-known warrior heroes. The sequence is of a series of stylized fighting gestures that are formally named as follows: (1) *ushiro kikake*, (2) *taregakushi* (two forms), (3) *jodan,* (4) *ashibiki*, (5) *kumiuchi* (two

**Figure 5.8 Warrior Dance Pattern**

*Makudashi* sequence:

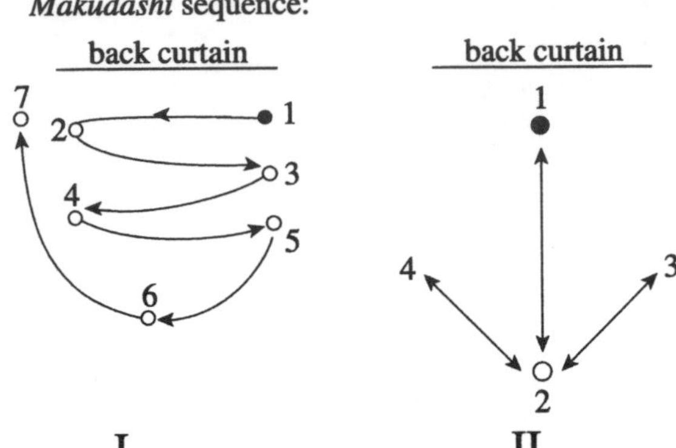


*Makuzuki* sequence:

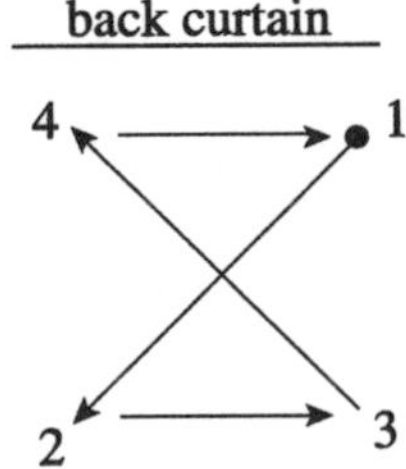


forms), (6) *kata otsuke*, and (7) *mae kikake.* Wood sticks, representing a type of halberd called *bō,* are the weapons manipulated in this fighting sequence. Mirrored movements of the two dancers in this series of gestures create choreographic symmetry. The formal designation of fighting gestures in this dance, as well as the poses in warrior dances in general, were evidently adopted from folk kabuki dance. The bold movements of kabuki dance are a distinct feature of the warrior dances. Borrowed elements from folk kabuki reinforce the characterization of *nōmai* as being more theatrical than *yamabushi kagura*, which is comparatively more subdued and ritualistic.

A distinctive dramatic feature of warrior dances is the unusual fashion in which the dancer enters the stage from underneath the back curtain. The series of movements performed by the dancer in the special stage entrance begin with: (1) standing with both feet firmly planted and spaced apart behind the curtain and holding the stage curtain up to the middle of his chest with both hands; (2) stamping his right foot and shifting his weight onto the right leg before stamping his left foot, then shifting his weight to the left leg and raising the right foot up to the knee of the left leg and; (3) kicking his right foot out to the right and stamping, followed by shifting his weight to the left leg again and lowering his pelvis. The dramatic entrance continues with the repetition of steps two and three; this time, however, the dancer begins by raising the left foot to his right knee, placing his weight on his right leg, then kicking his left foot out and stamping. Next, the dancer pulls the curtain with both hands, first to the left then to the right, followed by taking a step backward, first with his left foot, then his right foot and moving forward, stepping first with his right foot, then with his left foot, then again with his right foot, quickly lifting the curtain and completing a ninety-degree turn upon entering the stage with his whole body and landing on his left knee facing the curtain. The strong movements of this entrance pattern display the virility of the warrior characters. Stage entrances of *nōmai* dancers from underneath the stage curtain are a custom of relative antiquity, derived from rituals and now embodied in *yamabushi kagura* repertories (Hoff 1978: 169). Entering the stage from the sides of a curtain or stage, as seen in *nō* drama and other dramatic forms, is a later development.

### Comic Dances (Dōkemai)

The final category of *nōmai* pieces are the comic dances, or featuring humorous dialogues between the main comic character and the drummer who joke about people in the immediate community, situations, or some other matter ripe for ridicule. Comic characters perform gestures mimicking country bumpkin figures, rather than actual dance movements. Movements of the male comic characters include swinging the arms and legs and occasionally stamping to punctuate their sentences or otherwise emphasize the buffoonery taking place.

Some of the comic pieces in the repertoire—"Warabi ori," "Tengyō," and "Kitsunemai"—incorporate *onnamai* (women-character dances). The play, "Nenzu," includes *oiwake* folk dance at the end performed by people in the audience who are brought to the dance area by comic characters to dance in a circle. The audience participation in "Nenzu" is a unique feature enjoyed by all.

## ORGANIZATION OF MUSIC AND DANCE

The music and dance sections within a single *nōmai* piece occur as follows:

1. *Gobyōshi no iri*—the standard instrumental introduction played by the *hayashi*—*fue, taiko,* and *tebiragane*.
2. *Hairi no uta*—an introductory song which narrates the context, background, or story of the particular dance drama. The song begins, overlapping with the *hayashi* which continues to play the *gobyōshi no iri* instrumental introduction.
3. *Makudashi*—a song accompanied by *taiko* and *tebiragane* only. During or immediately following this section, the dancer enters the dance area from behind the stage curtain.

4. *Shitamai* (also *jimai*)—a dance section accompanied by the entire *hayashi*. The dancer sometimes emits *kakegoe* (punctuated calls).
5. *Makuzuki*—a song (sometimes called "Shamon," "Shamon-datte," or "Samadatte"). In many pieces, the dancer reposes at the back of the stage, fanning himself during the singing of this text. In some pieces, *shosa* (posturing and gesturing dance movements) are performed during this song.
6. *Makuiri*—an instrumental postlude played by the *hayashi*.

These six major sections form the basic structure of the dance dramas. Of course there are many variations of this format. The older ceremonial dances "Torimai" and "Henzai" do not include all of these sections. Then there are pieces which repeat certain sections, forming lengthy dramas that are divided into two distinct halves. Dialogue, a later addition to *nōmai,* is also added to the format in "Kurama" and "Watanabe." Finally, comic dances have their own structure, featuring dialogue between the comic character and the drummer or another comic character, with a section or two of dance.

This structural format features three primary instrumental compositions played by the *hayashi*: *gobyōshi no iri, sagari ha,* and *kiri. Gobyōshi no iri* serves as the opening statement of a majority of the pieces. *Sagari ha* is a slow instrumental piece that functions as accompaniment for both the dance of women characters and the choreography in the first halves of "Okina" and "Henzai." In the warrior dances, the fast-tempo *kiri* accompanies the *shitamai* sections of many pieces. *Kiri* is played particularly quickly when depicting battle scenes of heroic warriors. In addition to these instrumental pieces, the dance sections in the ceremonial piece "Sanba" and the comic piece "Kitsunemai" require special instrumental compositions (Kojima, 1965: 97). Special music also accompanies the songs for "Okina" and "Kanemaki." This additional music adds variety to the pieces.

Each of the song sections—*hairi no uta*, *makudashi*, and *makuzuki*—also have standard melodies, although special melodies are sung in certain pieces, such as "Kanemaki." The song melodies at times overlap with the instrumental accompaniment. Since the instrumental music and song melodies are performed in different modes, this practice results in a bitonal musical texture, a practice heard in *nagauta* music of the kabuki theater.

The arrangement of song, dance, and instrumental sections varies according to individual pieces. *Gireimai*, or ceremonial pieces, contain the most variables in format, while the warrior pieces, for the most part, are uniform and almost formulaic. The outlines of four representative dance dramas, two from the ceremonial repertoire and one each from the warrior and prayer categories, illustrate the various ways the dance dramas combine music and dance. I chose to outline the structure of two ceremonial pieces because of the importance of this category as the earliest and most representative type of dance drama in the original *nōmai* style.

The first piece, "Torimai," is one of the oldest pieces in the *nōmai* repertoire.

Its simple structure may reflect the older character of *yamabushi kagura* before the incorporation of the dramatic elements that now pervade *nōmai*:

1. *Gobyōshi no iri*—introductory instrumental composition.
2. *Hairi no uta* text—sung and overlaps with the latter portion of the *gobyōshi no iri,* which rhythmically changes and quickens in tempo. Two dancers enter the stage one by one and begin dancing the specific choreography for "Torimai."
3. Bridge—an instrumental bridge passage is played by the *hayashi*. Singing of the *hairi no uta* ends. The dance continues.
4. *Shitamai*—dance accompanied by the *kiri* instrumental composition.

The ceremonial piece, "Okina," is a symbolic dramatization of longevity and a prayer for abundant crops and the welfare of a community. This is a fairly long piece that is divided into two parts as follows:

**Part l**:

1. *Gobyōshi no iri* instrumental composition
2. *Hairi no uta* text—sung and overlaps with the latter portion of *gobyōshi no iri*, which quickens in tempo.
3. *Makudashi* text—sung without musical accompaniment.
4. *Shitamai*—dancer enters the stage and begins dancing to the *sagari ha* instrumental piece.
5. Bridge—*hayashi* plays an eight-beat musical passage.
6. *Shitamai*—the dancer shifts his movements to a faster tempo to synchronize with the faster *kiri* instrumental accompaniment.
7. *Makuzuki* I song text—sung without musical accompaniment; dancer exits the stage.

**Part 2**:

1. *Gobyōshi no iri* instrumental composition
2. *Shitamai*—*kiri* composition accompanies the dancer who enters the stage wearing the Okina mask, sits on the floor, and then stands to dance.
3. *Makuzuki* II song text—sung without musical accompaniment; the dancer rests at back center of stage.
4. *Shitamai*—*kiri* composition accompanies the dancer, who resumes dancing.

The outline of these two *nōmai* plays demonstrates the variances found in the format of the ceremonial dances. The warrior dances, in contrast, are more uniform in the progression of song, dance, and instrumental sections. The following is an outline of the warrior dance called "Shinobu":

1. *Gobyōshi no iri* instrumental composition
2. *Hairi no uta* text—sung and overlaps with the latter portion of *gobyōshi no iri.*
3. *Makudashi* I text—sung without musical accompaniment.
4. *Shitamai—kiri* instrumental composition accompanies the dancer who enters the stage and begins dancing. The dancer is unmasked for this section. He also occasionally emits *kakegoe.*
5. *Makuzuki* I text—sung without musical accompaniment. The dancer rests at back center of stage.
6. *Shitamai—kiri* instrumental composition accompanies the dancer who resumes dancing. Dancer exits stage.
7. *Makudashi* II text—sung without musical accompaniment.
8. *Shitamai—kiri* instrumental composition accompanies the dancer who reenters the stage wearing the mask of Shinobu.
9. *Makuzuki* II text—sung to the accompaniment of a *hayashi* composition particular to "Shinobu." The dancer changes to a different dance with movements that synchronize with the slower tempo *hayashi* music.
10. *Shitamai—kiri* instrumental composition accompanies the dancer who resumes the dance of the above *shitamai* sections while twirling a sword.

The last piece outlined in this section is "Kanemaki," a prayer dance that is essential to the repertoire and actively performed by all *nōmai* groups. "Kanemaki," a drama that extols the merits of Buddhism, is closely associated with *yamabushi* who created *nōmai.* Three characters are introduced: a steward of Kanemaki Temple (*betto*); a young woman who, on her religious pilgrimage to shrines and temples throughout Japan, becomes enchanted with Kanemaki Temple and decides to begin the austerities required to be a nun there; and a *yamabushi* who exorcizes the young woman-turned-demon due to the insufferable harshness of the 1000-day austerities. This piece is long and contains many sections. Special melodies are heard and much of the text is chanted, interspersed with phrases in heightened speech.

**Part 1:**
1. *Gobyōshi no iri* instrumental composition.
2. *Hairi no uta* text—sung to the latter portion of *gobyōshi no iri.* The *betto* character enters the stage and dances.
3. *Shitamai—sagari ha* instrumental composition accompanies the character of the young woman who enters the stage and dances.
4. *Makuzuki* text—sung to a special rhythm played by the *tebiragane* and *taiko* without flute. The dancer continues the dance, which symbolically depicts the young woman's attempts to complete her austerity training.
5. *Shitamai* of the young woman—the *hayashi* switches to the *kiri* composition. Singing of the *makuzuki* text ends.

**Part 2**:

1. *Gobyōshi no iri* .
2. *Hairi no uta* text—sung in tandem with the latter portion of the *gobyōshi no iri* composition.
3. *Makudashi* text—sung without musical accompaniment.
4. *Shitamai—kiri* instrumental composition accompanies the *yamabushi* character who enters the stage and dances.
5. *Makuzuki* text—sung without musical accompaniment. The dancer rests at back center of stage.
6. *Shitamai—tebiragane* and *taiko* rhythm heard in section 3 of part 1 above accompanies the *yamabushi* character who resumes dancing. Singing of the *makuzuki* text continues. Dance of the *yamabushi* character becomes more ceremonial. Dancer emits *kakegoe,* giving the dance more vigor. The young woman-turned-demon character enters the stage, and the choreography of her struggle with the *yamabushi* character ensues.
7. *Shitamai—kiri* instrumental composition provides the accompaniment. Dance of the *yamabushi* character and the young woman-turned-demon character continues. The last line of the *makuzuki* text is repeated over and over, bringing the drama to a climactic ending.

These pieces are carefully structured as dramatic presentations of sacred ceremonies, tales of heroic warriors, or didactic plays. Instrumental music, sung narration, and dance are effectively alternated to provide variety or combined to build intensity and drama.

## MASKS

Realism is created in *nōmai* through the use of masks, costumes, and props. The use of masks in Japanese theater can be traced back to *gigaku,* which featured masked dances, pantomime plays, and pageants. Masks became more widely used with the introduction of *bugaku* in the 7th century. In *kagura,* a major influence on *nōmai,* the widespread use of masks is relatively recent and limited to the entertainment portion of ceremonies intended to be offerings to the gods (Ortolani 1984 : 179).

Masks used in *nōmai* function to prepare the dancers in portraying various characters. "Dancers as artists and performers," Mr. Ōta expressed, "are expected to act out the character represented by the mask they are wearing." When dancers wear masks it helps to build their confidence, since they believe that the masks belong to the Kumano *gongen* and will therefore prevent them from making mistakes. Performers must memorize all the movements of a dance before practicing with the mask on, since wearing one restricts their vision and makes it difficult to judge their movements spatially. Mr. Ōtsuki of Iwaya commented that "it takes a good dancer to make the character of a dance come alive while wearing the mask—this is how a dancer is judged. So wearing a mask is important in assuming the role of a character and portraying a character to the fullest."

Most of the *nōmai* pieces require masks to provide realistic presentations of the character being featured. The pieces not requiring masks are those that focus on the enactment of a myth or ritual, rather than a particular character. Masks, for example, are not worn for the two ceremonial dances, "Torimai" and "Henzai," since the enactment of ritual purification in the former and the presentation of offerings to the deity in the latter is of primary importance, rather than the character performing the action. In "Okina," "Sanba," and all the warrior dances, masks serve a specific dramatic function. These pieces are divided into two main dance sections. A dancer performs unmasked for the first half, which represents the character's youth; in the second half, however, a mask is worn to depict the mature years of a character's life. In lieu of masks, makeup is worn by the dancer portraying the warrior-priest Benkei in "Kurama" and the warrior Watanabe in "Watanabe."

The donning of masks for the comic pieces enhances the comedy in exaggerating the foolish countenance of the character. Masks also help to realistically portray women characters, since *nōmai* is performed only by men. Other *nōmai* masks include ones for depicting demons, old men and women, the chief priest in the piece "Tauemai," and the fox in "Kitsunemai." The use of masks in *nōmai* is effective for creating realism. It corresponds to the art of *monomane*, a Japanese concept of mimesis that developed in various folk theatricals during the 13th and 14th centuries (Ortolani 1984: 171).

Masks are categorized according to the dance in which they appear. In Shishipashi, all the characters have individual masks except for those used in the comic pieces. In communities whose mask collection is small, there are single masks commonly used for many characters, such as one for all women characters and perhaps two for all warrior characters. All *nōmai* groups, however, have special masks for "Okina," "Sanba," and "Kanemaki," since these pieces are of a sacred nature and each of the masks has unique features.

Shishipashi's masks distinguish themselves as being of the same style, supposedly, as the original *nōmai*-style masks. All of the masks are carefully carved and lacquered, making them precious cultural treasures. Mr. Ōta mentioned that they are not considered valuable if they are repaired or altered, and are thus left in their present condition. There are no records of how old the masks are, but Mr. Ageji of Ōri and Mr. Ōtsuki of Iwaya surmise that many of theirs are at least one hundred years old. The fact that masks of certain characters are recognizable among the collections owned by various *nōmai* groups supports the existence of a definite style and method for making these masks.

In comparing *nōmai* masks to *kagura* masks, those of *nōmai* have stronger features, said to be an influence of *yamabushi* and the ascetism of Shugendō. *Kagura* masks, in contrast, are more somber in taste and are indicative of a style that became popular in later forms of drama after the medieval period. Inoura suggests that the features of both, despite their present differences, can perhaps be traced to those of Mibu *kyōgen* [8] masks (Inoura 1963: 1120).

The wooden lion's head, or *gongengashira*, is also a type of mask. Within the dance "Gongenmai," the lion's head symbolizes the presence of the Kumano *gongen* deity. Such use of a mask can be traced back to the art of *monomane*, which introduced masks to represent various deities and spirits (Ortolani 1984:172). As a mask, the *gongengashira* is not worn on the face but is held in both hands and rhythmically manipulated in a series of dance sequences. The lion's head is an example of theophany, in which masks of real or imaginary animals serve as visible manifestations of a deity. Strong animals such as lions, leopards, tigers, bears, crocodiles, deer, and bison were theophanic models to prehistoric man, who held these animals in awe for their might and prowess.

In prehistoric times, the totem animal was all important for the life of a clan. Man and clan, totem and ancestors, were all one. Totem animals were believed to possess *mana* power—the power of the elemental forces of nature embodied in an object or person. People chose strong animals as totems, since the *mana* power of the clan was understood to reside in the animal. Clans as well as individuals continually drew upon totems for new power. The shaman who put on the skin and head of an animal was the predecessor of the actor in costume and mask. Wearing the mask of the totem animal transformed the shaman into a deity, enabling him to "partake in the cosmic process" (participation mystique), and to use the deity's supernatural powers for the welfare of the clan.

Later on, mask and costume were simplified and stylized, but the wooden mask that replaced the real head is still regarded as the *tamashiro*, the receptacle of, and a real, not symbolic, presence of a deity (Immoos 1969: 407). The *gongen* makes its presence known in "Gongenmai," which usually concludes a *nōmai* performance, with a mighty clapping of its jaws and quick movements of its head in an expression of joy at having been entertained by all of the dances that preceded it.

The role of the lion's head is also important in *kado uchi,* in which the *gongen* deity is conjured to purify and bless all the homes in a community. Two *gongengashira*, the young *gongensama* and the older *inkyōsama* are carried from house to house, but only the young *gongensama* is employed for presenting an abridged version of "Gongenmai." From the preceding, it is clear that the *gongengashira*'s function as a mask is to represent the embodiment of the Kumano *gongen* deity, who is invoked for various acts of purification as well as for purifying the *nōmai* dance area and audience members at the beginning of performances.

## COSTUMES

Dancers don various types of garments and headgear to portray different characters. Materials now used for costumes include silk and cotton for the robes; yarn intertwined on pieces of stiff material, such as cardboard, to simulate the front and rear plates of a warrior's armor; and, for the hats, cloth pasted over ten or more layers of paper, which is then covered with several layers of lacquer. Two or three layers of a costume is customary: one or two layers of underwear and a formal outer garment, a *hitatare*[9] or kimono. To complete the costumes dancers wear hats of differing shapes and sizes that indicate the social status of the character being portrayed.

Costumes worn for the ceremonial dances are similar to those used in *kagura*, since the dances are borrowed from that genre. A garment called *kariginu*[10] (ancient official's robe) is worn; in many *nōmai* groups, this costume is often just a formal and elegant kimono worn over a *hakama*[11] (men's formal divided skirt). The hats used depend upon the particular dance: an *eboshi*[12] (noble's hat) is worn for "Henzai," a *tate eboshi*[13] (high noble's hat) is worn for "Okina," and either an *eboshi*, *tate eboshi*, or *chōtate eboshi*[14] (head noble's hat) is donned for "Sanba." For the piece "Torimai," dancers wear two unique *eboshi* with a figure of a rooster affixed to the top of one and a hen attached to the top of the other, with large flaps that hang down on both sides. These hats serve to portray the dancers as the chickens in the origin myth of this *kagura* dance. Even though the traditional color of the various *eboshi* is black, other colors are seen, perhaps for theatrical effect, such as the gold *tate eboshi* used by some groups for "Okina." In Shishipashi, a blue-gray color is used for the hats in "Torimai," and the two-dimensional figures of chickens attached to the top are hand-painted in an assortment of colors. The hat for "Sanba" is invariably black and is distinguished by a crest, consisting of a gold circle and two gold stripes both above and below the circle, and placed on both sides of the hat. Performers wear Japanese-style socks, called *tabi*, for the ceremonial dances. The costumes and hats in these dances closely match those worn in similar dances found in the folk *kagura* repertoire.

The costume worn for the dance "Bangaku" in the first half of the prayer piece "Gongenmai" includes a *hakama* worn over an informal kimono or *montsuki* (formal black kimono bearing one's family crest), *tabi*, and a white *hachimaki* (white headband tied around the head). For the *gongengashira* used in the dance in the second half, a rectangular piece of cloth is attached to represent the body of the lion. The dancer, who eventually transforms into the *gongen* deity, drapes his head and body with this cloth while holding the lion's head above his own to depict the transformation.

Characters in the warrior pieces have specific costumes that are traditionally fixed for separate characters. A suit of armor called *yoroi* is the central garment worn. Two or three layers of various garments include an under kimono (*juban* or *hadagi*); a robe with tightly fitting sleeves (traditionally called *teppo* but now referred to as *habaki*); and the suit of armor on top. A silk sash worn around the waist holds a sword and scabbard in place on the dancer's side.

*Eboshi* are used for most warrior characters. *Tate eboshi* are specially worn by the high-ranking warrior in "Watanabe" and the woman warrior in "Tomoe." Their family crests are affixed to both sides of the hat. In Shishipashi, special armor is used for the main characters in "Watanabe," "Tomoe," and "Kurama." In creating the illusion of a warrior's helmet, a gold-colored *kuwa* is attached to an *eboshi* to represent the metal ornamental piece placed on the front of warrior's helmets during feudal times. The combination of garments and hats used for warrior characters varies according to the wardrobe available in each *nōmai* association.

The costumes of women characters vary according to their age and rank. Women characters wear full-length outer kimonos called *kinagashi* or kimono jackets called *uchikake*. The kimonos of young women are usually colorful and have bold designs, while those of older women are more subdued in color and design. A wide silk sash (*obi*) is wound around the middle of the torso and tied in front.[15] A black cloth is draped on the head to represent hair, while small tufts of hair are worn as a wig on the sides of the face. For the women characters in "Kanemaki" and "Tengyōmai," a gold-colored crown headpiece, called either *tenkan* or *yūraku*, is placed atop the cloth hairpiece to signify their upper rank. The women's costumes in some of the associations are the oldest. They are also, in some cases, the most valuable, since they are expensive to replace.

The costumes for the comic plays have changed somewhat as the old-style garments have worn out and been replaced with more modern attire. For male comic characters, a loincloth-like apron made from a padded material (*dotera*) was once considered standard. Other old-style costumes included an article of underwear, called *mijiga*, worn from the waist down, and a short coat, made from coarse cotton and tied with a sash, called *nunokogi*. Inoura asserts that the old-style costumes are prototypes of clothing dating from before the Meiji period (1963: 1124). Today, thermal underwear used for leggings, a kimono-style short coat tied with a sash (similar to the traditional *nunokogi*), and sometimes an informal *hakama* are worn by male characters. Their headgear consists of a cloth that wraps around the head with long pieces that hang on either side of the face, tied with a headband. Costumes for female comic characters have changed little. An informal kimono with a wide sash tied in front is standard.

## PROPS

The use of small stage properties also enhances the sacred value and realism of *nōmai* performances. A *shakujō* [16] (priest's staff) is held by dancers in the ceremonial pieces, by the *betto* and *yamabushi* characters in "Kanemaki," and by the dancer in "Gongenmai." The woman character in "Kanemaki" holds a *heisoku* (Shinto offering of cut paper). The dancer in the first half of "Gongenmai" and the mother character in "Suzuki" hold a *juzu* (Buddhist rosary). A *katana* (long sword) is worn and manipulated in dance movements of all the warrior pieces to depict a warrior in battle. A wood rod used by the warrior Benkei in the fighting scene in "Kurama" is a simplified version of a halberd said to have been used in the training of warrior-priests. From the lyrics of the song sung for "Kurama," it is evident that such a *halberd* was used in the actual fight between the two well-known warriors Benkei and Ushiwakamaru.

Other typical props include: (1) a four-foot wood rod, representing the oar of the boatman, in the comic play "Warabi ori"; (2) a small black wood carving in the shape of a cow's head to depict the riding beast of a man, also in "Warabi ori"; (3) a desiccated bear's arm to represent the arm of the demon in "Watanabe"; (4) some type of prop to serve as a foxtail in "Kitsunemai"; (5) a long piece of cloth manipulated by the dancer and wound around a square piece of wood with a handle to symbolize an actual *kane no o*[17] in "Kanemaki"; and (6) a gold-plated square of wood, approximately 8.4 inches in length and width, with a handle approximately 1.2 feet long and the Japanese characters *kinsatsu* (prohibition notice board) written on it, used to ward off the devil in "Watanabe."

The use of props is minimal, but they are visually and sometimes symbolically important in enhancing the drama.

All the dances except the comic pieces include the use of a white paper fan held by the dancer. A white fan is customary, although Mr. Ōta pointed out that in Shishipashi a special gold paper fan is used together with a *shakujō* for the prayer dances because the dance is offered to the Kumano *gongen* deity. In the warrior dances, the fan is a traditional component of a warrior's garb. Many movements utilize the fan in various postures that accentuate the bold movements characterizing the virility of warriors in battle. The use of a fan is customary in the Shinto ritual of divine inspiration or possession in *kagura*. Scholars suggest that the use of the fan in *nōmai* ceremonial dances may actually be based on the Shinto idea of the possessing spirit residing temporarily in the object held by the performer. This idea connects to the "deeply-rooted Japanese belief in shamanic possession and the consequent veneration for the temporary abode of the possessing spirit." (Raz 1981: 10-11). A white fan has additional symbolism. It is called *suehirogari* or *suehiro*, which emcompasses the meanings "develop" and "future." A fan is considered an auspicious object because of the association between the structural design of a fan and the concept that it suggests of "developments (folds of the fan) leading to one's future." From this interpretation, the use of a fan in the ceremonial dances symbolizes good fortune and blessings.

## AUDIENCE REACTION AND BEHAVIOR

An audience's rapport with performers relates to the genre's sacred origins. In sacred forms of folk performing genres in Japan, such as *nōmai,* spectators are generally part of the ritual. Proposed earlier was the idea that the backstage area where the *gongen* deity is enshrined, the dance area, and the audience are an integrated whole, establishing a relationship between the villagers in the audience and the Kumano *gongen* itself. Although this relationship is now obscured due to the addition of secular influences such as folk kabuki, it is intrinsically the basis for the close ties between the audience and performers that still exist today. During a performance of "Gongenmai," for example, the stage curtain is lifted to expose the backstage area, where the singers sit facing the audience. This action integrates the audience, dance floor, and backstage area as a prerequisite to summoning the *gongen* deity; united, the people in the three areas receive the deity.

The fact that the performers are residents of the community and the audience essentially consists of their relatives and neighbors reinforces their connection. Audience members hold similar sentiments and interest toward the dancers, creating an important support system for performances. One way in which audience support is expressed is through a custom in which individuals in the audience make monetary donations (*hana*) to the *nōmai* association. While a dancer is performing, money wrapped in a handerkerchief or *furoshiki* (piece of cloth used to wrap and carry objects) is thrown onto or brought to the stage. This custom offers opportunities for individuals to express their appreciation of a dancer's skill, show support for a dancer if he is a relative, or to provide encouragement for young men who are performing a particular dance for the first time in public.

Audience reaction and behavior during performances is participatory and active. When one walks into the community assembly hall where performances take place, the amount of audience activity is striking. As in many folk performances in other parts of Asia, such as the *wayang kulit* (shadow puppet plays of Indonesia) audiences are not strictly attentive, since the event is also a social one in which people converse with one another and children play. People constantly come and go during *nōmai* performances. They converse with their friends and relatives, mothers chase after their babies, shouts are heard from children playing in the back of the hall, and teenagers congregate. The attention of the audience to the performance drifts in and out. It is not constant and intensive.

Spectators do, however, actively respond to performances. Dancers receive enthusiastic ovations for their bravado performances. I also witnessed shouting and cheers for a skilled dancer during a performance of "Kanemaki." When the young dancer came out on stage as the popular *yamabushi* character, the crowd cheered and clapped in response to the enthusiasm and energy of the performance. Every time the dancer held a pose and emitted a robust "*ya haaaaa...*" the crowd responded. Other judgmental responses are the jeers and laughter heard when performers forget their lines in plays that contain dialogue. During the presentation of the warrior dance "Watanabe," for instance, the performer who portrayed the demon disguised as Watanabe's nursemaid elicited a response of hilarity and ridicule to the lines of dialogue he forgot, to his amusing speech imitation of an old woman, and his other actions on stage resulting from his not being able to see too well with a mask on. Audience reactions in general are spontaneous and supportive. Disapproval is subtle and more likely to be expressed by not clapping and not offering monetary contributions.

Audience behavior correlates with both the religious and entertainment functions of *nōmai* performances. Reactions and accompanying behavior correspond to the intent of specific pieces. For the solemn and sacred ambience created by the ceremonial and prayer dances, audiences exhibit more reverential behavior than for the warrior and comic pieces that are intended as entertainment. The symbolic and abstract choreography of the older ceremonial dances elicit less of a response than the theatrical and heroic performances of the warrior dances or the humorous slapstick of the comic pieces. The strong bond between performers and their audiences in small villages like Shishipashi reflects the unity and cooperation, both economically and socially, that exist among members of the community. Traditionally, these ties are spiritual as well. Audience responses to performers are social interactions that strengthen the social and familial bonds of everyone in the community.

## OCCASIONS FOR PERFORMANCE

Several occasions call for *nōmai* performances. During the New Year's season, the young men's association traditionally makes several formal public appearances in their *makubiraki* (curtain opening), *makuosame* (curtain closing), and *kado uchi* (door-to-door) performances. The first two appearances are usually full-length events lasting up to six hours. The third is a ritual in which the prayer dance "Gongenmai," performed at the door of each house in the village wards off evil for the coming year. Other occasions for performance include Haru Matsuri (Spring Festival), Aki Matsuri (Fall Festival), dedication ceremonies for newly built houses, called *shinchiku*, and the annual concert of the Higashidorimura Native Folk Performing Arts Association. *Makubiraki*, *makuosame*, Haru Matsuri, Aki Matsuri, *kado uchi*, and *shinchiku* are all traditional occasions, while the Performing Arts Association's concert is a contemporary context created twenty years ago for the purpose of preserving *nōmai*. In this joint concert, all thirteen *nōmai* associations perform for one another, creating competition among the groups. This has revitalized the tradition and helped to uphold performance standards.

The first *nōmai* performance during the New Year's season is the *makubiraki* event that, according to Mr. Ōta, serves as a ceremony to the Kumano deity in requesting the care and protection of the community. Not all *nōmai* associations give *makubiraki* performances and those that do set their own dates.

The next *nōmai* event during the New Year's season is *kado uchi*, a carry-over of the New Year's tradition in which *yamabushi* of local Shinto shrines visited villages to collect contributions.[18] *Yamabushi* collected contributions after performing a prayer dance that exorcised a home from evil influences. This was part of the old system of support that shrines received from communities.[19] Today, the young men's association practices this tradition. Younger members of each association usually take responsibility for this activity.

*Makuosame* is the next *nōmai* performance during the New Year's season. Each village sets the designated day for this event. It is traditionally a ceremony thanking the Kumano *gongen* deity for the care and protection of the community. *Makuosame* is also the time when the Kumano *Gongen* returns to the village shrine or *betto*'s home. Mr. Ōtsuki mentioned that the *nōmai* association in Iwaya performs the *kagura* dance "Kami okuri" (sending away the gods) to symbolize the return of the deity. Villages also present auspicious dances for this occasion, such as "Kitsunemai," "Suzume oi," "Ebirisuri," or "Ebisumai." "Kitsunemai" (fox dance) is especially propitious in Higashidorimura, where all villages do some farming. The fox represents Inarisama, the god of the rice plant, and the dance symbolizes hope for a bountiful harvest in the year to come. *Makuosame* performances feature such dances, since they signal the final *nōmai* presentation for the New Year's season.

Brief *nōmai* performances provide entertainment for the spring and fall festivals at the shrine of a village's guardian deity (*ujigami*). In Higashidorimura, both festivals are closely bound to the agricultural cycle of planting and harvesting. In many villages, rice cakes (*mochi*) and *saké* are offerings given to the guardian deity as a ritual during the spring festival in hopes for favorable crops and during the fall festival as a thanksgiving for plentiful harvests.

Although Shishipashi does not present *nōmai* as part of the spring festival, other villages such as Iwaya perform the prayer dances "Kami okuri" (their designation for the dance commonly known as "Bangaku") and "Gongenmai," as well as some folk *te odori* dances. The fall festival appears to be a more important event and many *nōmai* associations perform as part of the festivities. Mr. Ōta mentioned that the Shishipashi group used to perform *nōmai* for this event when, according to the lunar calendar, it fell during the farmer's slack season. At present, fall festival performances are omitted, since adapting the festival schedule to the Gregorian calendar sets the event almost one month later, falling during the time farmers are busy. Groups that do perform during the fall set their own date for the festival. The pieces chosen by *nōmai* groups for this event vary, although the prayer dances "Gongenmai" and "Bangaku" remain standard.

Another traditional occasion requiring a *nōmai* performance is *yagatame*,[20] a dedication ceremony for newly constructed houses. *Shinchiku* (new construction) is the ritual for this event. All *nōmai* associations enact the *shinchiku* ritual for newly built homes in their respective communities. The set dance is "*Mōtari*," although slight variations of this name exist; in Shishipashi, "*Mōtari*" is called "Modaru." Even if a house was completed in the earlier part of the year, the New Year's season, considered auspicious, is the time reserved for *yagatame*.

The Higashidorimura Native Folk Performing Arts Assembly is the most recently created context for *nōmai* performance. It is held annually in January as a joint concert organized by the Higashidorimura Federation for the Preservation of the Native Folk Performing Arts, whose membership includes all the *nōmai* and *kagura* groups in this area. The assembly features performances by many of these groups, which perform one piece each. The concert also includes interludes of *te odori* folk dances and lasts up to seven hours. The federation was created by Mr. Ōta of Shishipashi, with the intention of maintaining *nōmai* and *kagura* in Higashidorimura.

## NOTES

1. Community assembly halls are multipurpose and often function as schools (usually kindergarten) and meeting places for various community groups.

2. *Tatami* are thick rectangular mats made of tightly woven rice-straw covered with woven rush grass with the edges bound in cloth. The standard dimensions of these mats are six feet by three feet and two inches thick. They are used as a standard of measurement for Japanese-style rooms.

3. Placing the two *gongengashira* in the backstage area is believed to be the original practice. A different arrangement is seen in the villages of Iwaya and Shiriya, where a single *gongengashira* is placed on a *kamidana* (deity shelf). In Iwaya, the *kamidana* is affixed to a wall above the curtain separating the dance and backstage areas, in full view of the audience. The idea of placing the *gongengashira* where it can be seen by the public is considered to be a later development. It is suggestive of the Buddhist custom of placing an image of Buddha in a position in the temple where it can be seen from above or through an opening of the *sanmon*, a large two-storied gate situated at the entrance of all temples. The placement of only one *gongengashira* on the *kamidana*, as practiced in Iwaya and Shiriya, is also considered to be a recent practice.

4. *Sarugaku nō* was a theatrical art performed by villagers in services at the festivals of temples and shrines from about 1300 to 1450. This genre was a later development of

*sarugaku*, a performing art imported from China that included song and dance, acrobatics, magic, and conjuring. In the tenth century, *sarugaku* became *shin sarugaku* (new *sarugaku*), a performance of fragmentary songs, dances, and imitative acts of various kinds, characterized by the emphasis of speech and action. *Shin sarugaku* matured further into the dramatic form of *sarugaku nō*. A program of *sarugaku nō* consisted of ceremonial music and dance, dramatic plays, comic plays, a prayer dance of exorcism, and various other pieces from the allied arts (Inoura and Kawatake 1981: 9, 11, 65-66).

5. *Mushofushi in* is formed by joining the palms of the two hands; the middle, ring, and little fingers are raised and touch at the ends. A space is left between the hands. The indexes are flexed and at their tips they join the thumbs, which are erect side by side. To this grouping of the fingers the following symbolism is applied: the erect fingers represent the six Original Substances; the thumbs and index fingers designate the Three Mysteries (*sammitsu* )—word, thought, and body (action)—which form the Triple Unity, the basic principle of Esotericism. This mudra is peculiar to Dainichi Nyōrai, the supreme principle of esoteric Buddhism, and is known as one of the gestures of the ultimate mystery of Dainichi (Saunders 1960: 115).

6. *Kuji o kiru* is a gesture that symbolizes the Buddhist concept of the "nine realms" derived from Taoism. The "nine realms" refer to realms of the three worlds: (1) the world of desire, whose inhabitants have appetite and sexual desire; (2) the world of form, whose inhabitants have neither appetite nor sexual desire; and (3) the formless world, whose inhabitants have no physical form. The world of desire is equivalent to the realm of the present physical world. The world of form consists of four realms of "meditation-heaven," and the final formless world is equivalent to four realms of "heaven" (*Japanese-English Buddhist Dictionary* 1979: 185, 252).

7. *Yamabushi* used *kuji o kiru* when they wanted to concentrate their power. This ritualistic gesture of magic was introduced to *yamabushi* through the Shingon Buddhist sect, which adopted many rituals first used in Taoism. *Yamabushi* interpreted *kuji o kiru* as a stance between this world and the universe. In creating this gridlike configuration in midair, the vertical lines are created before the horizontal lines.

8. Mibu *kyōgen* was a folk theatrical performed in the compound of Mibu Temple in Kyoto. It featured pantomime plays that were either comic, religious, or historical (Malm 1974: 106).

9. A *hitatare* is an ancient court garment worn by warriors on ceremonial occasions.

10. *Kariginu* literally refers to a hunting garment. It was an informal robe worn mostly by nobles or court officials in the Heian period (794-1192).

11. A *hakama* is a divided skirt similar to culottes that reach to the ankles. It is worn only over a kimono on ceremonial occasions chiefly by men. Nowadays, it is rarely used other than at traditional wedding ceremonies or festivals.

12. An *eboshi* is a black-lacquered, brimless hat worn by nobles or those holding rank from the Nara period (710-794) to feudal times.

13. A *tate eboshi* is slightly taller than an *eboshi* and it was worn by noblemen or court officials to designate a higher rank.

14. A *chotate eboshi* is even taller than a *tate eboshi* to designate the top rank of the person wearing it.

15. In ancient times, Mr. Ōta relayed that an *obi* was tied in the front. Before the Genroku period (1688-1703), young women used to tie it in back, while married women

wore it tied in front or on the side. In the latter half of the Edo period (1600-1868), an *obi* was worn tied in back only until the age of thirty. After the Meiji period (1868-1912), the custom of the *obi* tied in front remained in costumes worn by geisha (professional entertainers) or prostitutes.

16. A *shakujō* is a staff of a Buddhist monk. It was one of the eighteen possessions of a monk. As paraphernalia peculiar to *yamabushi*, the *shakujō* used in *nōmai* is a shortened version of a priest's staff and includes only the top portion. Metal rings are affixed to the top ring forming a rattle.

17. *Kane no o* is a long, thin piece of cloth with stuffing inside and it is attached to a hanging bell placed in the front entrance of a temple or shrine and pulled to activate the bell.

18. *Yamabushi* were forced to make their living as Shinto priests during the Meiji period (1868-1912) due to the Japanese government's ban on Buddhism, forcing the closure of Buddhist temples.

19. A certain percentage of what was collected would go to the main shrine in the area and the remainder was kept by the branch shrines.

20. *Yagatame* is believed to have originated from a dance of exorcism, called *hogotame*, which is performed in *sarugaku nō*. The dance was intended to be a prayer to subdue the evil spirits in the four directions on the occasions of divine rites and the dedication of new houses. According to the *Suzuka Monjo* (Document of the Suzuka Family), *hogotame* is cited to be a piece in the repertoire of *miko sarugaku* of Kasuga Shrine in 1349 (Inoura and Kawatake 1981: 66).

# 6

# Sacred Chronicles, Tales of Valor, and Humorous Yarns: Repertoire

The *nōmai* repertoire derives from that of the more ancient *yamabushi kagura*. The oldest and most central compositions of *yamabushi kagura* are the ceremonial and prayer dances that date back to the middle of the 13th century. In the 14th century, archaic comic dances were added to increase the entertainment value of this folk drama. The adaptation of warrior dances, depicting the valor of warriors in battle or other heroic or tragic undertakings, further enriched this form of *kagura* in the 15th century (Inoura and Kawatake 1981: 75-76).

In chapters 2 and 3, I noted that scholars coined the term *shugen nō* to refer to the theater genre developed by *yamabushi*. In this chapter the appellation *yamabushi kagura* takes precedence over *shugen nō* for several reasons. First is the claim made by Zeami in his writings, connecting the origin of *sarugaku* to *kagura*. In following this connection, as discussed earlier, theater scholars hold that *nō* theater originated in the shamanistic music and dance of Shinto (*kagura*). *Shugen nō* as a particular form of *nō*, therefore, derives from *kagura*. Another argument favoring the designation *yamabushi kagura* is the fact that central pieces in this genre derive from that of folk *kagura*, again pointing to *kagura* origins. Finally, the *ennen* dance that *yamabushi* learned as part of their training is thought to issue originally from the Shinto *chinkon* funeral rite. One could say the designation *shugen nō* changed to *yamabushi kagura* as the genre continued to evolve in the regions of Iwate and Aomori prefectures and passed on to the local people. All these aspects support Honda's use of the term *yamabushi kagura*.

*Nōmai* emerged in the first half of the 17th century as a type of *yamabushi kagura*. This accounts for *nōmai*'s shared repertoire with this older form of *kagura*. As *nōmai* evolved, changes in the repertoire occurred. Gradually omitted were dances depicting mountain gods, which are now retained by *okajishimai* folk performers in Higashidorimura. Some dances were added, such as the comic dance "Kitsunemai" (Fox Dance) and the prayer dances "Sanbon guchi" and "Kenmai." These two prayer dances, however, are rarely performed. Another change, according to Japanese folklorist Yamaji Kōzo (1983), is the influence of kabuki theater in the warrior pieces. Other than these alterations, the repertories of *yamabushi kagura* and *nōmai* are fundamentally the same.

## TRADITIONAL CATEGORIES OF PIECES

Traditional categories of the *nōmai* repertoire distinguish four groups. The oldest category is *gireimai*, or ceremonial dances, and they function to purify the performance area and pray for abundant harvests and long life. Five pieces fall into this category:

1. "Torimai" (Chicken Dance)
2. "Henzai" ("Kagomai" or "Senzai")
3. "Okina"
4. "Sanba" ("Sanbasō")
5. "Bangaku"

The second traditional category is *kitōmai*, or prayer dance, which serves to exorcise evil influences, tell stories of mountain gods and Buddhist deities, or give allegorical accounts of *yamabushi*; all are meant to educate villagers about the merits of Buddhism. The two pieces in this category are:

1. "Gongenmai"
2. "Kanemaki"

A third group of dances is classified as *bushimai*, or warrior dances, encompassing eight pieces:

1. "Shinobu"
2. "Watanabe"
3. "Soga"
4. "Yashima"
5. "Jūbangiri"
6. "Suzuki"
7. "Kurama"
8. "Kiso" ("Tomoe Gozen")

The final category is *dōkemai,* or comic dances, embodying eleven compositions:

1. "Nenzu"
2. "Warabi ori"
3. "Tengyō"
4. "Ebisumai
5. "Tsuna hiki"
6. "Kitsunemai"
7. "Nenshimai"
8. "Jizōmai"
9. "Suzume oi"
10. "Ebirisuri" ("Tauemai")
11. "Dekōsuke"

The current repertoire consists of twenty-six pieces in all. There are other prayer dances and comic dances that were originally part of the repertoire, but they are not included here since they are either retained by only one village, or are no longer transmitted or performed at all.

Shishipashi's repertoire does not contain all of the above pieces. They perform all of the *bushimai* dances except "Soga." Out of eleven *dōkemai* pieces, they perform six: "Nenzu," "Ebirisuri," "Warabi ori," "Tengyō," "Nenshimai," and "Kitsunemai." The dance dramas perpetuated by the other twelve villages also differ slightly from the above list, and vary according to their *nōmai* lineage and the popularity of particular pieces.

## CEREMONIAL PIECES

*Nōmai* performances commence with ceremonial dances beginning with "Torimai" and followed by "Henzai" (Divine Protection Dance), "Okina," and "Sanba." These *gireimai* form the oldest and most sacred portion of the repertoire. Traditionally, other pieces cannot begin until these dances are presented.

### "Torimai" (Chicken Dance)

"Torimai" is an enactment of a portion of the *Heavenly Cave Door* (*Ama no iwato*) myth, in which the call of two chickens is heard just before the Sun Goddess, Amaterasu, is coaxed from the cave where she has hidden. From their role in this myth, Mr. Ōta of Shishipashi believes chickens came to be regarded as sacred, particularly in sacred rites performed before *kami*.

To villagers, this dance between a rooster and a hen symbolizes prayer for fertility and new life. "Torimai" is also associated with the Shinto *chinkon* rite, in which spirits of the dead are pacified (Gorai 1972b: 5). In order to be pacified, spirits had to be invoked first. The form of a bird in this dance symbolizes the belief in Japan, as well as other cultures such as Egypt, Greece, and Rome, that the spirit of a deceased person would take on the form of a bird (Immoos 1969: 408).

According to Shinto practices, the invocation of *kami* described in Chapter 2 is called *kami oroshi*, a ritual that forms the basis of ancient *kagura* performances (Ortolani 1984: 176). *Kami oroshi* is related to the phenomenon of *kami gakari* in Japanese shamanism, in which a spirit takes possession of the shaman-medium, usually a *miko*, and through her communicates directly with the faithful (Honda 1960-61: 109). "Torimai" is a type of *kami oroshi*, forming an implicit connection between shamanism and early *kagura* (Immoos 1969: 408).

As an invocation in calling down the spirits, "Torimai" is always presented as the first piece in a *nōmai* performance. It is an elegant dance, carried out with steady stepping movements by two dancers who hold a fan in one hand and a Buddhist sistrum in the other during the first half. *Yamabushi* adapted this Shinto ritual dance from the local region and superimposed the Buddhist *gongen* deity as a manifestation of the ancestor deity that was originally consecrated. "Torimai" is just one example of the coalescence of Shinto and Buddhist elements that characterize *nōmai.*

In the latter half of "Torimai," the two performers enact a request for an abundant harvest of the five grains (wheat, rice, beans, and two kinds of millet). Rice, carried on a tray, is sprinkled on the stage by the dancers (*Higashidorimura no nōmai* 1984: 11).

The costumes (particularly the design of the hats) and choreography greatly resemble those of *bugaku* of Kasuga Shrine in Nara. The adoption of *bugaku* elements occurred at a time when both the court and major Shinto shrines and Buddhist temples shared *bugaku* and other court performing traditions. The fact that masks are not worn by the dancers is evidence of the ancient nature of this dance, since the use of masks reflects the later influence of *sarugaku.*

### "Henzai"/"Kagomai"/"Senzai" (Divine Protection Dance)

"Henzai," also referred to as "Kagomai" and "Senzai," is the second ceremonial piece presented. It is a dance of purification that serves to prepare the dance area for the remainder of the program. Equivalent dances in other genres are "Tsuyu harai," in *yamabushi kagura* of Iwate Prefecture, and "Senzai," in the version of "Okina" seen in classical *nō*. Reference to this ritual is found in the *Konjaku monogatari,*[1] *Nichiren ibun,*[2] and *Kongo myō saisho ōkyō* (Buddhist chant book). In the word "Kagomai," *ka* means add, *go* is translated protection, and *mai* is dance. Literally, the title means "protection by the addition of god's sympathy dance" and is thus referred to as a "divine protection dance."

"Henzai" has Shinto origins, but it is recorded in the Buddhist texts given above. Mr. Ōta describes it as a dance that symbolizes the connection between people and *kami*. Regarding this dance as one created from the heart and mind of the *kami*, people express their thanks and pray for divine protection.

In many Shinto ceremonies in Japan, the day before celebrating is called *yomiya*. On the day of *yomiya* at large shrines, abundant offerings of grain and other goods are presented to *kami* in solemn and large-scale ceremonies. Mr. Ōta believes "Henzai" is a dance version of these ceremonies. The dance is performed by one person; the masks of the characters Okina and Sanba are placed as an offering on top of a small offering stand (*sanbo*) held by the dancer. Offering *nōmai* before the *kami* is a means of praying for the health and safety of the united villagers in the audience. Mr. Ōta related that "Henzai" is a performed ritual, not entertainment.

"Henzai" is danced without the use of a mask and performed in a meditative manner with steps that are also reminiscent of *bugaku* court dance. The choreography includes dancing in the four directions, similar to that in "Torimai," and is said by performers to be a difficult dance, since it consists of a complex number of foot movements that are performed slowly.

### "Okina" (Old Man)

It is difficult to talk about "Okina" as a separate piece, since it is one of three ceremonial dances—"Henzai," "Okina," and "Sanba"—which together form one piece known as "Shiki sanba" or "Okina sarugaku." This composite piece was originally part of the *sarugaku* repertoire, where it featured an actor with an Okina mask, who danced and told stories (*Kabuki jiten* 1983: 76). These dances are said to have been in existence toward the end of the Heian period in the 10th century.

Throughout its history, "Okina" has retained its religious significance. It combines song and dance designed to gain the favor of gods in obtaining peace and prosperity throughout the land and long life for its people (O'Neill 1958: 73).

One of the original purposes of this piece is to ask for longevity. In rice-planting ceremonies of the Heian period, references to the characters of an old man and an old woman were expressions of a wish for long life.

One prototype of "Okina" was included in the *daijōe,* the emperor's enthronement ceremony, and it came to be known as "Inanomi no Okina" (Okina of the Rice Crop). Ritual prayer practiced in ancient agricultural communities by farmers in their hopes for abundant harvests is the source for this court ceremony (Nakamura 1971: 58).

The character of an old man in "Okina" dates back to a custom described in the ancient chronicles. These written sources tell of the conquering of one tribe after another by the early Yamato race of people, until all Japan was united under a single system of laws. It is said the conquered tribes showed their submission to the Yamato court by hanging the bells they used in their festivals on branches of a *sakaki* tree; proclaiming their loyalty and obedience in words of blessing and by performing *kagura*-like songs and dances that had been handed down to them since ancient times. The words of blessing were always intoned by the oldest and most respected man *(okina)* in the village. This tradition, asserts Nakamura Yasuo, is the origin of the Okina role and dance (1971: 56-57).

Closely related to this assertion is Honda Yasuji's analysis of "Okina" as a danced version of a blessing (Hoff 1977: 50). According to Carmen Blacker, the figure of Okina symbolizes a corporate spiritual entity of the "Ancestor," in which all past forebears of the family are believed to be encapsulated. This corporate being is represented by the "beaming, anonymous, and beneficient old man known as Okina" (Blacker 1975: 44). As such a representation, the "Okina" dance gained an auspicious and congratulatory character. "Okina" is, therefore, a celebratory piece for commemorations, special occasions, and for the New Year.

Toward the end of the Heian period, esoteric Buddhism and *shushi* priests adopted the "Okina" dance. Within the Buddhist context, occasions for performing "Okina" included the national celebration of prosperity that took place annually from February first to the third or seventh. In similar celebrations, Okina *sarugaku* served as part of a Shinto ceremony for consoling spirits of the dead at Kasuga Shrine.[3] These religious contexts mark the transferrence of the performance of "Okina" from court ceremonies to temples and shrines, resulting in the Buddhist and Shintoist associations of the dance.

Medieval *sarugaku* troupes participated in festivals and celebrations at local shrines and temples, performing sacred Okina *sarugaku* as a central piece. At this time elements of parody and imitation, called *modoki*, were also added, further enriching "Okina" (Inoura and Kawatake 1981: 50).

Performances of "Okina" changed throughout its development. Prior to the Kōan period (1278-1287), three old men characters were featured: Chichi no jō, Okina, and Sanba. During the Kōan period, the character Enmei Kanja was added, together with the introductory dance "Tsuyu harai." A further development took place in the Okina *sarugaku* performed at Kasuga Shrine, expanding to five segments: (1) *Tsuyu harai* (a young harbinger), (2) *Okina omoto* (a bearer of the mask of Okina, the holy old man), (3) *Sanba sarugō* (interpreter of Okina's dance), (4) *Enmei kanja* (old man character), and (5) *Chichi no jō* (another old man) (Inoura and Kawatake 1981: 66). Until the 15th century, the above style was maintained and transmitted. Gradually omitted were the characters Enmei kanja and Chichi no jō. In the mid-Muromachi period (1338-1573) "Tsuyu harai" became known as "Senzai" and its present-day performance style was established (*Kabuki jiten* 1983: 76).

*Nōmai* preserves the sequence of the three pieces "Senzai," "Okina omoto," and "Sanba 0sarugō." "Henzai" or "Kagomai" is equivalent to "Senzai"; "Okina" is the counterpart of "Okina omoto"; and "Sanba sarugō" is presented as "Sanba."

The "Okina" dance is binary in structure. The subdued and ceremonial first half features a dancer holding a white fan while dancing. When the first half is over, the dancer goes to the rear of the stage, kneels, and juts his head under the curtain into the backstage area to put on the mask of Okina. In contrast to the former half, the humorous facial expression of the donned mask helps in creating a light-hearted, genial atmosphere in the latter half. After the dance is well under way, the audience whistles and points at Okina, saying "ya ya," at which time the dancer leaps off the stage into the surrounding audience. This begins the abduction scene in which Okina kidnaps a child from the audience, creating a commotion sending children running in all directions screaming. The kidnapping scene is the comic portion of the dance, and children who have been kidnapped by Okina are said to grow to be healthy within a year's time (*Higashidorimura no nōmai* 1984: 11-12).

> *Long, long ago there was a person called Okina, not enfeebled but youthful even at the age of one hundred years old, and when he exceeded the age of two hundred years old, was still vigorous. It was at the age of two hundred that Okina had his first child; his joy could not be expressed enough and he was very thankful to the kami. But, since he had a child after he was two-hundred years old, Okina was looked upon with the cold eyes of envy and jealousy by other people. Gradually, even children made fun of him and treated him with contempt. Okina, feeling chagrined, chased the children. After his child was born, Okina's body became suddenly weak, and he was not able to chase after children. Then Okina's child, Sanba, died suddenly before reaching the age of ten, in spite of the attention the child had received. Because of his distress, Okina lost his mind and cried for many days. In his grief, Okina took the corpse of Sanba from the grave, put flesh made from ashes onto the skeleton of his son, placed clothing on the body and held him as though he was alive. Okina was not, however, able to find the jawbone and so made a jaw out of wood (this accounts for the reason the mask of Sanba has a jaw which is separate and attached with a cord on either side). Okina's life came to a close when he prayed to the* kami, *asking it to be merciful by taking his life force and giving it to Sanba.*

> *His request was granted and Sanba came to life and danced a celebratory dance of the human world and the* kami *world.*
> (Ōta 1980: 16-17)

### "Sanba" (Son of Okina)

"Sanba" is the third and final ceremonial dance of the composite "Okina" piece. This dance depicts Sanba after he is raised from the dead through the transference of the life force from Okina. The black color of the lacquered mask conveys Sanba's reincarnation from the soil of the earth. The dancer, in addition to donning the Sanba mask, wears a nobleman's hat and a ceremonial court robe with a white fan held in one hand and a Buddhist sistrum in the other. In contrast to the more serious and ceremonial "Okina" dance, the choreography of "Sanba" is an example of comical *modoki* elements that serve to delight and entertain the audience. The *hayashi* accompanies the dance with a rhythmically lively melody, "Shiokumi," particular to "Sanba."

Hoff proposes that the relationship of "Okina" and "Sanba" is one of a "straight" number and its "parody." This coupling exemplifies *modoki* in the technical language of ritual and performance in Japan. Hoff contends that "Okina" expresses the concept of the everlasting, while "Sanba" characterizes human impregnation and birth (1977: 50).

"Sanba" concludes the ceremonial repertoire presented in *nōmai*. Villagers still revere the ceremonial dances for their sacred content. There is much ritual attached to these pieces. "Torimai" functions to ritually summon the *kami*, to whom requests for prosperity and welfare of the community are made. "Henzai" symbolically serves to purify the performance place for the dances that follow, while "Okina" and "Sanba" dramatize an ancient legend presented as a prayer for longevity and abundant harvests.

### "Bangaku"

"Bangaku," which is also listed under ceremonial pieces, is actually a prayer dance since it is an exact duplication of the dance performed in the first half of "Gongenmai"—a prayer dance—and is not *kagura*-derived as the other ceremonial dances. This basis is substantiated by the fact that the dancer's costume for this piece, which includes a *hachimaki* (cloth headband) and a *katana* (sword), is that worn in "Gongenmai." The piece is categorized as ceremonial, however, because the accompanying music is the same as that used for both "Torimai" and "Henzai," and the contexts requiring this piece are ceremonial in nature: *buchi komi* (short ritual *nōmai* performance), *makuosame* (final curtain) performance of the New Year, and Aki Matsuri (Fall Festival).

## PRAYER PIECES

*Kitōmai,* or prayer dances, are distinguished from ceremonial dances. Exorcisms were called *kitō*, which literally means "prayer." This designation draws from the Buddhist term *kaji kitō* which denotes prayer by drawing on the strength of Buddha. *Yamabushi* used *kitō* to cure people by driving out the demon or spirit believed to cause sickness. The pieces "Gongenmai" and "Kanemaki" both contain displays of ritual exorcism.

### "Gongenmai" (Lion's Dance)

The lion's dance is a ubiquitous tradition found throughout Japan. It was imported from Central Asia by way of China around the 6th century. The combined Buddhist and Shinto significance of the lion's dance gave it broader appeal, making it a perfect vehicle for *yamabushi.*

In *nōmai,* the Buddhist elements of the lion's dance, referred to as "Gongenmai," are dominant. *Gongen* is a Buddhist term defined as "the fact or image of a Buddhist saint appearing in a temporary state to save the public," and it is the name ascribed to the deity that is revered and summoned in *nōmai.* This term is derived from the Sanskrit word "Avatara," designating a historical incarnation of the Buddha. There are three *gongen* spirits (incarnations of Buddha) associated with Kumano Shrine, headquarters of the Shugendō sect: Buddha of the Pure Realm (Honchi Amida Nyorai), Buddha of Healing (Honchi Yakushi Nyorai), and the Buddhist saint of great compassion, mercy, and love (eleven-headed Kannon). Villagers in Ōri believe that the Buddha of Healing is manifested at the end of a "Gongenmai" performance, when a *nōmai* performer goes into the audience and touches every person with the Buddhist sistrum he is holding in his hand as a gesture of healing and protection from evil influences that cause illness.

Within the district of Higashidorimura, many occasions call for a performance of "Gongenmai": fall festivals in September; *buchi komi*, an event marking the arrival of the *gongen* deity for the New Year's season; full-length New Year's *nōmai* performances; and dedication ceremonies of newly built homes. A performance of "Gongenmai" for house dedication ceremonies varies slightly from that given in *nōmai* presentations. Instead of taking a Buddhist sistrum and rosary in its mouth, the lion dancer takes a firebrand of pine slivers bundled together (*taimatsu*). According to local beliefs, fire itself symbolizes the presence of a deity, and when the *gongen* deity, manifested in the lion's head, takes the pine torch in its mouth, it changes into a dragon with seven heads and seven tails whose steps are as large as eight mountains. In this context, "Gongenmai" serves to exorcise evil influences in a newly built house that might cause damage by fire or water.

"Gongenmai" contains elements of both Shugendō and Shinto. The athletic movements of the dancer manipulating the lion's head suggest *tombogaeri* and other acrobatic feats that were performed in earlier versions of this dance. Acrobatic movements in the dance have some relation to a genre of sword dances (*tsurigimai*) and to rigorous movement found in ascetic practices of Shugendō (Inoura 1963: 1138). Use of the Buddhist sistrum and rosary is also representative of the influence of Shugendō. The lyrics to the song accompanying this dance, however, are believed to be prayers of Shinto origin. The combined elements of both Shugendō and Shinto in "Gongenmai" reflect the fact that Shinto deities are closely associated with Buddhist ones as a result of the inter-association of these two religions in medieval Japan (Inoura 1963: 1139).

### "Kanemaki"

"Kanemaki" is the second of two prayer dances in the *nōmai* repertoire. Judging from the song texts and performance style, this piece probably dates back prior to the middle 1300s (Inoura 1963: 1144). The legend "Dōjōji," a story taken from the book *Hokke Genki,* forms the basis of the dance drama "Kanemaki." Fourteen versions of this story appear in *Konjaku monogatari,* a collection of Buddhist tales, many of which are based on folk tales. The framework and structure of *nōmai*'s "Kanemaki" is very similar to *nō* drama's "Dōjōji" and Kurokawa *nō*'s "Kanemaki" (also a folk version of the classical form), although the latter two are enactments of different versions.

Mr. Ōta proposes that *nōmai*'s version of "Kanemaki" originated during the Heian period, when Buddhism was at its peak and was transmitted to Japan through China via Korea. He relates the story of "Kanemaki" as follows:

> *In Kyoto, the only daughter of a famous village headman became a strong believer in Buddhism. Free to do anything she liked, she travelled and worshiped at shrines, Buddhist temples, and other famous sites. By chance, she went to Kanemaki temple and, while praying there, decided to enter into that temple's priesthood to become a nun. When she expressed her desire to a steward of the temple, he told her that Kanemaki temple was very sacred and to enter the priesthood one had to learn ascetic practices regulated by Buddhist law. The steward stressed that a man was required to practice asceticism for a hundred days, but women had to complete ascetic practices that lasted for a thousand days. He related that there was no precedent for women entering the priesthood of Kanemaki temple because of the severity of the prolonged period of asceticism, and many women became demonesses in their attempt to do so. Despite the steward's words of advice, the young women's heartfelt desire was firm and she presented a* kane no o *(cloth or straw bell cord found at entrances to shrines or temples) as a symbolic offering in commencing the religious practice of a thousand days. But meanwhile, sad to say, the practice was not the kind a young woman could bear; she became insane and turned into a demoness wandering around Koya (a mountainous area in the historical Kii province of Wakayama Prefecture, famous for its numerous Buddhist temples). In the meantime, her father, who was in Kyoto, heard the rumor about his daughter, and in wondering what he could do to aid her found a* shugenja (yamabushi) *known to have superior divine powers. The father immediately asked him to rescue his daughter. It is said the* shugenja *went into the*

> *mountains in Koya to meditate. He lured the daughter, who had changed into a demoness, with his divine power and a violent battle unfolded. But as expected, the demoness could not overcome the* shugenja's *divine power, steeped in the merits of Buddhism, and the daughter returned to her original state.* (Ōta, 1980: 20)

The variety of dances and characters portrayed in "Kanemaki," as well as the use of all of the accompanimental music pieces played by the *hayashi*—*gobyōshi no iri*, *sagari ha,* and *kiri*—make this piece a popular one among villagers. Singing and chanting alternate in effectively dramatizing the song text. Melodies, according to Inoura, are based on those found in the manuscript *Dōjōji engi emaki* (1963: 1141).

The beginning of the piece features a dance by the *betto* character (the steward of Kanemaki temple) who holds a white fan in his right hand and a *kinsatsu* (hand-held prohibition notice board) with the *kane no o* wrapped around it, in his left hand. This stately, ceremonial dance is identical to the choreography in the first half of "Okina." The *betto* departs, leaving the *kinsatsu* on the stage; it is believed that the *kinsatsu* represents a bell with the *kane no o* wrapped around it.

Next, the character of the young woman enters the stage and elegantly performs in the style of *onnamai* (women's dance) to the slow tempo accompaniment of *sagari ha* played by the *hayashi*. The musical accompaniment then stops and singers weave the story about Kanemaki temple, introducing the woman. During the song, the dancer portraying the woman sits at stage center performing a series of ritualistic movements with a Shinto paper wand offering *(gohei)* in her left hand and a Buddhist rosary (*juzu*) in her right hand. The dancer then claps her hands twice, performs three mudra-like gestures with her hands, again claps twice, then stands up and takes the end of the *kane no o*. The rhythm, which up until this point has been slow and calm, changes to a faster tempo, and the dance takes on a more vigorous character. The dancer then alternately takes steps toward and away from the *kinsatsu*, which functions as a spindle and is held by someone sitting at stage left front. This portion of the dance symbolically depicts the anguish of the young woman, who slowly begins to go mad from her attempt to complete the rigorous ascetic training. To help portray this important scene the singers chant:

| | |
|---|---|
| *Shogyo mujō* | Evanescence of all worldly things |
| *zeshometsu po* | This law of birth and death |
| *shometsu metsu mi* | My law of birth and death |
| *jakumetsu iraku no kane no* | Rest at the place of the *kane no o* |
| *o yasumikeri* | of peaceful Nirvana. |

The song continues:

| | |
|---|---|
| *Tachimachi kishin ni naraba nare* | In an instant she became a demoness. |
| *Mairasu kane no o wa san to suru* | Worshiping *kane no o* and praising it. |
| *Sue wa tomare kakumo are* | In any case, what could be the future (of the young woman) |
| | |
| *Kakumo are* | In any case, |
| *Mairasu kane no o wa san to suru* | worshiping the *kane no o* and praising it. |

The quicker rhythm of the *taiko*, *tebiragane*, and *fue* resound as the woman unwinds and winds the *kane no o* around the *kinsatsu*. At length, she turns into a demoness and exits off the stage (*Higashidorimura no nōmai* 1984: 18).

In the second half of the dance, a virulent *yamabushi* character enters the stage and proceeds to exorcise evil influences in the five directions and symbolically display the merits of Buddhism. While the *yamabushi* (*shugenja*) dances, the singers repeatedly sing:

| | |
|---|---|
| *Namu seiho ni mo gyoja gyoja* | Hail to Buddha to the west, devotee |
| *Namu hoppo ni mo gyoja gyoja* | Hail to Buddha to the north, devotee |
| *Namu nanpo ni mo gyoja gyoja* | Hail to Buddha to the south, devotee |
| *Namu toho ni mo gyoja gyoja* | Hail to Buddha to the east, devotee |
| *Namu chuo ni mo gyoja gyoja* | Hail to Buddha to the center, devotee |

To these words the *shugenja* continues a vigorous dance in which he emits his power and strength to the five directions. The singing stops and the demoness enters the stage to struggle with the *shugenja* in the form of a dance. In the end, the *shugenja* overpowers the demoness and leads her "to the righteous path of Buddhism" (*Higashidorimura no nōmai* 1984: 18).

"Kanemaki" is the most dramatic piece of storytelling in the *nōmai* repertoire. It is a compelling combination of a didactic play that espouses the strengths and virtues of Buddhism and an entertaining story that contains both a hero and a villain. Somewhat misleading is its designation as a prayer dance. Sacred in nature, the exorcism that takes place in this piece symbolically serves to exorcise the community of any evil influences that might bring illness and misfortune to its inhabitants. It is not so much a request or prayer directed to some deity, but an active drama that extols Buddhism.

These two prayer dances are the most Buddhist-influenced pieces in the *nōmai* repertoire. Evidence of this lies in the designation of these dances as *kitōmai*, which is derived from the Buddhist form of prayer called *kaji kitō*.

## WARRIOR PIECES

To balance the more serious and ritualistic ceremonial and prayer dances, *yamabushi* incorporated pieces that were designed to entertain their provincial audiences. In the 15th century, they included *bushimai* or warrior dances based on the two-part structure of the older ceremonial and prayer pieces. Most of the pieces in this category depict the battles between the Genji and Heike clans in their struggle for power in the latter part of the 12th century. Other pieces feature the vendetta of the Soga brothers or the warrior known as Shinobu no Taro. The popularity of these pieces reflects the empathy people had for defeated warriors such as Yoshitsune of the Genji clan, or the Soga brothers, who were killed while avenging the murder of their father. Stories about Yoshitsune were of particular interest to *nōmai* audiences, since this infamous warrior fled to and was exiled with his men in Ōshu, an area that at present includes all of Aomori Prefecture and one district in Iwate Prefecture. Warrior dances appealed to the romantic tastes of rural audiences and served to immortalize well-known historical heroes.

As *bushimai* evolved, a number of influences merged: (1) *kōjakumai*, a type of acrobatic dancing; (2) *kyokumai*, a narrative art with drumming accompaniment, which occasionally included dancing; (3) *nō* plays based on stories of warriors; (4) *heikyoku*, an epic ballad recited to the accompaniment of the *biwa*; and (5) *kōwakamai*, a narrative art with a minor element of dance.

Chronologically, the oldest warrior dance drama is "Shinobu," which dates back to 1300. "Yashima" originated around 1500 and "Watanabe" came into being after 1600. "Watanabe" is a later form of *bushimai* that includes dialogue (*serifu*). The source of influence for the addition of dialogue is folk kabuki performed in the Tōhoku region (Aomori, Akita, and Iwate Prefectures). Nanbu *kagura* is another source from which *yamabushi* borrowed from in adding dialogue and more imitative elements to the dramatic presentations of *bushimai* (Inoura 1963: 1156).

*Yamabushi* had opportunities to see *sarugaku nō* performances in Yoshino, where the exiled Emperor Go Daigo established a court separate from that of the capital of Kyoto in 1331, known as the Southern Dynasty. Performing arts of the capital, such as *sarugaku nō,* accompanied the steady stream of guests and visiting members of the Kyoto imperial court to Yoshino. Itinerant *yamabushi* exposed to these performing arts then incorporated elements of this *nō* form into *yamabushi kagura.* The influence of *sarugaku nō* also spread as a consequence of Southern Dynasty members' frequent visits to northern Ōshu (districts in Miyagi, Iwate, and Aomori Prefectures) in the early 1400s (Inoura 1963: 1149).

### "Shinobu"

"Shinobu" is a highly respected dance drama considered to be the oldest *bushimai*. In Shishipashi, this dance often immediately follows the presentation of the four ceremonial dances. It is a typical *bushimai* and the first warrior dance learned by performers.

According to the lyrics, this title refers to a warrior named Shinobu no Taro, but obscurity surrounds the identification of this historical character. Inoura offers a couple of possibilities for the character's origin. The fifth chapter of *Ama no ko no monogatari* (*Tale of a Child from the Heavens*), a literary source for a ballad drama form (*jōruri*) of the Okuni school in Idzumo, mentions a character named Shinobu. In this tale, Shinobu is the guardian of Sato Sugunobu, who is one of the four bodyguards of Yoshitsune of the Genji clan.

A person named Shinobu is also found to be related to the Sato family in the *Maruyama monogatari (Tale of Maruyama)*,[4] also used in the Okuni ballad drama repertoire. This tale includes an episode in which the well-known Genji warrior, Yoshitsune, names the son of Sato Tadanobu (brother of Sato Sugunobu), Shinobu Genta Yoshinobu. Later episodes of the story describe the maturation of Shinobu into a fine warrior. It is possible that the Okuni ballad texts for these episodes serve as the source for the *nōmai* song text of "Shinobu." A third possibility is that Shinobu is a fabrication of people living in the northern area of Ōshu, who created this story to emulate feudal lords of the Sato family (Inoura 1963: 1145). In any case, the piece expresses the courageous battling of Shinobu no Taro.

**"Watanabe"**

"Watanabe" focuses on the legendary fight between Watanabe no Tsuna, a retainer of Yorimitsu of the Genji clan, and Ibaragi Doji, the demon of Rashomon. The background of the fight between the two characters is as follows:

> *The demon, Rashomon, appears inside the southern gate of Kyoto and commits many bad deeds against the local people. Watanabe has posts put up with messages telling the demon to stop. The enraged demon challenges Watanabe to fight. In the ensuing battle, Watanabe cuts off the devil's arm. The story continues with the demon disguising himself as an old woman who claims to be the nursemaid of Watanabe. Watanabe's retainer Gunzo knows that the nursemaid is the demon and tells his master. Watanabe does not believe him until the old woman transforms herself back into the demon, which regains its arm.*

Watanabe performs a robust warrior dance in the first half. The singers introduce him, explain his objective to conquer the demon of Rashomon, and narrate the ensuing fight. In the midst of the main character's dance, Ibaragi Doji, the demon, comes out on stage and jumps at Watanabe. In their scuffle Watanabe cuts off the demon's arm. This portion ends with the demon running offstage and Watanabe exiting afterward. A dialogue between Watanabe and his retainer, Gunzo, begins the second part:

> *The retainer warns his master that Ibaragi Doji might come in disguise to retrieve his arm. At this time an old woman appears, telling Gunzo that she was Watanabe's nursemaid, and enters Watanabe's house. The old woman says, "If I worship the arm of the demon cut off by Watanabe, I will become a Buddhist saint*

> *(bodhisattva). So, please let me look at it." Watanabe shows the nursemaid the arm and she says "Awful! Awful!" at which time the demon character takes off the mask and costume and reveals itself as the demon.* (Ōta 1980:45)

After the demon leaves the stage with its arm, Watanabe and Gunzo pose in a *roppō* position (pose of suspended action characteristically seen in kabuki) that shows they are ready to chase the demon.

"Watanabe" follows the two-part structure of warrior plays, but it is atypical in that it includes dialogue spoken in a stylized manner, new choreography, the use of facial makeup rather than a mask for the Watanabe character, and a certain uniqueness in costuming. These features point to the strong influence folk kabuki had on *nōmai* in the latter part of its development. This is the most contemporary piece in the *bushimai* repertoire. Its use of dialogue makes it less abstract than the other warrior dances, which use only song to narrate the background and plot.

Well-known stories, characters, and legendary tales come to life in the warrior pieces. These plays are not religiously didactic in content, but they appealed to *yamabushi* perhaps due to a connection drawn with the Heike, who achieved their prosperity and glory through the special blessings of the Kumano Shrine—headquarters of the Shugendō order.

### "Yashima"

The dance drama "Yashima" centers around two famous battles between the Genji and Heike clans, who vied for power of the central government in medieval Japan. It is presented in the typical binary structure of warrior dances, with the first half an enactment of the battle at Yashima[5] and the second half depicting the historically important battle at Dan no Ura,[6] in which the reigning Heike clan is vanquished.

"Yashima" features the Sato brothers, Tadanobu and Tsuginobu, who served as bodyguards to the Genji leader Yoshitsune. The *makuzuki* song section in the first half relates the story of Kagekiyo, head of the Heike clan, and his attempt to capture Yoshitsune. The song continues to tell how Kagekiyo's attempt fails, and how Sato Tsuginobu dutifully protects Yoshitsune and is killed by the arrow intended for his master. The *makuzuki* song in the second half narrates the famous sea battle at Dan no Ura, with the Heike army coming from the sea and the Genji officers and men coming from land to engage with one another in a fierce battle. The synchronized movements of the two dancers in this dance strive to portray the depth of a warrior's passionate devotion to his master.

### "Suzuki"

This warrior dance dramatizes the sad parting of Suzuki Saburo Shigeie, retainer of Yoshitsune of the Genji clan, and his mother. This piece is unique in its emotional expression of the tenderness between a mother and her child. The *Taiheiki* (*Chronicle of the Great Peace*), is the literary source for this story, which relates the fighting between Yoshitsune and his brother Yoritomo, head of the

Kamakura feudal government. Yoshitsune passes through the Ataka boundary gate near Sendai, but tells ten of his twenty retainers to return home. Suzuki, being one of the ten to continue with Yoshitsune, is greeted by his mother, who has come from Kishū in southern Wakayama Prefecture to meet her son, since it will be her last chance to see him. Yoshitsune tells Suzuki to return home with his mother, but Suzuki refuses, saying he would follow Yoshitsune wherever he went. The mother tries to change her son's mind, saying that Yoshitsune has enough good retainers such as Musashi Bo Benkei and Kamei Rokuro. The son is nonetheless firm in his decision to accompany Yoshitsune and risk his life if need be. So the mother gives in to his wishes and enourages him to be courageous (*Higashidorimura no nōmai* 1984: 15-16). The story is a didactic one that highlights the devotion of a warrior to his master and stresses that mothers must be strong (Ōta 1980: 39-40).

"Suzuki" begins with the main character, Suzuki, dancing a vigorous warrior dance accompanied by the fast tempo *kiri* instrumental music. During the singing of the next *makudashi* song, the mother character enters the stage and dances a woman's style dance (*onnamai*) to the slower tempo *sagari ha* music. Her son Suzuki joins in the slow, meditative movements of the *onnamai*. and the duet is a moving scene that portrays the agony of the final parting of a mother and her son. After the duet ends, the *makuzuki* song narrates the grief and sorrow of the two characters, and the play finishes with a vigorous warrior dance by Suzuki. Audiences find this sentimental one-act play appealing.

### "Kurama"

"Kurama" narrates the story of the battle between Ushiwakamaru (the medieval warrior-hero Yoshitsune when he was a young boy) and the famous warrior monk Musashi Bo Benkei[7] on Mount Kurama, which is located to the north of Kyoto. Mr Ōta relates the story as follows:

> *Ushiwakamaru plans to raise an army and wants Benkei to be his advisor, since the monk is known to be a good strategist. In order for him to approach Benkei to request that the warrior monk be his advisor, Ushiwakamaru feels he must challenge him, but Benkei refuses. After repeated challenges, he finally accepts. During the actual fight, it is said that Benkei used seven kinds of martial arts and the knowledge of forty-two volumes of strategy. During their battle Benkei realizes the young boy's ability and decides to become his retainer.* (Ōta 1980: 55-56).

Ushiwakamaru, entering the stage wearing a mask during the singing of the *makudashi* song section, begins the one-act "Kurama" dance drama. The succeeding *makuzuki* song introduces the main character Ushiwakamaru, who dances to the full accompaniment of singing and instrumental music in a section called *uta-gakari*.. Next, the young warrior takes off his mask and declares his challenge to the warrior monk. This is Benkei's signal to enter the stage, at which time he appears playing a shell trumpet, paraphernalia characteristic of *yamabushi*. Swords and sticks are the weapons used in the choreographed battle scene. Sound effects of the weapons striking one another punctuate the scene, featuring acrobatic movements and somersaults. At the end, Benkei loses the fight and leaves the stage followed by the triumphant Ushiwakamaru (*Higashidorimura no nōmai* 1984: 16-17). "Kurama" is fast-paced and most often performed by younger actors.

## COMIC PIECES

Presented last in a *nōmai* program are *dōkemai*, or comic pieces. The addition of *dōkemai* increased the popular appeal of *yamabushi kagura* in the 14th century. Within Shintoism, comedy was associated with spirit appeasement. People believed that if one could induce laughter in the spirit being approached for a request, the request would be granted. Therefore, when deities were invoked for favors, they had to be entertained and humored. Entertainment of such kind was often earthy, even bawdy. The dance of the goddess Ame no Uzume in the *Heavenly Cave Door* myth has been interpreted as a form of such salacious entertainment (Garfias 1965: 11).

An important element of the comic pieces is *modoki*, or the art of imitation, which is often satirical. *Modoki* was an important developmental influence on *dōkemai*, with its focus on current topics and public figures of interest and ridicule. The outline and plot of each piece is fixed, but within this context the comic character is given the freedom to improvise by rearranging words and phrases of the dialogue in satirizing current events or village members.

*Dōkemai* comic pieces reflect the local color of village life through use of the local dialect and by audiences' response of laughter or cheers to what is being said. Audiences enjoy the gossip (*mono ii*) about individuals or situations lampooned in the plots of these comedies. Actors speak in traditionally prescribed inflections and speech patterns of the local dialect in their dialogues with the *taiko* drummer, who often accents punch lines of the comic character with the strike of a drumhead, adding to the humor of the plays.

*Dōkemai* incorporate less dance than the other types of *nōmai* plays; instead, a major portion of the plays have the main actor pose as a stand-up comic wearing special masks (*hyottoko*[8]) that are humorously moronic. Various masks depict other characters, such as an *okame* (fat-faced woman) or the beaming face of the god Ebisu.

These plays are pure entertainment, in which anyone can be the target of ridicule and fun. Socially, the shared humor in viewing *dōkemai* serves to renew the exuberance and community spirit of a village.

*Dōkemai* is a form combining elements from a number of different sources. As plebeian parody and satire, it is believed to derive from the lineage of *shin sarugaku*, a dramatic tradition dating from the 10th century, featuring mimicry and comic gestures of a more rustic nature. Two folk performing genres that influenced the use of dialogue in *dōkemai* are Nanbu *kagura* in Iwate Prefecture, which developed during the same time period as *dōkemai*, and *Futo kagura* of Edo (now Tokyo), another rurally based performing tradition, which also contributed dramatic elements. Additionally, the comic pieces "Suzume oi" and "Tauemai" derive from the narrative genre *kyokumai*. *Yamabushi*, from the time they incorporated comic pieces, had villagers perform them. Villagers, thus, were responsible for any changes and additions made in *dōkemai*, and *yamabushi* tacitly permitted them (Inoura 1963: 1156-1158).

### "Nenzu"

"Nenzu" is one of the oldest and most representative *dōkemai* that Mr. Ōta believes dates back to the Heian period. It is a popular piece transmitted among most of the villages. It is curious that the dialogue between the comic character and the *taiko* drummer has very little if any connection to the background story of this piece. Mr. Ōta relates the background story as follows:

> *A long time ago there was a daughter of a wealthy man in a certain village who went to the capital (Kyoto) to study Buddhism. There she grew into a beautiful woman and, upon finishing her studies, decided to return home. The rich man was overjoyed and held a celebration inviting even the nursemaid, but the young men in the village were even more overjoyed. This dance expresses the joy in the return of the beautiful, fine daughter.* (Ōta 1980: 60).

In the dialogue between the comic character and *dōtori*, or *taiko* drummer, there is no reference to the character of the daughter or her return home. A woman character, however, does appear on stage and dances at the beginning of the piece. The comic character, in a burlesque fashion, focuses on two topics: women as demons in disguise, and making a lot of money as a lumberjack and spending it in the entertainment quarter. He continues the dialogue and tells of appeasing his wife, after his profligacy in the gay quarter, by bringing her rice to make rice cakes (*mochi*). The husband and wife end up eating too much *mochi* and, feeling uncomfortable, decide to go with their friends to dance at the Obon Festival. The disjointed dialogue also includes a reference to the *gongen* deity, and the woman's dance in "Nenzu" is meant to be interpreted as "dance as prayer." Both aspects appear to be superimpositions based upon Shugendō beliefs that were forced upon the piece by *yamabushi* to give it some sacred meaning.

The action of the play does correspond to the dialogue. The piece commences, as mentioned above, with a dance by the woman character (*onnamai*). After the dancer retreats behind the curtain into the backstage area, the *dōke* and *dōtori* begin their dialogue. The *dōke*, upon ending his story of being a lumberjack and spending the money he made, remembers the woman who left the stage and goes back behind the curtain to look for her. At this point, live folk music is played and the comic character fetches people from the audience to go on stage to dance *bon odori*.[9]

**"Tengyō"**

Only three villages continue to perform "Tengyō," which is translated "heavenly maiden." The background story seems to have little connection to the actual dialogue and action of the play. The appearance of a woman character as the heavenly maiden is reminiscent of the *nō* play "Hagoromo," which also features the character of a heavenly maiden. The piece begins with the dance of the *tengyō,* featuring a pose that uses two fans to depict the feathers of the maiden. The male comic character comes out in the middle of the *tengyō*'s dance and the dance becomes a duet. Then the woman character exits offstage and the comic actor and drummer perform their dialogue (*Higashidorimura no nōmai* 1984: 20). The distinguishing and most enjoyable portion of "Tengyō" is the duet danced by the *dōke* and the heavenly maiden.

**"Nenshimai"**

"Nenshimai" takes place on New Year's Day. It is an amusing story about a man who goes to his wife's parent's home to offer them a New Year's greeting and dance for them. The father-in-law tells the man to let his daughter stay with them for a while, although the reason is unclear. The man agrees, but after drinking to celebrate the New Year he forgets his promise and ends up taking his wife home (*Higashidorimura no nōmai* 1984: 22). This story is related in the dialogue between the comic character and the *dōtori,* and the main male character dances his New Year's greeting to his in-laws.

**"Kitsunemai"**

The original text of "Kitsunemai" (Fox Dance) is based on the legend of a white fox in Shinoda Forest. The central theme of the play concerns the trapping of a white fox:

> *The hunter appears and tells the* dōtori *that he has come to catch a white fox and ask it about the future. The* dōtori *says the white fox will come out with the sound of a certain musical rhythm. A woman then appears on stage and interacts with the hunter. The hunter asks the woman to take him to the forest, whereupon the woman requests that he offer her an oil-fried rat (evidently a favorite food of a fox). The hunter does not grant her request, so the woman leaves. Next, the hunter asks the* dōtori *to play the special rhythm that the fox likes when dancing folk dances called* te odori. *During the playing of this rhythm, the white fox character comes onto the stage wearing a fox costume on his front side and a woman's costume on his back side. Dancing to the rhythm of the folk piece "Shinnai," the fox and woman characters alternate in a beguiling dance to show that they are the same being. This dance is the most entertaining scene in the*

> *piece. After the fox leaves the stage, the hunter appears again and makes a trap using an oil-fried rat. The white fox reappears and falls into the trap. The hunter then asks the fox about this year's harvest and fishing industry, and the fox responds saying* "hōnen tairyo," *which means successful harvest and fishing. The piece ends with the hunter and fox dancing a duet.* (*Higashidorimura no nōmai* 1984: 21)

Animals play an important part in both Japanese mythology and legend, not just in their own right, but also because of their relationship with humans or, in the earliest narratives, deities. An example is the fox, which is believed to be a messenger of the rice god or goddess (there are conflicting ideas of actual gender) Inari, itself sometimes depicted as a fox.

The aspect of the fox as a messenger of the rice goddess is evident in the above story, where the hunter captures it to have the fox predict the outcome of the rice harvest and, in association, the fishing industry. Like other animals, the fox is able to transform itself into human form and, in "Kitsunemai," disguises itself as a woman (Piggott 1893: 109, 120). The deception of foxes appearing as women is seen in a famous woodblock print by the artist Kuniyoshi, in which foxes can be seen turning into young women in the background, while peasants revel around a haystack.

### "Ebirisuri"

"Ebirisuri," also called "Taue," is performed on January 16 for *koshōgatsu,*[10] which is literally translated "little New Year." The cast of characters includes a hard-working man and his wife and the man's younger brother. All three wear masks, with the younger brother's smiling mask the most distinct. The story of this comic piece unfolds as the older brother receives a rice paddy from the government because he is known to be a hard worker. He works even harder after receipt of this land and tries repeatedly to get his younger brother to help. The younger brother, however, is very lazy and sleeps a lot. The older brother uses various ploys to wake him and ends up throwing a party to arouse his idle brother from sleep. "Ebirisuri" is a satirical piece about agricultural life, and it is particularly popular among villages whose economies are based primarily on agriculture (*Higashidorimura no nōmai* 1984: 21-22).

## SUMMARY

The programmatic sequence in which *nōmai* pieces are presented is traditionally set. Performances by *nōmai* groups always begin with "Torimai," followed by "Henzai," "Okina," and "Sanba." Prayer dances, in contrast, occur in a less set pattern. Shishipashi performs "Gongenmai" as the final piece. The village of Iwaya, however, presents this dance at both the beginning and end of a performance. There are also instances in which "Gongenmai" is featured in the middle of a program or in between warrior dances if a program is getting too long and people in the audience begin to leave. The second prayer dance, "Kanemaki," also occurs in the middle of a program, either in between individual warrior dances or immediately following them just before the comic pieces.

Warrior dances are dramatized next, with either "Shinobu" or "Yashima" (the oldest dances in this category) often presented as the first *bushimai* piece. The number of warrior dances staged varies from two to six, chosen from a total of eight pieces in the repertoire. One or two comic pieces operate to conclude a complete program.

The intent of the program order is to progress from serious ritualistic pieces to light parody and from songs and dances to conversation and mimicry. This ordering represents a model of the diachronic development of programming in Japanese drama, which customarily commences with ritualistic pieces and ends with light entertainment.

An early model for such programming is *kagura* performances, which open with a ritualistic enactment of purification, followed by the conjuration of desired deities and ending with a segment of entertainment for the conjured gods.

The traditional composite construction, referred to as the "banquet form," is a progression from both ritual to comic and from song and dance to dialogue. This program construction characterized performances of *ennen nō* and *sarugaku nō,* particularly of *shushi* priests.

Since it is difficult to substantiate, scholars have proposed theories that could account for such continuity in programming between these performing genres. Kawatake presents his theory more as a relationship between the serious element in *nōmai* —the ceremonial and prayer pieces, having sacred origins— and the comic parody of that seriousness expressed in the comic dances. It is also appropriate to reiterate Hagen Blau's hypothesis that a standard pattern to all Japanese festivals has prevailed from ancient times—the coupling of serious ritual with comic entertainment (cited in Ortolani 1984: 170).

The sequence of pieces described above not only displays a certain dramatic effect intended to entertain, but also forms a pattern of acts that creates social cohesiveness among people in a village. The ceremonial and prayer pieces symbolically represent ancient prayers of renewal for both economic prosperity and health for the entire community. The succeeding warrior and comic pieces generate a jovial atmosphere in which people renew their bonds with one another. A *nōmai* performance thus provides an opportunity for community members to share both sacred and social moments together.

## NOTES

1. *Konjaku monogatari* is a collection of didactic tales firmly based on the teachings of the two major Buddhist sects of Heian period Japan, Tendai and Shingon, with strong influence from the Amida cult of Pure Land Buddhism, which became very popular in the 10th century (Kato 1979: 200).

2. Posthumous documents of the monk Nichiren, founder of the Nichiren Buddhist sect.

3. Kasuga shrine is one of the most ancient and most venerated Shinto shrines in Japan. It is located on a hill east of Nara and was erected in 710 by Fujiwara Fuhito as a

shrine dedicated to his ancestors.

4. The *Maruyama monogatari* is a literary work believed to have originated in the area historically known as Ōshu in the 16th century, a date which corresponds to the development of *bushimai*. According to historical documents of the region, this story contains a great deal of verifiable historical information.

5. Yashima is in Sanuki province on the northern coast of the island of Shikoku. It is the place where the Heike clan settled and dispatched their armies to the fourteen neighboring provinces after fleeing the capital.

6. The battle of Dan no Ura took place in A.D. 1185 in the bay in southern Yamaguchi Prefecture (which at the time was known as Nagato) located at the westernmost tip of the island of Honshū and across from Fukuoka Prefecture on the island of Kyūshū.

7. Benkei was the son of a Buddhist priest at Kumano temple (Shugendō headquarters). Contrary to his calling, he always evinced a greater taste for fencing and other military exercises than for the monastic life. Legendary accounts have embellished Benkei's adventures and popularized his strength, stratagems, and devotedness to Yoshitsune (Papinot 1984: 45).

8. *Hyottoko* (literally, distorted male) is one of several masks used by comic characters.

9. *Bon odori* are folk dances performed by men, women, and children who dance in one big circle at the summer Obon Festival, in which the souls of ancestors are commemorated.

10. *Koshōgatsu* falls on January 16, and it is an event celebrated by women in a village. Since women are very busy cooking and entertaining relatives who are visiting for New Year's celebrations, they do not have a chance to relax and enjoy the holiday. When family and village activities for the New Year are over, women gather to dance and eat together.

Photo 1. *Taiko*

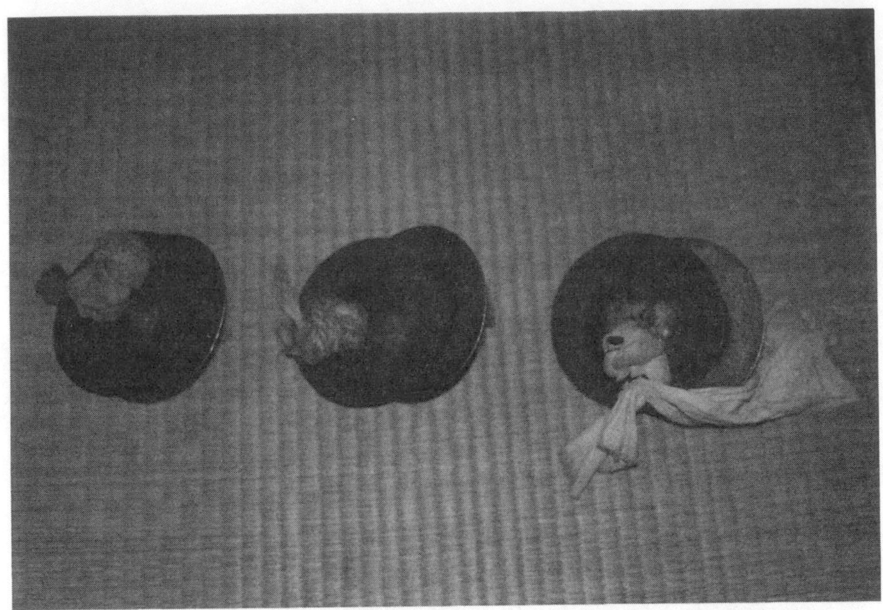

Photo 2. *Tebiragane/Kane*

Photo 3. *Fue*

Photo 4. *Nōmai* instrumentalists: *taiko* drummer and *tebiragane* players.

Photo 5. Altar, in the village of Ōri, dedicated to *nōmai's gongensama* (*gongen* deity). The lion's head on the left represents the "old *gongensama*" and the one on the right is the "young *gongensama*."

Photo 6. From left to right: *yamabushi*, *oni* (demon), and young woman's masks used in the play "Kanemaki."

Photo 7. Dance of young woman in "Kanemaki."

Photo 8. Warrior dance by Soga brothers in “Soga monogatari” play.

Photo 9. Dance by Ebisuri (God of the Sea) in the comic play “Ebisuri.”

Photo 10. Warrior dance by the character Shinobu in the play "Shinobu no Taro." The pose (*kata*) held by the dancer is referred to as *sashi ogi*.

Photo 11. *Nōmai* rehearsal of *gireimai* (ceremonial dance) in the village of Ōri.

Photo 12. *Yamabushi* character in "Kanemaki." Note the entrance of the dancer onto the stage from behind the rear curtain. This way of entering the stage is characteristic of older theater forms.

Photo 13. The village of Shishipashi's *nōmai* mask collection. Masks shown include Okina (beneficient old man), a fox, a young woman, an old man, a warrior, and comic characters.

Photo 14. Shishipashi village in the district of Higashidorimura on Shimokita Peninsula. This village served as the research base for studying *nōmai*. The population is about 253 people.

Photo 15. *Haiden* (shrine sanctuary); the first of two Shinto shrine buildings in the village of Shishipashi.

# PART III

## *NŌMAI* MUSIC

# 7

# Drum, Cymbals, and Flute

Instrumental music is an essential component of *nōmai*. The *hayashi*, or instrumental ensemble, plays an accompanimental role in performances, functioning to: (1) open each piece with introductory music, (2) accompany both singing and dancing, (3) bridge the various song and dance sections, (4) create the mood of a particular scene (such as battle scenes in the warrior dances), as well as (5) conclude each piece.

An important Shinto influence in *nōmai* music is the *hayashi* instrumentation of drum, cymbals, and flute. This combination of instruments parallels the instruments used not only in local folk *kagura* forms such as Okunai *kagura* or Nanbu *kagura*, but also in folk *kagura* throughout Japan. An example of the direct connection between *nōmai* and folk Shinto music is the great similarity of the *kai no kudari* instrumental piece, which accompanies both the lion's dance in *nōmai* and the lion's dance of Okunai *kagura*.

The instrumental music of *nōmai* generally follows the same musical structure as folk *kagura*, in which a certain number of set pieces are repeated as often as necessary, and the music is continuous and organized around rhythmic cadences. The adoption of these folk *kagura* elements points to the tendency of *yamabushi* to draw upon local Shinto performing traditions as a means of making *nōmai* accessible to the local population.

## INSTRUMENTS OF THE *HAYASHI*

*Hayashi* actually means "musical accompaniment," accurately defining the instrumental ensemble's role. Principal musical instruments of the *hayashi* include a *taiko* (cylindrical drum), *tebiragane* (cymbals), and *fue* (a bamboo transverse flute) (see Photos 1, 2, 3). Both sacred and secular folk performing traditions in Japan commonly use this instrumentation. The accompanying ensemble of *gigaku*, which included one transverse flute, hip drums, and brass cymbals, is the origin of this instrumentation (Araki 1978: 36).

Each instrument has religious significance. In *odori nembutsu*, a genre of Buddhist invocation with dance, the *taiko* is said to reflect the spiritual background of human nature. In Buddhism, the sound of the *taiko* and a conch shell trumpet are believed to embody the sound of spiritual enlightenment itself. Other religious associations in *nōmai* include the belief, mentioned earlier, that the music of the flutist and singers performing from behind the stage curtain emanate from the *gongen* deity itself enshrined backstage. The religious symbolism of the musical instruments is significant in providing accompaniment for the ceremonial and prayer dances. An instrument not considered part of the *hayashi* is the *horagai*, a conch shell trumpet used to herald the beginning and signal the end of the prayer dance "Gongenmai." The *horagai* has long been an instrument of *yamabushi*, who at one time used it to announce their entrance to villages, particularly for ritual or dance performances given in exchange for donations.

### *Taiko*

The *taiko* is a cylindrical drum with two drumheads. Each drumhead has a wide rim with up to twelve holes, through which ropes (*himo*) are strung. *Dō* is the term for the drum body and *wa* or *mimi* refers to the rim. According to Mitsuo Ageji of Ōri, a device inserted inside the drum body divides the single sound chamber, so that when both drumheads are struck the sound from either side does not interfere with the other.

In Shishipashi, dimensions of the *taiko* are as follows:

| | |
|---|---|
| Length of drum body | 13.96 inches |
| Diameter of drum body | 15.6 inches |
| Diameter of drumhead (including rim) | 19.1 inches |

The length of the drum body varies from one village to the next. In Shishipashi, the length is made to match the width of a man's shoulders; in Ōri, the width of a man's lap determines the length.

The bodies of the *taiko* used to be made from slat wood barrels used to store pickles and wine. Now they are carved out of one piece of *sugi* (cedar plutomeria), which makes the drum heavier but improves the sound quality. The drumheads are made of stretched horseskin; until the middle of the Taisho period (1912-1926), however, bearskin was customarily used. The tautness of both drumheads requires strength and endurance of drummers.

Both drumheads are struck with a pair of drumsticks called *bachi*. The length of the *bachi* normally match the diameter of the drum body before the rim is attached. In Shishipashi, for example, where the diameter of the drum body is 15.6 inches, the *bachi* are of an equivalent length. The drumsticks are narrow and approximately .6 inch thick. Woods used to make *bachi* include paulownia and maple.

*Nōmai* associations carefully maintain *taiko*, many of which are quite old.

Maintenance by the drummers involves tightening the drumheads when the instrument is in use and loosening the heads when they finish playing. In Shiriya, the young members clean and repair the drums, but the drummers themselves are responsible for tightening and loosening the drumheads. Oil or *saké* is applied to the drumheads to protect the leather, especially when the weather is cold and dry. This makes the heads more pliable and increases their resonance. Drum making has become a specialized craft, so all the *nōmai* groups hire professional drum makers to attach new skins for the heads as needed.

Mr. Ōta of Shishipashi stated that the desired timbre of the *taiko* is a rich, sonorous sound. He described the ideal sound quality to be a combination of the soft and soothing drum sound of the Buddhist Hoke sect, which uses frame drums called *uchiwa*, and the harder, sharp sound of the *shime daiko* drum used in Tsugaru folk music of northern Japan.

Neophyte drummers learn *taiko* techniques by using mnemonic syllables called *kuchi jamisen*. In Shishipashi, beginners learn drum stroke rhythms played directly on the drumhead, using the syllables *don, kon, tan, dan, dakasuku,* and *sutaraku dan.* These syllables are rhythmic verbalizations of subdivisions of beats and syncopations, as well as onomatopoeic representations of the different tone qualities obtained by striking different areas of the drumhead. The mnemonic syllables used in learning strokes played on the rim of the *taiko* include *sucharaka* and *chaka chaka.* Damping strokes learned utilize the syllables *zuki* and *tsuku.* One of the first instrumental pieces that apprentices learn is the ensemble piece *kai no kudari*, since it is used in a number of contexts: "Gongenmai," *kado uchi,* and processions.

The traditional position while playing *taiko* is sitting on one's knees Japanese style, referred to as *seiza*. The drummer sits in an upright position and strikes both sides of the drum, alternating right- and left-hand strokes. His placement at stage center (in the case of Ōri to stage left) enables him to carefully watch the dancer and successfully accent the dancer's movements.

Good drummers learn to dance many of the *nōmai* dances. Their familiarity with the dances equips them to anticipate the movements of the dancer, as well as to handle idiosyncratic movements of individual dancers. In Shiriya, it is said that anyone can learn to play the drum as soon as he becomes a member of the young men's association, but that until he knows how to dance *and* sing, he cannot play rhythms accurately. Even though the rhythm and tempo are set for each *nōmai* piece, the drummer adjusts tempos by watching the dancer. If the drummer is rhythmically inconsistent, the cymbal players take control to stabilize the tempo.

The *taiko* player has a number of functions. Besides learning all of the musical pieces that accompany dance and song sections, drummers also learn transitional rhythms used to bridge two different instrumental pieces. Traditionally, drummers are also responsible for learning the dialogue of comic pieces, in which they converse with the main comic character and accent their slapstick movements with various drum strokes. In addition, dance movements in the warrior piece "Watanabe," which is more theatrical than older *nōmai* pieces, require specific accented rhythms.

### *Tebiragane/Kane*

Small hand-held cymbals made from stainless steel are important instruments of the *hayashi*. Played in pairs, these knobbed cymbals, formally known as *tebiragane*, are generally called *kane*. Iron was the original material used to make these instruments until steel became more widely available. Some groups make *kane* from steel electric chain-saw blades. Steel's greater resonance, making it more desirable a material than iron, improves the sound quality of the cymbals. Most *nōmai* groups hire blacksmiths to make new cymbals when old ones deteriorate. Dimensions of those used in Shishipashi are as follows:

| | Diameter (from rim to rim) | Diameter of knob |
|---|---|---|
| 1st pair | 5.03 in. and 4.99 in. | 2.92 in and 2.73 in. |
| 2nd pair | 5.1 in. and 4.99 in. | 3.12 in. and 2.76 in. |
| 3rd pair | 5.18 in. and 5.14 in. | 3.23 in. and 3.12 in. |

From these dimensions, there seems to be a tendency to make one cymbal in each pair slightly smaller. One slightly small cymbal probably facilitates playing and creating a fuller sound.

Musicians hold one cymbal in each hand by grasping handles made from strips of cloth or rope. A thin piece of metal is inserted through a small hole in the center of the knob and shaped into a loop with the ends braced against the inside of the knob. Cloth or rope is threaded through this metal loop and a knot is tied. A loose, flexible grip facilitates playing and is less tiring.

The desired sound quality is a full, hard, brittle sound that is not too tinny or high-pitched. *Kane* now made from stainless steel are apparently less tinny-sounding than the original iron cymbals. Timbre is in part determined by how a player holds the *kane*—handles held lightly produce a good, clear sound, while handles held tightly create a poor, muffled sound.

The role of the *kane* is threefold: (1) to maintain a steady tempo, (2) to create excitement when fast rhythms are played, and (3) to play *ai-no-te,* a kind of call-and-response with the *taiko* and *fue*. The *kane* part contains less rhythmic variety compared to the more extemporaneous *taiko* and flute rhythms. The steady pulse of the cymbals provide simple rhythms that clearly delineate each beat.

All members of a *nōmai* group learn to play *kane*. They alternate playing these instruments during performances, since it is tiring to play for long periods. Taught first are hand motions without holding the cymbals; then, when the motion is learned, instruments are held. The angles at which *kane* are held vary from vertical (perpendicular to the floor) to slanted (approximating a forty-five degree angle to the floor). The angle may change according to the particular rhythm being played, since it is important to find a comfortable hand position that does not sacrifice the desired sound quality, but still allows one to play for long periods of time. The two cymbals are deflected off one another in a forward direction, followed by a backward stroke when playing the characteristic dotted eighth- and sixteenth-note rhythmic figure. Straight quarter notes are played with the two cymbals striking each other head on. Novices learn set rhythmic patterns before improving the sound quality. Playing *tebiragane* also includes mastering two levels of dynamics: *kyōjaku*—*kyō* meaning strong and *jaku* meaning weak.

### *Fue*

The *fue* (pron. "fwee" in Zuzu dialect) is a transverse flute made from one piece of bamboo without joints. It is a type of Japanese flute with seven finger holes formally referred to as *shinobue*. The flute gives voice to the *gongen*, and it is played from behind the stage curtain in the backstage area that symbolically serves as the abode of this deity during performances. In a *nōmai* presentation, the flute music emanating from behind the stage curtain reflects the belief that a dancer enters the stage as a reincarnation of the *gongen*. Its sacred symbolism coupled with being the only melody instrument in the *hayashi* makes the flute an essential instrument.

This instrument is made by *shinobue* makers in Kyoto and purchased in retail stores in nearby Mutsu City. There are various sizes of *shinobue*. *Nōmai* uses a *san-go* (No. 3) flute. The four flutes listed below are all *san-go* flutes used in Shishipashi:

| Diameter of flute body | | Length |
|---|---|---|
| At end close to mouthhole | At farthest end | |
| .7 in | .7 in. | 19.13 in. |
| .78 in. | .62 in. | 19.09 in. |
| .7 in. | .58 in. | 19.09 in. |
| .78 in. | .66 in. | 19.01 in. |

Red lacquer is applied on the inside walls of the *fue,* apparently to refine the tone quality. The first and seventh finger holes are closed permanently with electrical tape trimmed just wide enough to cover the hole, then wrapped around the circumference of the flute. This adaptation of the *shinobue* is required in order to produce only those pitches used in *nōmai* flute music. *Yamabushi kagura* and, subsequently, *nōmai* adopted the use of the *shinobue*, since it was already in use at the time these genres evolved. Thin strips of bamboo bark wound around both ends of the *fue* serve as decoration and prevent the bamboo body from cracking.

The *nōmai* flute sound is bright but resonant and well supported. The high range of the flute melodies and the overblowing needed to produce harmonics at the fifth or octave above sustained tones require good breath support.

The flute plays highly embellished melodies that require more training than either *taiko* or *tebiragane*. Flute playing is a special skill, yet many flutists also dance and play *taiko*. All flutists learn by watching fingerings and listening. Master flutists use mnemonic syllables devised especially for *nōmai* flute. The mnemonic syllables include *toro*, *tere, tero, torori, torira,* and *tororirori.* Each syllable—*te, to, re, ro,* and *ri*—represents a specific pitch. When combined they form melodic motives which are then linked to create an entire melody. Ornaments, which are an essential element of the *nōmai* flute style, are learned next. They color the line and create rhythmic momentum toward sustained tones. Embellishments include trills, grace notes (*kobushi*), tremolos, and melismas, collectively categorized as *korobashi*. Flute melodies help to create atmosphere. Quiet and energetic are the two moods achieved by changes in tempo and timbre.

There is at present a shortage of flutists, both because of the dwindling number of young people who stay in their villages and because of the relative difficulty of playing the instrument. Flute playing was once passed down within certain families. Now, however, due to the decreasing number of performers, it is taught to anyone who is willing to learn. Shishipashi village is fortunate to have three competent flutists, while Iwaya and Shiriya must ask flutists from other villages to play for their performances.

## JAPANESE CONCEPT OF THE TONE SYSTEM

The tetrachordal structure and theory of *nōmai* music is based on a tonal system that is applicable to all genres of Japanese folk and traditional music. A general theory of a tonal system for all traditional Japanese music did not exist until the introduction, in the 20th century, of the tetrachordal structure as a theoretical model. Instead, each genre such as *gagaku* (court music), *shōmyō* (Buddhist chant), *yōkyoku* (*nō* drama songs), and *sōkyoku* (*koto* music), had its own tonal theory and terminology (Koizumi 1977:76).

At present, scales in traditional Japanese music can be analyzed based on a system in which nuclear tones and accompanying musical pitches are organized into tetrachordal structures. This tonal system is based on Robert Lachmann's analyses of *nō* songs and Siberian shaman songs. In Chapter 1, "Tonsysteme," of his book *Music des Orients*, he proposes that the framework of the melodies is composed of tones a fourth interval apart, and that the relationship between the tones coincides with his *Konsonanzprincip*, or consonance principle. In this principle, he describes the melodic function of main tones, called *Kern* or nucleus tones, and their neighboring tones, *Nachbartöne*. Following World War II, this tonal system was adopted by Japanese musicologists in analyzing Japanese folk melodies and *nō* songs.

The original tetrachord in Greek music theory designates four tones: two nuclear tones that form the interval of a fourth and two inside tones. In the Japanese tone system, however, only one inside tone exists within the tetrachord (Kakinoki 1975: 60, 62). This tetrachordal structure correlates well with the melodic movement of many Japanese melodies, especially *shōmyō*, *heikyoku* (epic-ballads sung to the accompaniment of the Heike *biwa*), and *nō* songs, in which the interval of a fourth is a dominant feature. It is relevant to note that these song genres all flourished during the medieval period.

In 1958, the well-known musicologist Koizumi Fumio applied the tetrachord principle to Japanese folk melodies in his book *Nippon dentō ongaku no kenkyū* (A Study of Japanese Traditional Music). From his analyses, he established that Japanese folk melodies are composed of conjunct or disjunct tetrachords, in which the position of the inside tones varies according to four different intervals (Kakinoki 1975: 62). Koizumi also states that not only a fourth, but an interval of a fifth or any other interval may occur according to the tonal nature of the melody. In Japanese melodies, especially of *nō,* kabuki, genres of *shamisen* music, and folk music, he maintains that it is more appropriate to consider two tones similar in function in determining the tonal center, rather than a single tone. He calls these nuclear tones *kakuon* and states that in forming an interval of a fourth or fifth, they form a melodic frame within which other tones occur. These intermediate tones form either a minor second, major second, minor third, or major third interval above the lower nuclear tone. Based on these four intervallic relationships, four kinds of tetrachords emerge and in the following examples they appear in order of the frequency in which they are used.

Tetrachord I, referred to as the *minyō* tetrachord, is found mostly in folk songs and children's traditional game songs. This tetrachord is characterized by the interval of a minor third between the lower nuclear tone and the intermediate tone.

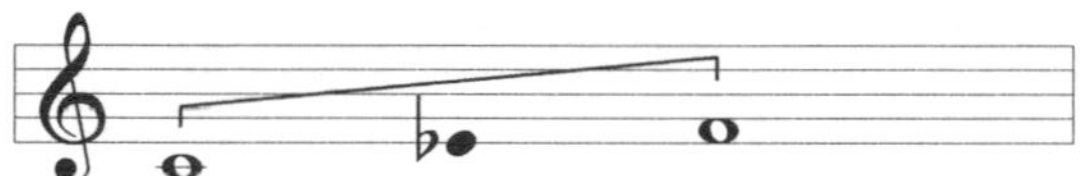

Tetrachord I—*Minyō*
(Koizumi 1977: 73)

Tetrachord II occurs primarily in art music such as *sōkyoku*, *nagauta* (narrative songs in kabuki), *shakuhachi*, and *biwa* music, and some folk melodies that originated in urban areas. It is called the *miyakobushi* or *in* (pron. "een") tetrachord, since its intervals correspond to those found in the *miyakobushi* scale that were identified by the Japanese theoretician Uehara Rokushiro (1848-1913) in his study of pentatonic melodies of urban genres played by professional *koto*, *shamisen*, and *shakuhachi* players. Uehara contrasted this scale with the *inakabushi* scale of folk song melodies heard in rural areas. The minor second interval between the lower nuclear tone and the intermediate tone gives this tetrachord its distinctive sound.

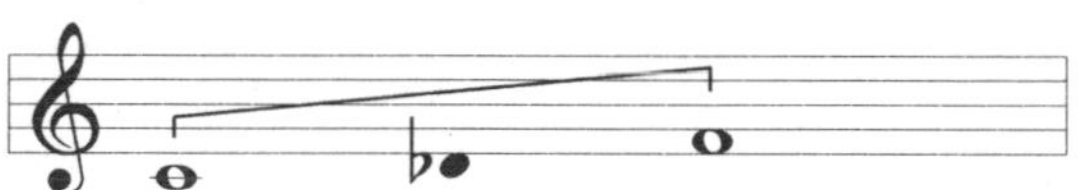

Tetrachord II—*Miyakobushi* or *in*
(Koizumi 1977:74)

Tetrachord III is the *ritsu* tetrachord. The pitches in this tetrachord correspond to the *ritsu* scale, which according to traditional *gagaku* music theory consists of two tetrachords. Tetrachord III occurs mostly in *gagaku* and Buddhist chant, including folk songs it influenced. In actual use, the intermediate tone tends to be slightly flatted. When it is flatted to the point of forming a minor second interval to the lower nuclear tone, it becomes Tetrachord II.

Tetrachord III—*Ritsu*

(Koizumi 1977: 75)

Tetrachord IV, called *ryūkyū*, is characteristic only of melodies of the Ryūkyū culture area in the southern Japanese islands of Okinawa Prefecture. The unique sound of tetrachord IV is due to the interval of a major third between the intermediate tone and lower nuclear tone.

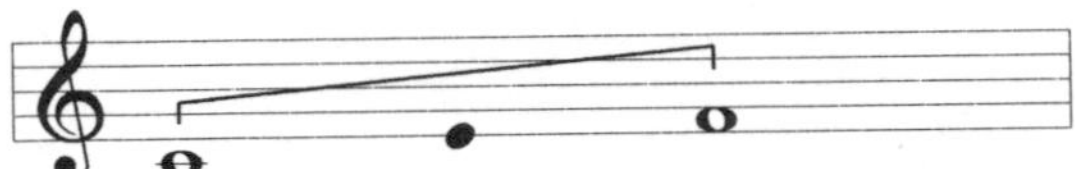

Tetrachord IV—*Ryūkyū*

(Koizumi 1977:75)

The range of two consecutive tetrachords forms an octave-scale when they are adjoined at an interval of a major second. The following are four kinds of octave-scales formed from the combination of two disjunct tetrachords of the same type:

*Minyō* scale—Nuclear tones: C-F-C

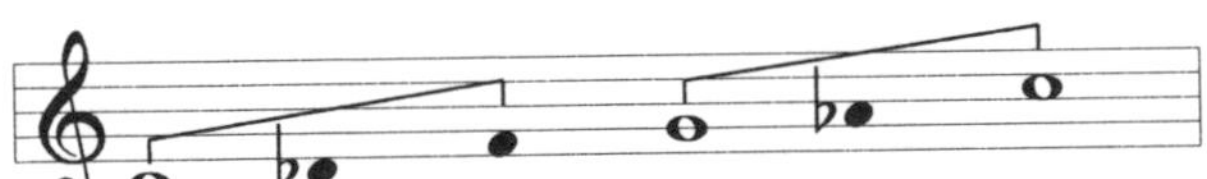

*Miyakobushi* scale—Nuclear tones: C-G-C

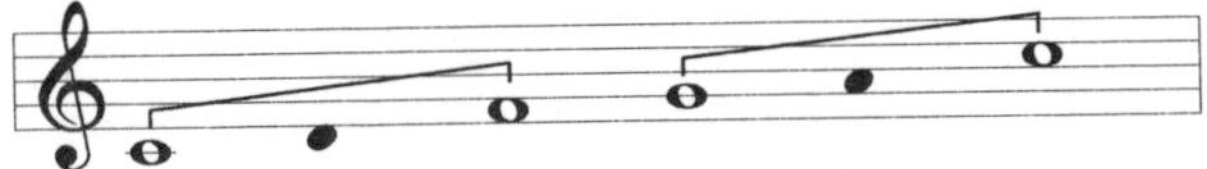

*Ritsu* scale—Nuclear tones: C-G-C or C-F-C

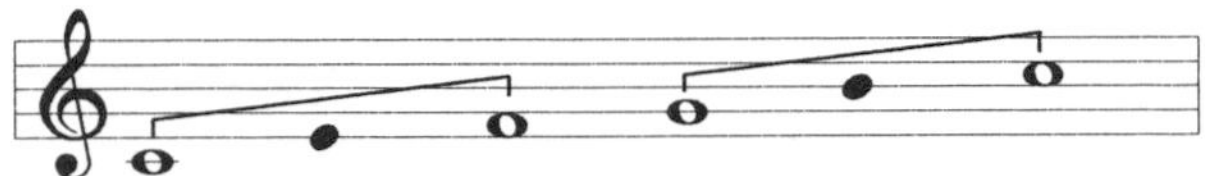

*Ryūkyū* scale—Nuclear tones: C-F-C or C-G-C
(Koizumi 1977: 76)

I applied the above tonal concepts to the scales found in both the *hayashi* music discussed here and in *nōmai* song melodies covered in the next chapter. The application of these concepts developed by Japanese musicologists, as opposed to analyzing scales according to western models, is essential in understanding the function of tones and their interrelationships that dictate the melodic characteristics of *nōmai* music.

## THE CONCEPT OF RHYTHM IN *NŌMAI*

In studying the music of any culture, conceptualizations of a music by those who perform it provide an important perspective on how one theorizes about the music. Rhythm in *nōmai* instrumental music is based on that of *yamabushi kagura*. Performers maintain that rhythm in *yamabushi kagura* occurs in patterns of seven, five, and three beats; it is said *nōmai* uses the five-beat pattern called *gobyōshi* (Kojima 1965: 98). In the district of Higashidorimura, the terms *gobyōshi* and *sanbyōshi* (three-beat) occur. It is unclear exactly what is meant by "five-beat" and "three-beat," since rhythmic analyses presented in this chapter show that *nōmai* music is basically duple meter. Confusion arises over the use of these terms, since "*hyōshi* " is technically defined as "meter" and it has numerous meanings depending upon the context in which it is used.

Besides meaning meter, *hyōshi* designates: (1) the name of an instrument, (2) a percussionist, (3) the playing style of percussion instruments, or (4) foot stamping (Sasamori 1969: 144). Mr. Ōta mentioned that the word *hyōshi* in the above terms (*hyōshi* changes to *byōshi* when occurring in a compound) is used in Higashidorimura in a number of ways. Among the local people, *hyōshi* means "beat," and is used in reference to rhythm as it occurs in music. The term also refers to musical instruments in the phrase *hyōshi o tsukero*, which is translated as "let the instruments sound." *Hyōshi* is also the name, in the village of Ōri, for an episodic section in the *sagari ha* composition, which has a different melody, rhythm, and slightly faster tempo than the principal *sagari ha* melody and rhythm. It is played a number of times during the course of a dance as contrasting material. *Hyōshi* in this sense is defined more generally as a sequence of notes.

*Gobyōshi* is distinguished as the musical style of the eleven villages that perform *nōmai,* while *sanbyōshi* is the music of the two villages, Iriguchi and Horobe, that practice the folk dance drama *okajishimai*. *Okajishimai* is considered to be a divergent form primarily because of its *sanbyōshi* musical style. This style is said by the local people to be faster in tempo and brighter sounding compared to the slower tempo and dense sound of *gobyōshi* in *nōmai.*

In terms of musical style, the local people offer various meanings of the word *gobyōshi*. Some say it refers to five musical compositions of the *hayashi*: *kiri*, *sagari ha*, *gobyōshi no iri*, *kai no kudari*, and Sanba *byōshi*. Another explanation of the term is that five phrases within one *hayashi* composition are repeatedly stated in creating the overall form.

There apparently is no real musical connection between *nōmai* music and the term *gobyōshi*, which is described as five-beat. *Gobyōshi* is incongruent with the actual rhythm of *nōmai,* whose basic unit is equal to two beats. It instead may just be a term loosely used in differentiating tempos of varying musical styles: *gobyōshi* to describe the slower tempo of *nōmai* music and *sanbyōshi* to describe the faster music of *okajishimai*. The vagueness of this terminology does not communicate a clear concept of rhythm in *nōmai* music. The fact that these terms do exist, however, is evidence of conscious efforts to conceptualize and distinguish one musical style from another.

## ACCOMPANIMENTAL MUSIC

Music of the *hayashi* is organized into four fundamental compositions played for particular dances, characters, or scenes, and one special composition performed only for the play "Sanba." *Nōmai* performers distinguish them as follows: *gobyōshi no iri*, *kiri*, *sagari ha*, *kai no kudari*, and Sanba *byōshi*.

The following in-depth study analyzes the four basic accompanimental pieces with transcriptions provided in the Appendix. Flute melodies of each of the *hayashi* compositions vary according to the skill of the flutist, the musical style of a particular village, and playings from one performance to the next, even within a single village. The prevailing melodic and rhythmic freedom in the flute line makes it sound spontaneous and improvised. These same qualities, however, make it difficult to capture the elusiveness of the melody in the limited number of transcriptions provided. My analyses, therefore, are merely representative and not comprehensive of all the variables that occur in *nōmai* flute melodies.

The same is partly true for *tebiragane* and *taiko*, too. The loose framework of the *hayashi* compositions allows for some variables in rhythm as well. The compositions exhibit flexibility in accompanying individual dancers. The improvisatory nature of this instrumental music makes analysis difficult, but I will identify its characteristic melodic and rhythmic principles.

### *Gobyōshi no iri*

*Gobyōshi no iri* is a *hayashi* composition that serves as an instrumental prelude to a majority of the dance dramas. An analysis of melody, rhythm, and form was made from a 108-beat sample (see Appendix Figure A.1.) representing only a portion of the accompanimental piece as played for the ceremonial dance "Torimai." *Gobyōshi no iri* is composed of two sections; the initial portion segues into a section that is faster in tempo and employs different rhythms played by the *tebiragane* and *taiko* and a slightly different flute melody. I have chosen to analyze the first section only, since this is the portion that is most readily recognized by the audience as a signal that the performance of a piece is about to begin.

**Form** The overall form of the first section consists of seven phrases: an introductory phrase and six succeeding phrases. The introductory phrase functions to establish pitch F as the primary nuclear tone. Phrase F acts as a kind of cadence or bridge into the second section of *gobyōshi no iri*. There are no repeated phrases within this first section. Phrase lengths vary from twelve to sixteen to eighteen beats and consist of subphrases of four, six, eight, or ten beats as shown in the following:

| Phrase | Number of beats | Subdivisions of phrases |
|---|---|---|
| Introductory | 16 | 8 + 8 |
| A | 18 | 8 + 8 |
| B | 12 | 8 + 6 |
| C | 16 | 8 + 8 |
| D | 12 | 6 + 6 |
| E | 18 | 10 + 10 |
| F [Bridge] | 16 | 10 + 4 |

The eight-beat unit appears to be the basic phrase unit, which is then expanded into ten beats or abbreviated into four or six beats. The variety of beat groupings fosters a flexibility in phrasing, giving the music an extemporaneous quality.

**Rhythmic Organization** The *tebiragane* players provide a steady pulse in straight quarter-note beats. The only deviation from this steady stream of quarter-note beats is the three beats of eighth notes in the opening phrase, which serve to accelerate movement toward phrase A. The moderato tempo of the given sample is one quarter note ranging from M.M. 104 to 108, and the fundamental rhythmic unit consists of two beats. There are no dynamic or tempo changes in this portion except for the accelerando in the opening phrase.

The *taiko* drum plays in unison with the *tebiragane* in the opening phrase. After that point, however, the *taiko* plays a sparser rhythm in phrases that combine quarter notes and quarter note rests. These note values combine, creating the following rhythmic phrase and its variants:

This and variations of this rhythmic pattern occur as *taiko* accompaniment to phrases A, B, D, and F. They are not played at regular intervals due to the varying lengths of phrases, but they do delineate the beginnings of phrases. In addition, the *taiko* has the colotomic function of playing the last beat to signal the end of the introductory, C, and E phrases.

Rhythmically, the flute melody is quite complex. It employs a wide range of note values from a sixty-fourth note to a double-dotted half note. The thirty-second note occurs the most frequently (45 percent of all the note values employed) because of its extended use in embellished figures. Four groupings of rhythmic motives are shown below to illustrate the rhythmic complexity and variety of the melody:

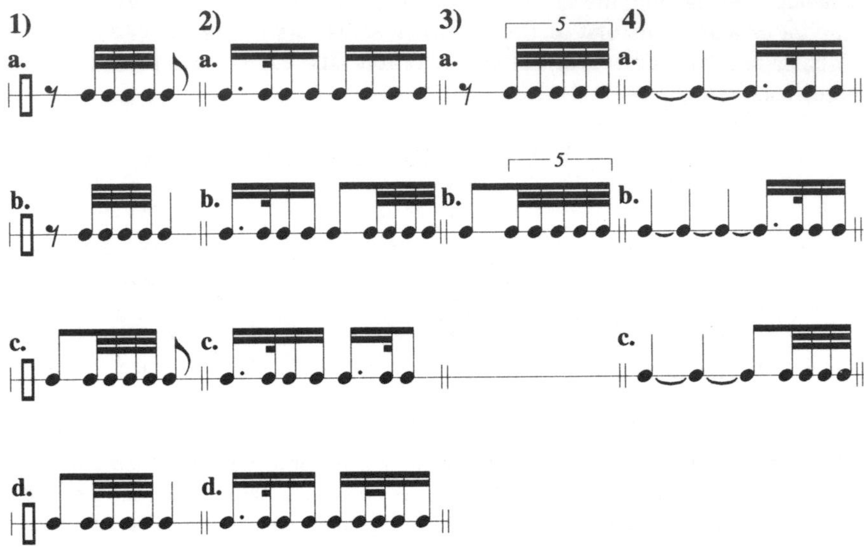


These short rhythmic motives are played in numerous combinations to form longer rhythmic phrases, which are for the most part organized into four-beat or eight-beat groupings. Groupings of four thirty-second notes frequently appear as rhythmic embellishments to sustained tones of durations of an eighth note or longer. The figures

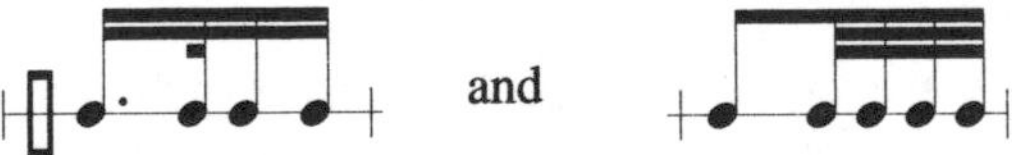


frequently appear as endings to sustained tones of a half note or longer. The melodic rhythm is rubato with a lot of give and take in note durations.

**Tonal Organization** The melody played by the flute is based on an octave-scale formed by a combination of the *miyakobushi* and *minyō* tetrachords which are shown in relative pitch as follows:

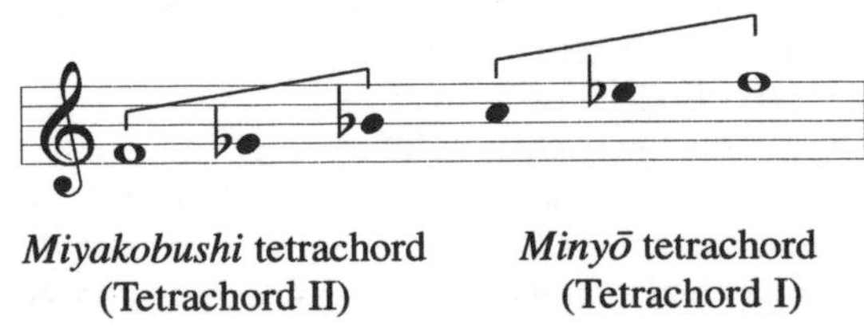

*Miyakobushi* tetrachord (Tetrachord II) *Minyō* tetrachord (Tetrachord I)

These tetrachords emerged from the following weighted scale, illustrating the frequency of occurrence of tones heard in the flute melody:

Pitches F, B♭, and C appear to be important nuclear tones based on not only their frequency of occurrence, but by their function as beginning and ending notes of phrases and as sustained tones held for two or more beats. Also, notes E and F are heavily weighted because of their frequent use in embellishments. Last, one can see from the above scale that the range of the flute in this accompanimental piece spans over three octaves.

The phrases of this melody utilize all five pitches of the octave-scale—F, G♭, B♭, C, and E♭--as tonal centers. The introductory, A, and B phrases establish pitches F and C. Phrases C and D eventually end on pitch F, further reinforcing it. Meanwhile, phrases E and F are less stable, but more varied, in tonally fluctuating between secondary pitches B♭, E♭, and F. The bridge section functions as a transitional passage to the second section of *gobyōshi no iri,* fluctuating between pitches G♭ and B♭.

| Phrase | Tonal Center |
|---|---|
| Introductory | F |
| A | F - C - F |
| B | F - C - F |
| C | C - G♭ - F |
| D | B♭ - F |
| E | B♭ - F - B♭ |
| F | F - E♭ |
| Bridge | B♭ - G♭ |

Melodic movement is primarily conjunct with minor seconds, major seconds (use in embellishments), minor thirds, and major thirds forming 87 percent of the total intervals used. Melodic leaps created at the perfect fourth, perfect fifth, major sixth, and octave add up to 13 percent of all the intervals used.

The melody contains both ascending and descending melodic motives that provide variety to the melodic line, while their many variants create a certain unity. Similar ascending melodic motives include:

Similar descending melodic motives that emerge are:

Ornamentation is an important melodic feature that includes trills, upper and lower neighbor grace notes, and harmonic tones at intervals of a perfect fifth and an octave above the fundamental tone. The following transcription illustrates these embellishments as they occur in the *gobyōshi no iri* melody. Trills function to decorate nuclear pitch F; grace notes ornament notes F, B♭, C, and E♭; and harmonic tones embellish nuclear tones F, B♭, and C.

Trills:

Grace notes—Approached from above:

Grace notes—Approached from below:

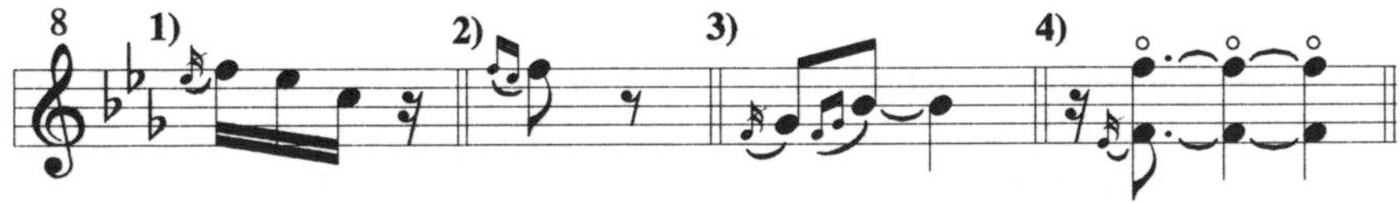


Harmonic tones:

### *Kiri*

The *kiri* instrumental composition is a fast tempo instrumental accompaniment with a quarter note ranging from M.M. 208 to 216. It is heard as accompaniment to dances in the latter half of ceremonial pieces and to battle scenes in the warrior pieces. The rhythm and melody of the *kiri hayashi* composition varies slightly from village to village and, within a single village, from performance to performance. *Kiri*'s form, rhythm, and melody were analyzed from a 154-beat sample (see Appendix Figure A.2.).

**Form** The form of the *kiri* accompanimental piece is a series of four basic phrases and their variants. An introductory phrase establishes the primary nuclear tone F and twelve phrases follow:

Intro-A-B-C-B1-C1-B2-C2-B3-C3-D-B4-D1

Each phrase represents a tonal area whose center is either pitch F, B♭, C or E♭. The sustained use of these pitches reinforces the notes of the octave-scale. The use of pitches F and B♭ outline the lower *miyakobushi* tetrachord and tones C, E♭, and F complete the upper *minyō* tetrachord. Tonal centers for each phrase are as follows:

| Phrase | Tonal Center |
|---|---|
| Introductory | F |
| A | F - C - F |
| B | F - C - F |
| C | B♭ |
| B1 | F - E♭ |
| C1 | B♭ |
| B2 | F - B♭ |
| C2 | B♭ - F |
| B3 | F |
| C3 | B♭ - E♭ |
| D | E♭ |
| B4 | F - B♭ |
| D1 | E♭ - F |

The introductory phrase firmly plants note F as the primary nuclear tone. Phrase A evolves around pitch C, confirming its importance as a nuclear tone. The dominant tonal area of all B phrases center around the pitch F. Pitch B♭ functions as the primary tonal center for all the phrases listed as C, and pitch E♭ is the central pitch for tonal areas in the D phrases. Phrase B and its variants occur with the greatest frequency, functioning to firmly establish the primary nuclear tone F. As a result, the B phrases serve as a tonal frame of reference for all the other phrases.

**Rhythmic Organization** The fundamental rhythm is a two-beat unit played by the *tebiragane* throughout the piece.

This consistently played rhythm allows the *taiko* to perform a more extemporaneous line that adds rhythmic vitality and accents movements of the dancer. The sixteenth and dotted eighth notes in the above figure has a triplet feel with the sixteenth note sustained a fraction of time longer, as indicated by the tenuto marking, resulting in a slight shortening of the dotted eighth note. Rhythmic variations in the *tebiragane* part do occasionally occur, as in the introductory phrase, which begins with twelve quarter notes played in a sequence in measures 1-6 in the sample followed by a rhythm which is the inverse of the two-beat figure above. Later on in the composition, in a portion not included in the sample, another divergence occurs:

These rhythms maintain the basic two-beat unit, and quarter notes are used to substitute for the prevailing one sixteenth and dotted eighth note figure in forming combinations that give variety to the rhythmic line, while maintaining the steady pulse.

The most prevalent *taiko* rhythmic figure performed in unison with the *tebiragane* is

Other rhythmic motives employed are:

These motives show the rhythmic variety of the *taiko* part. They are, for the most part, short. The syncopated figures create rhythmic momentum and punctuate the bold dance movements of warrior characters. Accents on notes of a duration of a dotted eighth note or longer rhythmically enhance the bold postures and movements of the dancer. Emphasis on the beat, an important rhythmic feature of the *taiko* part, balances syncopated rhythms and reinforces the steady beat of the *tebiragane*. The freer *taiko* part creates an arbitrary rhythmic line, in which motives do not appear to be played in a strict progression. Instead they are left to the discretion and skill of the particular drummer as they follow the movements of the dancer.

The rhythmically complex flute melody employs a wide range of note values that range from a thirty-second note to a whole note. Sixteenth notes predominate (63.4 percent of all note values), since they appear in both ornamental figures and melodic motives.

Note values are organized into several motives, which occur in various combinations to create rhythmic unity. Such motives include:

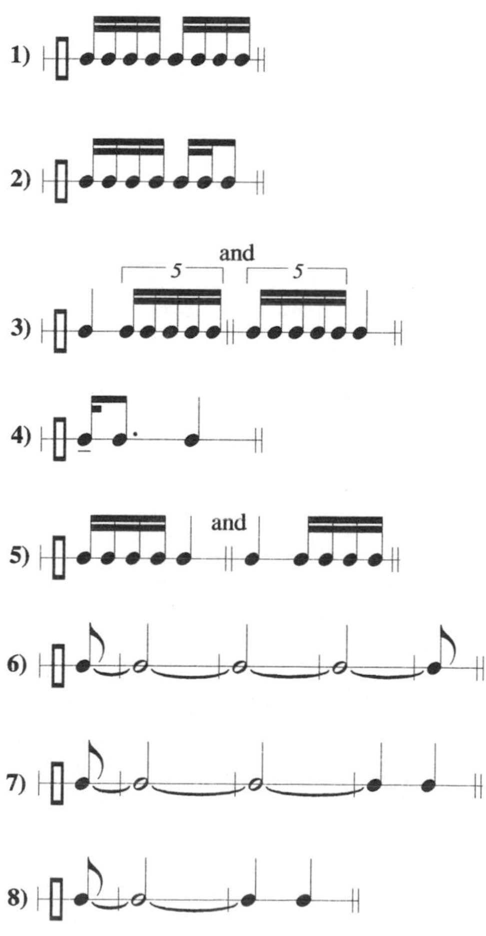

The triplet feel of the sixteenth and dotted eighth figure is the same figure played by both the *tebiragane* and *taiko*. The sixteenth note quintuplet figure characteristic of the *kiri* pattern occurs either as an approach to or movement away from a quarter note. Rhythmic figures shown in examples 1 to 5 above are combined in a variety of ways to form larger rhythmic units providing momentum toward sustained nuclear tones notated in examples 6, 7, and 8. Rhythmic movement is created by the alternation of rapid ornamental figures and sustained nuclear tones held for durations of two to six beats. This alternation shapes the rhythmic organization of the *kiri* pattern.

**Tonal Organization** The *kiri* melody played by the flute is a highly embellished, rather dense line that ranges over two octaves:

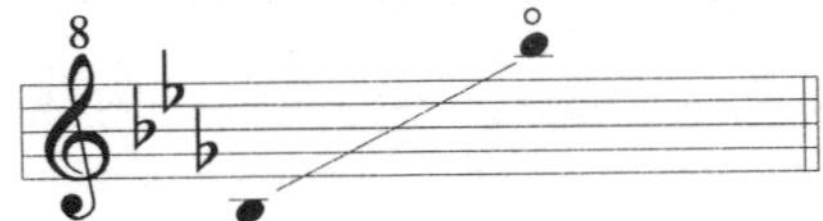


It is based on the same two tetrachords as that of the *gobyōshi no iri* melody: the *miyakobushi* tetrachord or Tetrachord II and the *minyō* tetrachord or Tetrachord I:

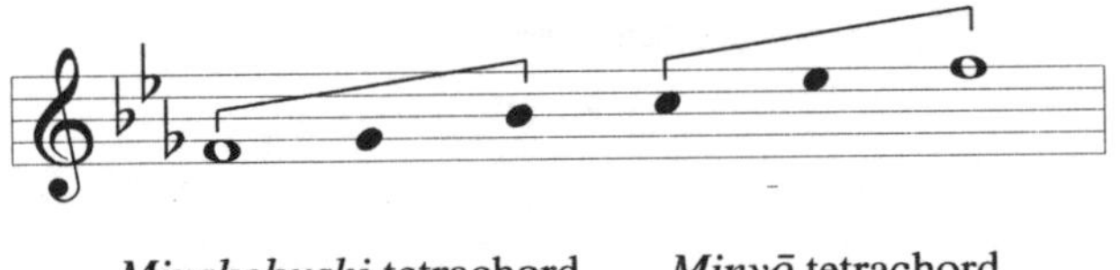

*Miyakobushi* tetrachord (Tetrachord II)   *Minyō* tetrachord (Tetrachord I)

From the tetrachordal structure and weighted scale provided, tones F, B♭, and E♭ emerge as the nuclear tones, with pitch C also having an important role:

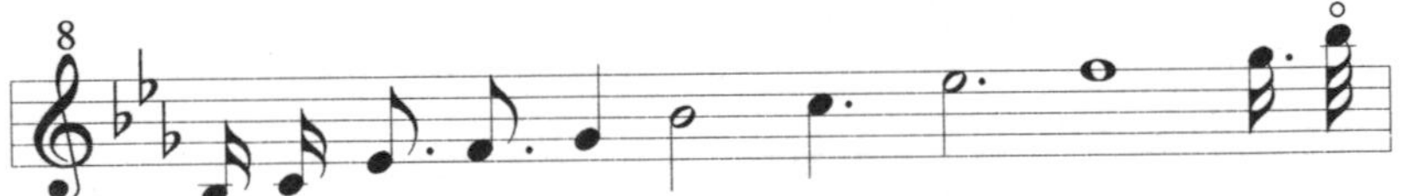


The nuclear tones operate to delineate phrases that have emerged in analyzing the tonal organization of this music. Phrase groupings and their respective tonal centers show that the melody is played in a definite progression of tonal areas, even though phrases are loosely structured over the rhythmic lines of the *tebiragane* and *taiko*. The undulating pitch descent that begins in the introductory phrase and ends in phrase D shows an alternation of pitch that centers primarily between F and B♭. An analysis of succeeding phrases and their tonal centers not included in the sample, however, does not repeat the progression I identified in the section on form above. The fact that this tonal sequence does not repeat indicates that the remainder of what is played is left to the discretion of the flutist, whose decisions may be influenced by his skill, musicality, or perhaps consideration of dramatic effect.

Melodic movement is primarily conjunct with a large number of major and minor second intervals featured in the numerous embellishment figures. Melodic leaps also occur, such as the ascending major and minor sixths that resolve in descending intervals of a minor second, major second, minor third, or perfect fourth interval. These intervals in turn usually resolve upward. Also, major and minor third intervals are frequently heard in tremolo melodic figures.

The melody consists of short motives that occur repeatedly throughout the *kiri* musical piece. Their frequency of occurrence unifies the melody, creating a coherent composition. Six such melodic motives are:

Melodic motives 1 and 2 are used regularly as endings to phrases.

Certain ornamental figures also occur regularly. Embellishments that serve as an approach to sustained tones include trills and tremolos:

Trills primarily decorate tones E♭ and B♭, while tremolos of a minor third interval regularly embellish tones G♭ and C. Harmonic tones sounded at a perfect fifth or octave create an added tonal dimension above sustained tones C, B♭, and F:

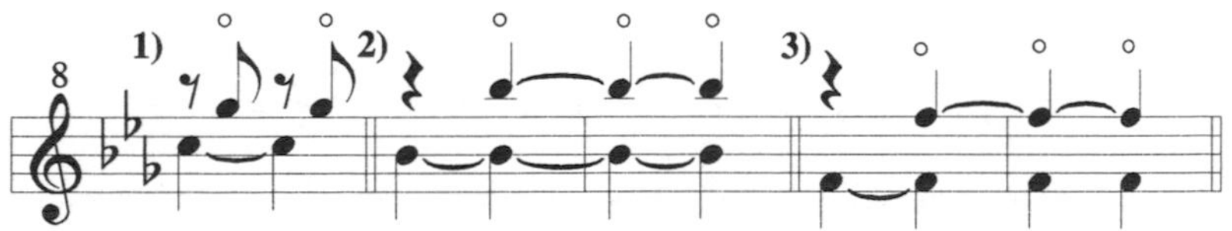


An important feature is the alternation of short melodic motives and ornamental figures with sustained nuclear tones. The results are melodic and rhythmic contrasts, in which the flurry of movement of the melodic motives and ornaments generates tension and momentum, and the sustained nuclear tones serve as a release and resolution.

### *Sagari ha*

Among all the instrumental music compositions, *sagari ha* has the slowest tempo, with a quarter note equal to M.M. 76-80. It is performed as an accompaniment for women characters portrayed in the *nōmai* dramas and for dance sections in the first half of the ceremonial pieces "Okina" and "Henzai." The slow tempo accommodates the dignified choreography of the ceremonial dances and the elegant, graceful movements performed by women characters. A complete statement of *sagari ha*, provided in the transcription (see Appendix Figure 3.A.), is repeated until the dance ends.

**Form** The repetition of two phrases and a bridge section form the continuous music of *sagari ha:*

| Phrase | Introductory | A | B | Bridge |
|---|---|---|---|---|
| No. of beats | 8 | 8 | 16 | 8 |

An eight-beat introductory phrase, played solo by the flute, opens this *hayashi* composition, followed by an eight-beat phrase A. A sixteen-beat phrase B and eight-beat bridge section complete one statement of this pattern. Phrase symmetry is achieved with the eight-beat phrase A and bridge section balancing the sixteen-beat length of phrase B. Tonally, the melodies in both phrases A and B center around the same pitches: E, A, and D. In phrase B, however, there is a cadence on the primary nuclear tone A, and the bridge section functions as a coda further emphasizing pitch A. Phrases are rhythmically delineated by accented beats played by the *taiko* and *tebiragane* and by cadentially sustained tones in the flute melody.

**Rhythmic Organization** Both the *tebiragane* and *taiko* perform eight-beat units, forming the rhythmic foundation for *sagari ha.* The eight-beat unit features a combination of quarter notes and the sixteenth and dotted eighth-note figure as follows:

The *taiko* also plays the above rhythm, but grace notes are added as embellishments to the first four consecutive quarter notes and the sixteenth and dotted eighth-note figure on beats five and seven. The tempo of the *tebiragane* and *taiko* rhythmic line fluctuates slightly with a quarter note averaging M.M. 76.

The eight-beat unit can be subdivided into two four-beat units, forming two distinct rhythmic motives:

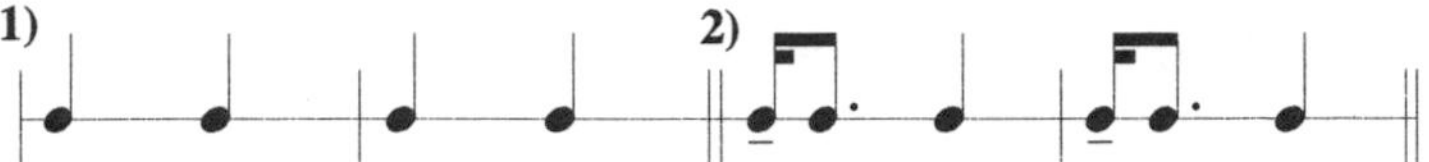


Together, they form one coherent unit. As seen in both the *gobyōshi no iri* and *kiri* accompaniments, the sixteenth and dotted eighth figure in example 2 is actually heard as a slightly sustained sixteenth note, resulting in a delayed attack of the dotted eighth note. The *taiko* rhythm is executed on the wood rim of both drumheads, as well as squarely on the drumhead itself. Grace notes, which embellish the quarter or sixteenth notes on beats 2, 5, 6, 7, and 8, are played on the wood rim. In Japanese drumming, the hard, wooden sound made by striking the rim of the drumhead is expressed by the onomatopoeic term *ka*, while the sound of the drumhead being struck is identified as *don*. The use of these contrasting timbres adds variety to the unison rhythmic line played by both *tebiragane* and *taiko*.

The note values employed in the rhythmically complex flute melody cover a wide range, from a sixty-fourth note to a dotted half note. Sixty-fourth notes and thirty-second notes form 57.7 percent of all the values used as a result of the highly embellished character of the melody. The sixteenth note occurs with the next most frequency at 16.3 percent, while eighth notes, dotted eighth notes, quarter notes, dotted quarter notes, one double dotted quarter note, half notes, and dotted half notes form the remaining 26 percent of the total note values. These notes are played in a rubato tempo, forming a free-flowing melodic line over the steady rhythm of the *taiko* and *tebiragane*.

The most prevalent rhythm is the dotted sixteenth and thirty-second note.

Other characteristics of the rhythm in the flute melody are the irregular rhythmic groupings of seven thirty-second notes and five thirty-second notes in embellished figures.

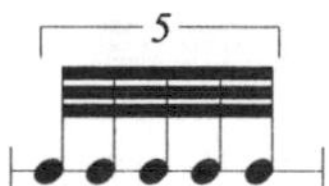


Another rhythmic grouping is that of six thirty-second notes or six sixty-fourth notes, which are actually formed from two triplet groupings of these notes combined.

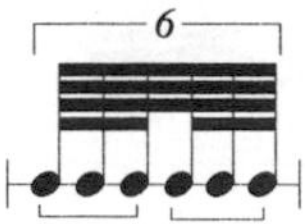


These groupings are used to ornament the final, sustained pitches of phrase B and the bridge section.

**Tonal Organization** The leading movement of embellished figures toward nuclear tones shapes the flute melody. It is based on an octave-scale consisting of two disjunct *miyakobushi* tetrachords:

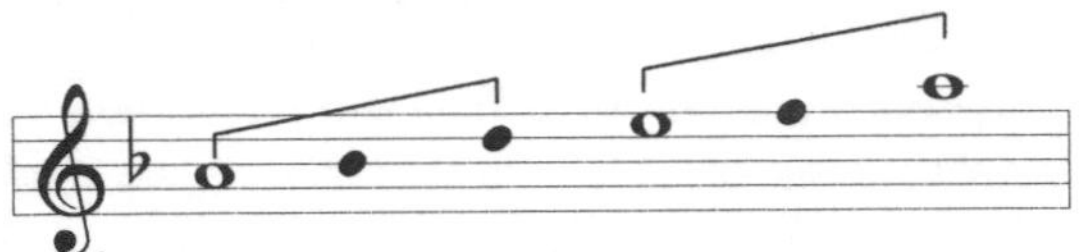

*Miyakobushi* tetrachord (Tetrachord II) *Miyakobushi* tetrachord (Tetrachord II)

The nuclear tones A, D, and E were determined from the weighted scale provided, while B♭ and F emerged as important pitches:

The tonal material from both tetrachords (A, B♭, D and E, F, A) are all well integrated in the flute melody. Melodic movement is generally conjunct with intervals of a minor second, major second, and major third occurring in embellishment figures, forming 91.7 percent of all the intervals employed in the sample. Some disjunct movement is created by skips of a perfect fourth, major sixth, major seventh, and perfect octave, which occur between phrases, subphrases, or at cadences.

The use of three melodic motives and their variants create unity in the melody:

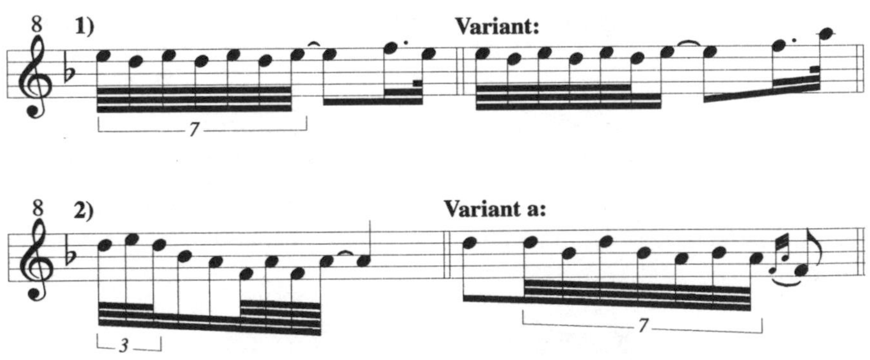

In motives 1 and 2 embellishing figures decorate nuclear tones E, A, or D. The ornamental figure in motive 3 functions to decorate the movement from nuclear tone E to D. These motives are only approximate representations of the types of melodic motives characteristic of the *sagari ha* instrumental piece, since factors such as the skill of the individual player and variations in tempo affect what is actually played.

A variety of ornaments—trills, tremolos, and grace notes—ornament the melody. Trills on pitch E function as an opening melodic figure to phrases A and B. Alternating pitches F and A occur in a tremolo figure serving to embellish pitch A. Grace notes decorate pitches A, B♭, D, E, and F from both ascending and descending directions in intervals that range from a minor second to a major seventh:

Harmonic tones an octave above the fundamental are heard above sustained pitch A at the end of phrase B and in the bridge section:

This figure functions cadentially to reinforce pitch A as the primary nuclear tone of the *sagari ha* composition.

### *Kai no kudari*

The final instrumental composition presented in this chapter is *kai no kudari.* A sixty-four-beat sample, equivalent to one full statement of the piece, is provided for an analysis of its form and rhythmic and melodic components (see

Appendix Figure 4.A.).

As told by Mr. Ōta, the melody of this instrumental piece is said to have originated when a son of the Kai family was adopted by the Nanbu clan, who ruled the western area of present-day Aomori Prefecture. The son was homesick for his family and in his loneliness played the flute. The melody he played was known as "Kai no kudari," which can be translated as "Coming from Kai" (Kai is a geographical designation as well as a family name). As the title of the melody infers, the music is primarily used for processions, that is, music to accompany travelling.

*Kai no kudari* is one of the first music pieces taught to neophyte instrumentalists, since it is frequently played for performances. It serves as an accompaniment to "Bangaku," the dance performed in the first half of the prayer piece "Gongenmai," which is the most central dance piece of the *nōmai* repertoire.

This piece also provides musical accompaniment for a number of ritual events. One is for processions transporting the wooden lion's head, or *gongen-gashira*, from its storage place to the home of the village *betto* (ceremonial leader), then to the community assembly hall, where it is enshrined during *nōmai* performances, and finally back again to the village Shinto shrine or private home where it is kept for the remainder of the year. *Kai no kudari* also accompanies the dance of exorcism performed for the dedication of new homes. Last, this composition accompanies the procession referred to as *kado uchi,* which was introduced earlier. In *kado uchi,* musicians play *kai no kudari* for *nōmai* dancers who process from house to house in their village, performing "Gongenmai" in the front doorway of each home.

**Form** An introductory phrase opens this *hayashi* composition. Four phrases are then combined to form one full statement of *kai no kudari* :

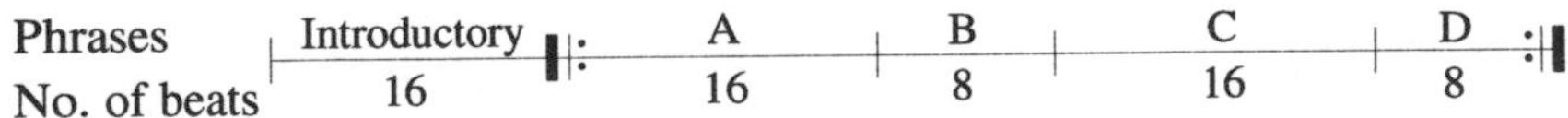


Phrases A, B, C, and D are repeated over and over as one complete unit until the dance ends. Each phrase begins with an ornamental figure on pitch F, and all phrases end on sustained pitches F establishing it as the primary nuclear tone. Unity among the phrases is achieved by repeated melodic and rhythmic motives, embellishments at the beginning of each phrase, and sustained tones that signal the end of each phrase. Diversity is provided by the variety of ornamental figures and the intervallic leaps in the flute melody.

**Rhythmic Organization** *Tebiragane* supply the fundamental rhythm of *kai no kudari,* as we have seen in the analysis of the other three *hayashi* pieces. The tempo fluctuates slightly with a quarter note ranging from M.M. 108 to 112. The *tebiragane* part employs three note values—sixteenth notes, dotted eighths, and quarter notes—in the following simple rhythm, which is repeated continuously throughout the piece.

The *taiko* part is also played in note values of sixteenth notes, dotted eighth notes, and quarter notes. The rhythmic motives in which these note values appear, however, are more varied than in the *tebiragane* part and four motives emerge as distinct units:

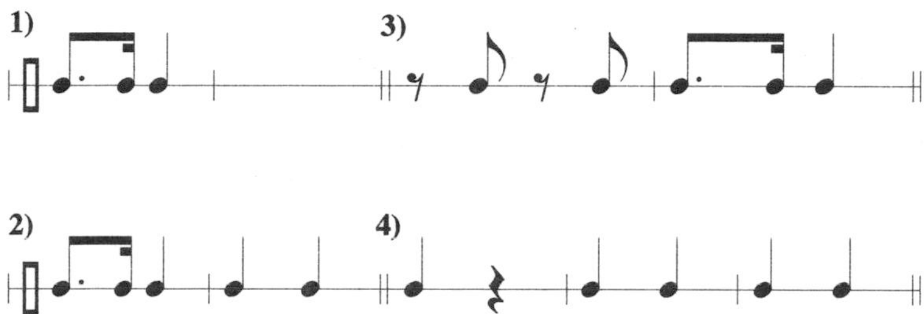


It should be mentioned that the *taiko* plays motif 1 regularly at the end of each phrase—a factor that was useful in determining phrase structure.

The flute melody is presented in note values that range from a sixty-fourth note to a whole note. Thirty-second and sixteenth notes in embellishment figures occur with the greatest frequency (65.2 percent of all the note values used), while eighth notes make up the next most frequently used note values (12.5 percent). Dotted sixteenth, eighth, quarter, and half notes are also important note values combined to form rhythmic motives. Half notes, dotted half notes, double-dotted half notes, and whole notes represent the values of sustained pitches, which occur cadentially at the end of phrases. These note values are played with a great amount of rubato within the tempo established and maintained by the *tebiragane* players.

Numerous rhythmic motives give the melody variety and momentum:

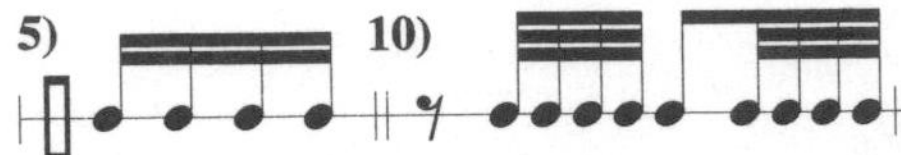


These short motives combine to form larger rhythmic units that are characterized by the movement of rapid rhythmic figures toward a sustained pitch. Some of these motives appear in embellishing figures that function to ornament important pitches F, B♭, and C. The rhythmic organization of *kai no kudari* features the alternation of rapid rhythmic figures that create tension and sustained notes that provide release.

**Tonal Organization** The flute melody is based on an octave-scale containing two disjunct tetrachords: the *miyakobushi*, or Tetrachord II, and the *minyō*, or Tetrachord I:

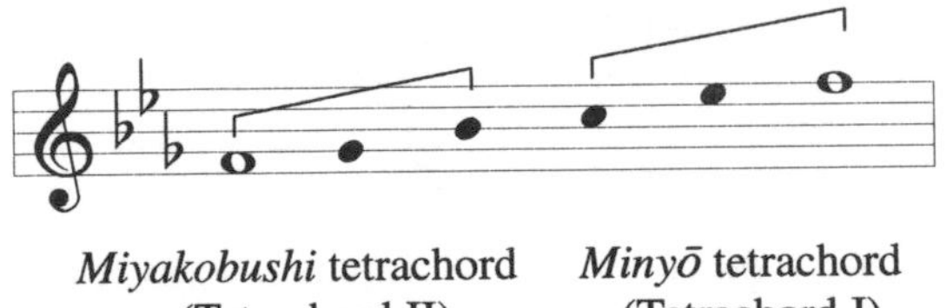

*Miyakobushi* tetrachord (Tetrachord II) *Minyō* tetrachord (Tetrachord I)

This tetrachord structure emerged from the frequency rate of the notes, as shown in the weighted scale below, and their melodic function:

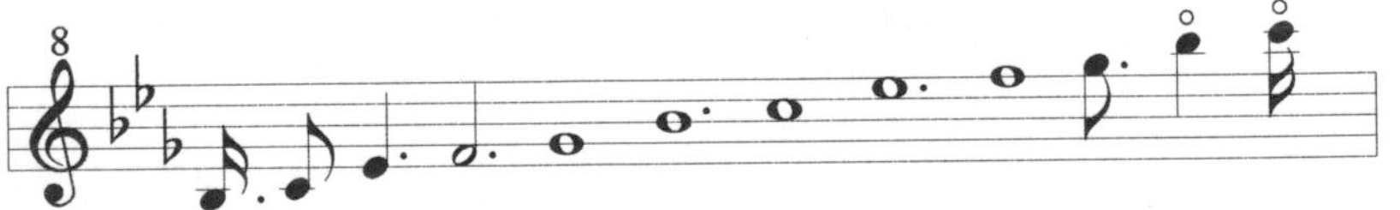


The melody, which has a range of just over two octaves, is composed of a series of tonal areas that evolve around nuclear tones F and B♭.

The wide range of melodic intervals used in the melody include those between a minor second and a perfect octave as well as major ninths and perfect elevenths. The predominantly conjunct movement of the melody is evident from the frequent use of major seconds, minor thirds, and major thirds, which make up 64.8 percent of all the intervals employed. There are, however, more intervallic leaps in this melody, in contrast to the fewer leaps found in the melodies of the other instrumental pieces. The frequent leap of a tone to its octave harmonic and the frequent leaps to tone F, in the introductory phrase and phrases A, C, and D, create a disjunct line.

A number of melodic motives serve to unify the melody. The majority are short and equivalent to one beat. None of the short motives provided below occur in the exact same rhythm or arrangement of pitches twice and the following variants emerge:

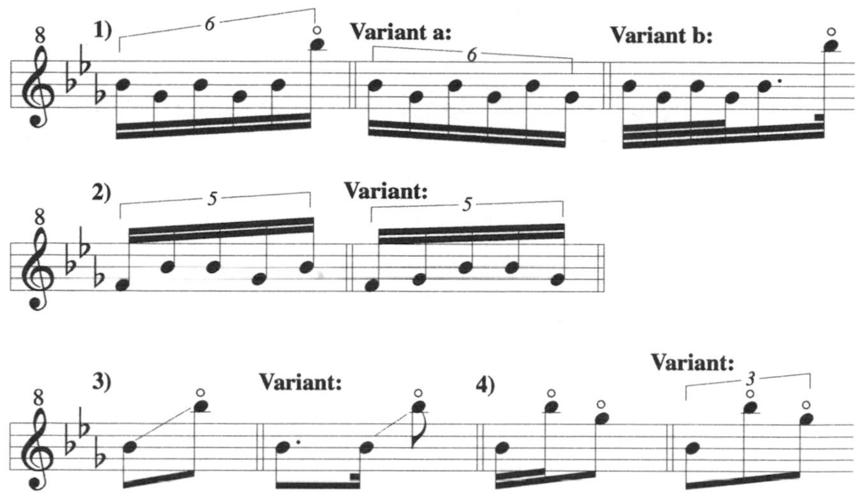


The following phrases are two versions of a melodic sequence that function cadentially at the end of both the introductory phrase and phrase B. Both sequences appear throughout *kai no kudari*, but they vary each time they are stated.

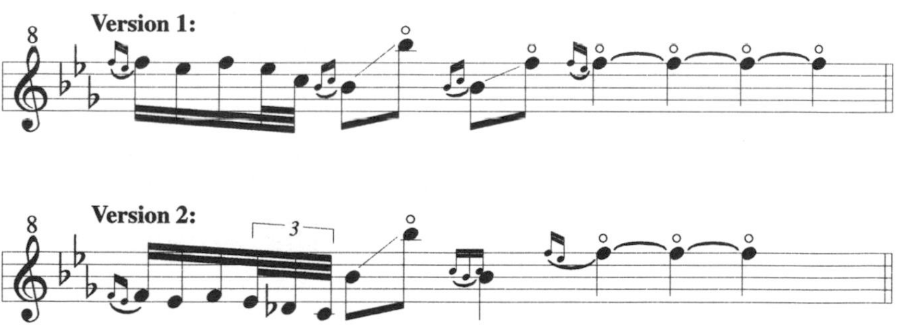


Numerous trills, grace notes, and harmonic tones embellish the flute melody. Trills function to ornament nuclear tones B♭ and F:

Grace notes are used as an approach to pitches F, B♭, and C from both above and below at intervals of a minor second, major second, or minor third.

Grace notes—Approached from above:

Grace notes—Approached from below:

Harmonic tones at both a perfect fifth and perfect octave are simultaneously heard above sustained pitches C, F, and B♭:

The extensive use of harmonic tones distinguishes *kai no kudari.* The technique of overblowing facilitates perfect fifth and octave leaps, in addition to creating a denser melodic line on sustained tones.

All of the ornaments above embellish pitches F, B♭, and C. This confirms the importance of these notes within the tetrachordal structure of the melody.

## OVERALL TEXTURE OF THE *HAYASHI* COMPOSITIONS

The three instruments of the *hayashi*—*tebiragane*, *taiko*, and *fue*—combine to form three layers of sound. The steady rhythm of the *tebiragane* is a layer that serves as a rhythmic foundation. The more extemporaneous *taiko* part forms a second layer of sound, and floating above the cymbal and drum parts is the rubato flute melody. The *tebiragane* and *taiko* sometimes play in rhythmic unison, but for the most part the *taiko* plays either a more sparse rhythm based upon that of the *tebiragane*, or a more decorated rhythmic line. In general, the *taiko* and *tebiragane* players listen to one another to synchronize their playing, especially when accompanying dancers.

The steady playing of the *tebiragane* is of particular importance for the flute player, who plays a highly embellished melody that results in a great amount of rhythmic variability. The sustained notes in the *fue* melody rely heavily on the consistent *tebiragane* beat as a time referent.

The overall texture is a loosely woven one; the *tebiragane* establishes a defined rhythmic structure within which liberties are taken by both the *taiko* and *fue* players. Variety and contrast result from these layers of sound. The three instruments of the *hayashi*, however, do not always perform together. In many of the song sections the flute drops out and the singers provide the melody; then when the song is finished the instrumental composition changes and the flute is heard again. On these occasions, the texture changes slightly, since the song melodies that replace the flute melodies are simpler and less ornamented.

## SUMMARY OF ORGANIZING PRINCIPLES

Rhythm is an outstanding feature of *nōmai* instrumental music. This is to be expected, since the primary function of the *hayashi* is to provide musical accompaniment for dance. The *tebiragane* players provide a steady beat and the *taiko* drummer plays a dynamic line that accents the movements of the dancer. The basic rhythmic unit in all of the accompanimental pieces is a two-beat unit. Rhythmic phrases, for the most part, form from the compounding of the two-beat unit into four-beat, six-beat, or eight-beat groupings.

The time-keeping function of the *tebiragane* requires simple rhythms. Quarter notes, a dotted eighth followed by a sixteenth note and its inverse are the rhythmic figures primarily employed. These note values occur in small units of two or four beats. An important rhythmic feature of *nōmai* music is the triplet feel of the above dotted rhythms heard in all the *hayashi* musical compositions. Needed research on the origin of this triplet feel may reveal some connection to the triplet rhythm heard in Korean music. Also, the *taiko* playing style of placing the drum horizontally and striking both drumheads from the right and left sides is reminiscent of the playing style of the Korean *changgo* and not commonly found in Japan.

The role of the *taiko* is varied. The freer rhythms of this instrument give the music a spontaneous quality. The *taiko* occasionally accents the last beat of a phrase to delineate phrases. The simpler and more regular rhythms of the *tebiragane* allow the *taiko* to follow the choreography of the dancer and accent certain movements. The often-syncopated rhythms played by the drum act to rhythmically propel the music forward and the timbre and loudness of the drum sound create excitement. The dynamics of strong and weak beats also adds to the excitement and energy created.

Additionally, the *taiko* has a leading role in the comic plays. The drummer accents the movements of the comic character and verbally responds to this character in the partly set, partly extemporized dialogue of the play.

Variables in the *tebiragane* and *taiko* parts do exist. Rhythms played by the *tebiragane* are set, although the tempo may vary slightly depending upon the dance being performed or the character being portrayed. There is some variability in the tempo of a single piece from one playing to the next as well. *Taiko* rhythms are also variable, depending upon the skill or playing style of individual drummers.

The rubato rhythm of the highly ornamented flute melody is also an important rhythmic feature. Many sections are played freely, with the flutist making the length of phrases at times indefinite, particularly in the *kiri* accompanimental piece (Kojima 1965: 102). Eight-beat phrases, where they occur, can be subdivided either into four two-beat units or two four-beat units, dictated in part by the phrasing of the flute melody.

A flurry of highly ornamented notes played in between sustained tones generally characterizes flute melodies. Tonal material is organized around nuclear tones, which often occur at the beginning, middle, or end of phrases as sustained tones. Nuclear tones are emphasized in phrases to provide melodic stability. The melody tends to be more intricate in the slower tempo pieces. Fast tempo melodies tend to be slightly less embellished. Ornamentation functions to decorate and emphasize pitches and create conjunct melodic movement. Embellishments used include grace notes, trills, tremolos, and harmonic tones. Harmonic tones overblown at a perfect fifth or octave above sustained tones are an important feature of *nōmai* flute melodies. The range of melodies is usually two octaves, although *gobyōshi no iri* composition employs a three-octave range.

The musicologist Kojima Tomiko proposes that the prolonging of certain notes by the flutist displays a strong influence of the folk music genre called *oiwake.* She believes that this prolongation increases the number of regulated beats in the rhythmic breathing of the flute player. This type of rhythmic sense is perceived in the folk songs sung by the local people on Shimokita Peninsula and the northern Tōhoku region (1965: 103).

The timbre and high-pitched melody of the flute functions to create tension and excitement in accompanying dance sections. The success in achieving this is predicated on the individual flutist's skill in phrasing, techniques of embellishment, and ability to control changes in tempo and dynamics (Kojima 1965: 102).

Within the loose structure of the instrumental music pieces, phrasing of the flute melody is not strict or set. It varies from player to player and even from one playing to another by the same musician. For example, among three transcribed examples of *gobyōshi no iri* played in Shishipashi, no two are identical, each slightly differing in rhythm and the execution of melodic embellishments. Less-skilled flutists play simpler embellishments. Other variables in the flute melody result from the differing melodic interpretation and playing styles transmitted in a particular village or of individual flutists.

*Nōmai* flute melodies are principally composed from octave-scales, with the *miyakobushi* tetrachord in the lower part of the conjunction and the *minyō* tetrachord in the upper part. The *miyakobushi* scale came into being around 1650. The development of *shugen nō* or *yamabushi kagura*, however, is traced to the 12th century. Kojima speculates that the original scale used in *nōmai* was the *ritsu* scale, which is found in other forms of *yamabushi kagura.* The *miyakobushi* scale, she adds, occurs in the flute music of a type of *kagura*, called *daikagura*, in Mena village in Higashidorimura, which had a strong influence on other music in the area. She proposes that the *ritsu* scale was modified into the *miyakobushi* scale as a consequence of the influence of Mena's *daikagura* flute music and the changing tastes of the people in the region (Kojima 1965: 101).

Three of the four *hayashi* compositions employ a scale comprised of both the *miyakobushi* and *minyō* tetrachords. The uniformity among the three compositions of using the same scale makes the use of a different scale in the *sagari ha* piece a glaring one. The melody in *sagari ha* is based on an octave-scale created by combining two *miyakobushi* tetrachords. This difference may point to *sagari ha* being a later addition to the *nōmai* music repertoire. The *miyakobushi* tetrachord's connection to traditional art music—that of the *koto*, *shamisen*, and *shakuhachi*—as well as folk melodies that originated in urban areas, gives us clues to its possible origin. The possibility that the *sagari ha* composition originated outside of the *nōmai* tradition is based on the existence of music of the same name in *nō* drama. The similar function of *sagari ha* music as accompaniment to women's dances in both *nōmai* and *nō* reinforces the probability that this composition stems from the same source, most likely that of *sarugaku*. Greater research is needed to make such a case.

The Shinto origin of *nōmai's* ceremonial and prayer dances suggests that *nōmai* instrumental music is also borrowed from Shinto, since music was adopted along with the dances it accompanied. The musical instrumentation and texture of the *nōmai hayashi* and local *kagura* groups are identical, and both share elements of rhythm and melody. A more detailed comparison of the music of these two genres requires a separate study, but I maintain that the musical foundation of *nōmai* instrumental music is *kagura* instrumental music, which was already in existence when *yamabushi* came to Shimokita Peninsula and developed *nōmai*. This is supported by the fact that *nōmai* is regarded as a type of *yamabushi kagura*. Use of the term *kagura* in *yamabushi kagura* substantiates the outright appropriation of elements of this genre by *yamabushi* as the musical foundation for their dance drama.

The musical pieces of the *hayashi* analyzed in this chapter alternate in creating continuous music that serves to unify dance and song sections within a single piece. Bridge patterns, not covered in the present study, function as smooth musical transitions made between dance sections and song sections. The instrumental music is the cohesive and musical force behind dance in *nōmai* dramas.

# 8

# Poetry and Narrative in Song

*Nōmai* dance dramas feature both singing and heightened speech. Song texts provide the context, background, or story of the pieces. Vocal production, as described by Junzo Hatanaka of Ōri, involves tightening the throat, inhaling, then exhaling slowly, while supporting the voice with the abdomen. The singers, called *utagake*, sing in a forceful style that is similar to the singing in *nō* drama. Mr. Ōta remarked that kabuki vocal techniques (*hassei hō*) are also incorporated.

Singers, Mr. Ōta added, do not have to have a good voice. Use of the abdomen is important, as in the singing style of *nō,* and breath is controlled from the chest. The desirable vocal quality is tense, forceful, and low in pitch.

One aspect of the singing style is the gradual rising in pitch of the melody. In the prayer dance "Gongenmai," for example, the singers intentionally sing sharper when the lion, symbolically representing the presence of the *gongen* deity, appears. Raising the pitch level creates tension, bringing the dance to a climax.

Responsorial singing between the leader and chorus in *nōmai* songs is a musical texture heard in Japanese folk songs, Buddhist chant, and *kagura* songs. The vocal parts overlap slightly in places where the chorus enters before the soloist finishes. There is not much dynamic variation in the voices. One exception is the slight crescendo heard in the final phrases of song sections in the warrior pieces, which are presented in heightened speech and serve as a kind of cadence.

Performers do not sing while dancing, but they occasionally vocalize *kakegoe.* These are short, rhythmic calls that dancers emit to accentuate their movements. Fellow performers also provide *kakegoe* at prescribed times to punctuate the music and to provide social reinforcement for the dancer. The points in a performance where *kakegoe* occur are traditionally set, and the words emitted depend on the particular rhythm of the musical accompaniment of the *hayashi.* In Shishipashi, for example, words used for *kakegoe* during the playing of the *kiri* accompanimental piece are *ha* and *cha.* In the warrior dances, *ha cha ha* or *ha* are heard. *Kakegoe* also include moans (*unari*) or growls (*igami*). Words to depict moans are *ya*, *yaa*, *wee*, and *oi*, while growls are sounded *hai do ha*, *haiya ha, ya haa....*, and *yoi do saa*. These words and phrases vary according to which of the three *nōmai* lineages villages belong. *Kakegoe* must be produced forcefully from the abdomen to be heard above the music of the *hayashi* or to be effective as a means of accentuation.

At least three singers perform from behind the stage curtain. They usually stand so that they can watch the dancer through the slits in the curtain, which are at eye level. Their voices also project better toward the audience through the slits. Often, microphones are used to amplify the singing, which would otherwise be muffled by the stage curtain. All members of a *nōmai* group are supposed to learn the songs. For performances, however, the older members sing, since younger members are busy dancing or playing *kane* and *taiko*. Songs are learned during rehearsals, when all members not dancing or playing an instrument are encouraged to sing. Fifty years ago, before the advent of songbooks, everyone memorized the song texts. Now, however, only a few older members in each group perform from memory. I did not observe any particular instruction or method for learning the songs. Instead, they seem to be learned through repetition.

There are three categories of songs: (1) *hairi no uta,* sung at the beginning of pieces, (2) *makudashi*, sung before the dancer enters the stage, and (3) *makuzuki*, which serve as accompaniment to dance or are sung between dance sections, while the dancer reposes at the rear of the dance area. In the longer pieces, the *makuzuki* song alternates with dance sections. A fourth context for singing is in the *utagakari* section, which combines the simultaneous performance of dance, song, and *hayashi* accompaniment to create a climactic ending in some of the longer pieces.

Song overlaps with dance in the *makudashi* and *makuzuki* song sections in many pieces. One example is "Kanemaki," in which singers provide extensive narration for the complex story of the dance drama. Singing occurs both with and without *hayashi* accompaniment. Flute parts often alternate with song. Only occasionally are both melodies simultaneously heard. Singing is both musically and textually a vital element that dramatizes the dance.

## BACKGROUND ON *NŌMAI* SONGS

*Nōmai* song melodies exhibit attributes of song styles from Japan's medieval period, including *yōkyoku* (*nō* recitation), *heikyoku* (epic-ballads), *saimon* (hymns used in Buddhist, Shinto, and Confucian rites), and a genre of song from a ballad drama called *kōwakamai.* The basis for these vocal styles and for medieval Japanese songs in general is Buddhist chant, or *shōmyō*.

The primary influence of Buddhist chant on *nōmai* songs is a result of the dissemination of folk music by Buddhist evangelists, who composed vernacular pieces that would be more accessible and appealing to the rural population. The existence of older folk song traditions that have a Buddhist overtone to their texts and sometimes a distinct *shōmyō* quality in their melodies is evidence of this influence (Malm 1974: 71). The predominance of *shōmyō* in *nōmai* songs is attributable to the *yamabushis'* Buddhist music orientation and training, as well as their desire to have *nōmai* serve as a didactic form of entertainment with which to proselytize to the provincial population.

The dominance of Chinese ceremonial and religious music, which began in the 8th century, receded as Japan by the 11th century began to compose sacred music that was distinctly its own. Two new forms of Buddhist psalmody that emerged as a result of Buddhist reforms at the end of the 12th century were *kōshiki* and *hyōbyaku. Kōshiki* hymns are didactic in nature and are sung as praises to deities and ancestors. These hymns are considered narrative *shōmyō*, since emphasis is placed on conveying the words, rather than the efficacy of tones sung. *Kōshiki* are half-sung and half-chanted on the same note and end in a melodic cadence (Tanba 1981: 49). *Yōkyoku* melodies closely resemble the melodic line of *kōshiki*. This fact indirectly links *nōmai* song melodies to *kōshiki* melodies. This connection is substantiated by *nōmai* performers who claim that there are similarities between *yōkyoku* and *nōmai* song melodies.

In the medieval period, *saimon*—a type of hymn used in Buddhist, Shinto, and Confucian rites—were adopted for use by *yamabushi* to interpret omens. In this capacity, the songs were referred to as *shōdō saimon* and their religious and didactic nature was retained. In the Edo period (1600-1868), *saimon* were integrated into various folk dramatic forms. One such example is the popularization by a man named Satsuma Wakadayū, who used it as accompaniment to puppet performances. *Shōdō saimon,* also known as *yamabushi saimon,* is still extant in the Hana Matsuri (Flower Festival) held on Mt. Mikawa in Yamagata Prefecture. The extensive use of the *saimon* by *yamabushi* and the integration of this song genre in folk dramatic forms makes it a likely musical source for *nōmai* songs.

It is important to mention the *saimon* sung by *itako* in their role as mediums. The coupling of *yamabushi* and *itako* in northeastern Japan give the *saimon* sung by these mediums significance. This connection requires further study and unfortunately it is not covered in this study.

Fragmented texts of songs in *nōmai*'s ceremonial pieces reveal their origins in ritual Shinto songs called *kagura uta.* These songs invited gods and consoled spirits to presentations of symbolic offerings and dances, intended as appeasing entertainment in exchange for the prolongation of life and continued welfare of the community. *Kagura uta* and the song types discussed above were most likely heard in *sarugaku* performances, given at major temples and shrines in the provincial regions of Japan by itinerant troupes. *Yamabushi* were likely exposed to these performances during their extensive pilgrimages to major temples and shrines throughout Japan. The coexistence of temples and shrines was common during the medieval period, when Shintoism and Buddhism coalesced into a hybrid religion called Ryōbu Shinto (Dual Shinto). This coexistence often brought many rituals, music, and dance of both Shinto and Buddhism together in a single event. Undoubtedly, the songs in these performances served as models for *yamabushi* in their development of *nōmai* songs.

## *NŌMAI SONG TEXTS*

*Nōmai* was originally an oral tradition, but today performers use songbooks that were first compiled in 1947 as an aid for memorizing song texts. The songbooks, *uta hon*, have helped to preserve *nōmai* songs; most singers use them during performance, although it is considered desirable for performers to memorize song texts. The *uta hon* of Shishipashi is written in the phonetic syllabary *hiragana*, which Mr. Ōta claims is the written form originally used for these songbooks. The librettos were first compiled and written in *hiragana* since many people could not read Chinese ideograms, *kanji*, which constitute the basis of written Japanese. Then in 1947, when librettos were formally compiled for all *nōmai* groups, *kanji* were inserted. This development has created problems, since many erroneous *kanji* now appear in the texts (many ideograms share the same word, but have different meanings), and the meaning of the lyrics is obscured even more.

Such problems stem in part from the ancient nature of the language, together with the fact that these songs have been transmitted orally for generations until fifty years ago. Adding to the difficulty is that the texts of the older ceremonial and prayer songs are believed to date back as far as the 8th century or earlier. Substitution of the standard pronunciation of words in the text with pronunciation peculiar to the local dialect of Higashidorimura, *zuzu-ben*, has also added to the corruption of *nōmai* song texts. Further complications in studying the song texts are owed to the differing content and sequences of textual lines among the thirteen villages.

I have not included entire song texts and their translations, since most of the songs are difficult to decipher. Some meanings of the songs were arrived at by consensus reached by comparing the texts of the thirteen villages that actively perform *nōmai* and then determining which meanings occurred most frequently or which fit into the context of a particular song. Singers, when asked if they understood the texts of the songs, replied that they do not literally understand much of what they sing, but that in some songs the general meaning can be derived from the underlying ritual, ceremony, myth, or well-known legend of a play.

Characterization is not a developed technique in *nōmai* texts or texts of other dramatic traditions in medieval Japan, in which an individual character is described only by a short epithet or a single descriptive adjective, since they are often well known historical or legendary figures (Araki 1978: 113). Araki also points out that there has been a tendency in the traditional dramatic arts of Japan to place an emphasis upon the stylized mode of delivery of song texts, rather than actual literary content. This may account for the fact that song texts for the ceremonial, prayer, and warrior dances form a patchwork of quotations and fragments from classical poetry, sacred Buddhist or Shinto song texts, or legends and epics, which are arranged in poetic form and sung to melodies borrowed from chants of the Tendai Buddhist sect or Shinto deity songs. These quotations or fragments were incorporated into songs accompanying ritualistic dances or into a loose plot in pieces intended to tell a story (Nakamura 1971: 65).

## *GIREIMAI* (CEREMONIAL DANCES)

### "Torimai" (Chicken Dance)

In the ceremonial dance "Torimai," sacred songs called *kami uta* (deity songs) provide accompaniment throughout the dance. In Shishipashi, five verses of *kami uta* are sung. The verses appear to be unrelated in content, but each consists of thirty-one syllables in the 5+7+5+7+7 grouping of the *tanka* poetic form that dates back to the 7th century. Much of the poetry in the "Torimai" song text is largely indecipherable, but it seems to include symbolic references to the invocation of spirits and the beckoning of spring (symbolizing renewal), as well as a description of movements in a *mikomai* dance, in which *miko* revolve from left to right, dancing in the four directions and shaking hand-held bell-tree rattles called *suzu*. This description portrays *mikomai* dance as it is still performed at Shinto shrines.

*Kami uta* formed the main body of Seishodo *mikagura* performances. Seishodo shrine celebrations held only once during the reign of an emperor for *Daijōsai,* an event that celebrated the ruler's first rice crop (considered to be an auspicious occasion), sponsored *mikagura* performances. *Kami uta* evolved as a component of Seishodo *mikagura*, a genre that played a major role in adding dramatic elements to rituals.

Literary sources for *kami uta* texts are poems found in the ancient records, *Kojiki* (A.D. 712) and *Nihon Shoki* (A.D. 720), which contain fragmentary myths and stories that originally were transmitted in the provinces, as well as ballads known at court and among the people at large (Kato 1981: 39). Another source, from the 10th century on, is the *Kokinshū* (Collection of Ancient and Modern Poetry, compiled in 905). This anthology features the classic *tanka* verse form described above. *Tanka*s were set to sacred melodies in *kami uta* because of the supernatural powers associated with this poetic form and the reverence attached to it as the noblest genre of Japanese poetry. The preface of the *Kokinshū* describes the power of *tanka* to move deities and demons. In his description of the *tanka*'s power in the *nō* play, Donald Keene states that "the knowledge of the *tanka* is declared to be a means of knowing the future, for poetry reflects the minds of the gods" (1966: 53). The *tanka* chosen for *kami uta* contain simple expressions of reverence to the gods and descriptions of nature.

## "Henzai"/"Kagomai"/"Senzai"

*Your age will continue forever,*
*The pine tree at Sumiyoshi (shrine)*
*testifies to that.*

These words are the opening lines to the piece "Henzai" in the villages of Ōri and Shiriya. According to Inoura, this wording corresponds to texts found in *kami uta.* He cites the *Ryōjinhishō* as a source for this kami uta. The *Ryōjinhishō* is a collection, compiled by Emperor Go Shirakawa in the Heian period, containing lyrics of popular songs, such as *imayō*, in addition to *kami uta* songs. This collection reflects the culture and religion of the populace during the Heian period (Inoura 1963: 1139).

The next portion of the "Henzai" text is a poem that begins with the words "*Agemaki ya.*" The two words form the title and first textual line of a song within the *saibari* [1] repertoire. *Saibari* were originally social songs performed by the common populace for their own entertainment, either in the streets or in open fields. They eventually became closely associated with *kagura*. *Mifume of Awaji* (compiled from A.D. 723 to 785) is the earliest collection of *saibari*. This collection appears to have included pure *kagura* songs, as well as *saibari* songs that were of a more unrefined, popular nature (Lombard 1966: 30). By the middle of the 9th century, *saibari* were one of two song types within the *kagura* repertoire. The first type consisted of *torimono* (offering) songs, meant to praise the gods and seek their aid, while *saibari* songs were sung to entertain the gods (Malm 1959: 43). The remainder of the "Henzai" song text is indecipherable, but it is probably a portion or fragment of either *kagura* or *saibari* texts.

**"Okina"**

The first two lines of the "Okina" song text are identical to that of "Henzai." The remainder of the text that follows this opening, however, differs. The introductory *makudashi* section is thought to be a portion of a *kami uta*, in which reference is made to the pine trees at Oda and Sumiyoshi, symbolizing longevity. There is also reference in this song to waterfalls, representing constancy or sustenance. The text of the following *makuzuki* section is slightly obscured, but it is seemingly composed of excerpts of various song texts that tell of the great age of Okina. Interspersed within this text are descriptions of the danced ritual, as well as celebratory phrases and references to prolonged life. Of particular interest are the phrases that tell of Okina's age:

> *At one hundred years old Okina is well protected.*
> *At two hundred years old Okina is at his prime.*
> *Okina's three hundred years of living is auspicious.*

These lines encapsulate the essence of this piece as prayer for prolonged life. This piece also prays for abundant harvests as a correlate to sustaining and prolonging life.

The second phrase of text in the *makudashi* section reveals yet another source for *nōmai* song texts. The line *Naru wa taki no mizu*, translated as "that which sounds is music from the waterfall," is taken from an *imayō* text (*Yōkyoku Taikan* 1931: 3). *Imayō* (literally meaning "present style") was a popular song genre of the late Heian period. The 6th century is traditionally the date of its origin, although the songs flourished only after the mid-Heian period. *Sarugaku* performances incorporated this song form because of its tremendous popularity (Araki 1978: 59-60).

Among the thirteen villages, four different texts appear for the first two lines of the song. I have singled out the above text, from Ōri and Shiriya, because these beginning lines are identical to those also found in the *nōmai* song texts of "Henzai" and "Sanba." This correspondence establishes a connection between the three pieces.

**"Sanba"**

The song text of "Sanba" is quite convoluted. The first two lines of text found in the Ōri village songbook correspond to the beginning lines of both "Henzai" ("Kagomai") and "Okina." Confusion, however, is created by the fact that among the other twelve villages, including Shishipashi, there are three different opening pairs of lines, from three different sources. The texts, however, conform more closely beginning with the following *makudashi* section. Portions of the texts vaguely describe Sanba's rejuvenation, while other fragments mention the waterfall at Yoshino, the crane and turtle (animals that symbolize longevity), and the sacred significance of the *shakujō,* a Buddhist sistrum. This dance represents long life symbolized by Sanba's reincarnation.

## *KITŌMAI* (PRAYER DANCES)

### "Gongenmai" (Lion's Dance)

Tracing literary sources of the lengthy "Gongenmai" song text is problematic, since the sequence of verses differs greatly from village to village and much of the language is obscured. The text appears to be a chain of fragmented sacred texts interspersed with portions of poetic verses. Mr. Ōta commented that the first half of the song instructs people about *kami* and Buddha. *Kami uta* are most likely the textual source for this portion of the song. Succeeding verses become more and more obscure, but seem to include more poetic references to nature than those of the first half.

*Saimon*, a Japanese song style containing congratulatory words of *kami* and Buddha originally used in worship events, is perhaps another textual source for "Gongenmai."*Saimon* of the Heian period reflected influences of Taoism (e.g., *Hokushin saimon*, *Jishingu saimon*, and others). In the medieval period, this song form was mainly adopted by *yamabushi*, who played an important role in its diffusion. The shaking of a Buddhist sistrum and the sound of a conch shell—part of the *yamabushi*'s regalia—accompanied the singing of *saimon.*

After the Edo period (1600-1868), *saimon* were performed at homes on New Year's Day. Since *yamabushi* performed "Gongenmai" at private homes on New Year's Day, it is possible that *saimon* were incorporated into the songs sung to accompany this piece. Sacred *saimon* texts are extant today in Yumi *kagura* performed in Hiroshima Prefecture and in the Hana Matsuri (Flower Festival) in Yamagata Prefecture (Yamaji 1982: 962).

Another possible source for the "Gongenmai" song text is the songs of *itako*, blind women mediums who sing formulaic songs intended to communicate with people's deceased relatives (*kuchiyose*), summon a tutelary-god (*kamiyose*), or recite holy ballads (*kami asobi*) (Karpati 1990:10). In the northern part of Honshū, *itako* have historically communed and today continue to do so at Mount Osore where people go to hire them in connecting them to deceased family members. *Yamabushi* practicing their austerities at the surrealistic sulfur surroundings of Mount Osore came into contact with *itako*, many of whom *yamabushi* travelled with in curing local villagers.

## *BUSHIMAI* (WARRIOR DANCES)

The song texts for the warrior dance dramas draw from early well-known literary works that narrate stories of the battles fought between the Genji and Heike clans and legendary tales of the warrior Yoshitsune. It is difficult to be certain which sources the song texts came from, but the following literary epic stories are the likely material: (1) *Heike monogatari* (*The Tale of the Heike*, c. 1202),[2] (2) *Gempei Seisuiki* (*The Rise and Fall of the Genji and Heike Families*, c. 1202),[3] (3) *Gikeiki* (*The Life of Yoshitsune*, c. 1400), and (4) *Taiheiki* (*Chronicle of the Great Peace* )[4] (Inoura and Kawatake 1981:157).

Song sections in both the first and second halves of each piece include *hairi no uta*, *makudashi*, and *makuzuki* songs. Storytelling is in the third-person narrative form. Textual lines in the opening *hairi no uta* are identical in all of the *bushimai*, except for the place name given in the first line, which is substituted according to the story. An example of the standard *hairi* verse is taken from the composition "Jūbangiri":

| | |
|---|---|
| *Hakone no yama ni haru wa kinikeri* | Spring has come to Mt. Hakone |
| *Haru wa kinikeri* | Spring has come |

In other *bushimai*, "Mt. Hakone" is replaced by other place names where the story unfolds.

The *makudashi* songs also are all identical among all the warrior dances, except for a substitution of the appropriate place name in the last line:

| | |
|---|---|
| *Yoi yoi isogi yuku hodo ni* | Quickly he (main character) goes |
| *Yoi yoi isogi yuku hodo ni* | Quickly he goes |
| *Hakone no yama ni tsuki ni keri* | He arrives at Mt. Hakone |

The *makuzuki* songs, on the other hand, are different for each dance. The texts for these songs describe the action of a particular battle being depicted. *Makuzuki* song texts provide details about the armor worn by the main character, names of other warriors being fought, and descriptions of the battle scene.

## *DŌKEMAI* (COMIC PIECES)

The only songs performed in *dōkemai* are *hairi* songs, used to signal the entrance of the comic character at the beginning of some pieces. A male comic character, *dōke*, customarily enters the stage by sticking his face out from the right or left edge of the curtain.

Women characters appear on stage in three plays: "Nenzu," "Warabi ori," and "Tengyō." *Hairi* songs also accompany the entrances and exits of women characters and their dances are treated semiseriously. The *hayashi* accompanies the dances of these characters with the slow tempo *sagari ha* music once they are on stage. Women characters customarily enter the stage in a kneeling position facing the audience.

*Dōkemai* consist mostly of dialogue. The dialogue spoken between the main comic character and the *taiko* drummer is called *serifu*, and it is spoken in the local vernacular. Mr. Ōta mentioned that accents and rhythms employed in the spoken dialogue are traditionally prescribed, but not formally designated. *Nōmai* groups keep written texts of the dialogues as guides for actors. The use of puns and double entendres enlivens the humor of the *serifu*, making it difficult to translate into English, since the play on words is lost and the spontaneity and humor of the text is flattened.

Although it is difficult to decipher exactly what the comic character is saying, his voice muffled as it is by the mask he is wearing, audiences understand the humor, responding with laughter since they are familiar with the plays. The dialogue's use of the local vernacular makes these plays locally exclusive. Those in the audience that are not from the area are often left baffled, but the levity of the audience soon compensates for the lack of understanding and everyone enjoys themselves.

## MUSICAL MODELS

The important influence of Buddhist chant on *nōmai* songs warrants a brief look at some of the underlying musical principles of this genre of chant. A survey of the melodic characteristics that constitute the evolution of *nō* drama songs also facilitates the study of *nōmai* song melodies. Since *nōmai* and *nō* drama share the same theatre lineage in medieval Japan, it is also useful to consult well-documented studies of *nō* drama's *yōkyoku* melodies to provide a framework for understanding the structure of *nōmai* song melodies.

An introduction to the general principles of both melody and rhythm in *shōmyō* provides a foundation for the analyses of *nōmai* song melodies in this chapter. Theoretically, three scales in *shōmyō* are distinguished: *ritsu*, *ryō*, and *chūkyoku*. Five basic tones and two auxiliary tones comprise these scales. *Ritsu* is the original pentatonic system described in *Shittanzō* written by Annen, the earliest Japanese *shōmyō* theorist:

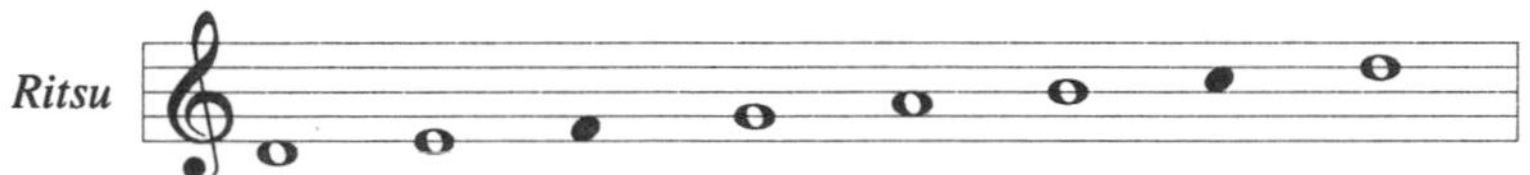


In the 12th century *shōmyō* incorporated the *ryō* system of *gagaku*:

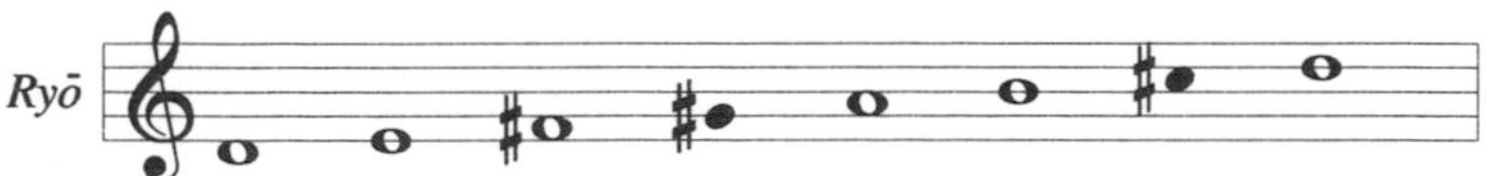


*Chū kyoku* is a combination of both *ritsu* and *ryō*, although which half is composed from what scale is a controversial matter among various theorists (Malm 1974: 66-67).

Short melodic fragments, *senritsu kei,* combine to form a melodic line. Among the various schools of *shōmyō,* each melodic fragment is fixed in form and given a special name, the exact meaning of which often varies with the par and *nō* songs—evidence of the widespread use of this method of melodic construction, which characterizes later developments of Japanese vocal music (Waterhouse 1984: 509).

Melodic ornamentation in Buddhist chant is based on standard musical patterns and melody types. A basic technique involves the use of a waver or slight change of pitch (*yuri*), which colors the melody (Kishibe 1962).

Categories of Buddhist melodies are taken from *Shōmyō Yōjinshu,* written in A.D. 1233 by a monk named Tanchi. Melodies composed in a pentatonic scale and containing a perfect fourth interval are called *ritsukyoku.* Two other categories established by Tanchi include *ryōkyoku,* which are pentatonic melodies having a major third interval, and *gakkyoku*, a chant containing intervals of both *ritsu* and *ryō* (Harich-Schneider, n.d.).

Rhythm and tempo in *nōmai* songs follow more closely *teikyoku* melodies in *shōmyō* that have a regular beat, rather than *jokyoku shōmyō* melodies in free rhythm.[5]

The musicologist Tanba Akira turns to the *kōshiki* Buddhist hymn style and the narrative *heikyoku* songs in reconstructing the tonal system he proposes served as the prototype for *nō* drama songs. Fundamental to the tonal system of *yōkyoku* is the modal style based on the nuclear tone system characteristic of *kōshiki* melodies. Nuclear tones a fourth apart designate tetrachords either in the form of an independent fourth, two conjoined fourths, or two disjoined fourths:

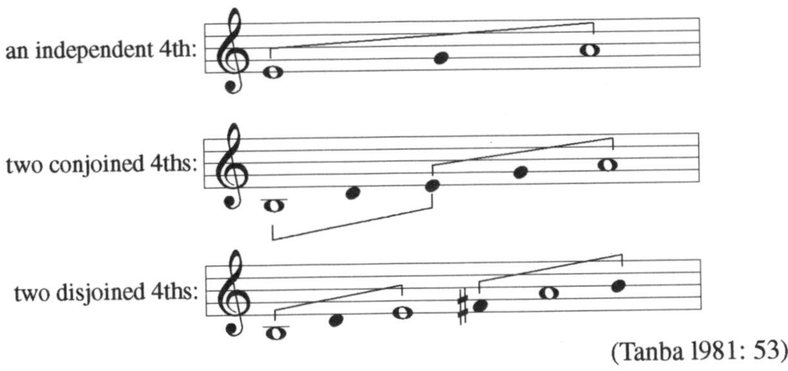


(Tanba 1981: 53)

Tetrachords in *kōshiki* melodies are divided by intervals in descending order of a major second and a minor third. Other intervals dividing a tetrachord evolved later and are seen in *yōkyoku* melodies. These intervals are viewed as mutations of those found in *kōshiki* melodies and they include, in descending order, a minor third followed by a major second and a major third followed by a minor second. A major third followed by a minor second division of the tetrachord developed in the 17th century when the interior, mobile note of the tetrachord had a tendency to be flatted forming a semitone and resulting in the emergence of the *miyakobushi* scale (Tanba 1981: 55). These elements create a melodic basis for the study of *nōmai* songs.

## RELATIONSHIP OF SONG TEXT TO MELODY

The poetic principle of classical Japanese poetry in which words are composed to fit into five- and seven-syllable units provides a frame for *nōmai* song texts. Classical poetry is organized into specific sequences of these two units. The order of these units in *tanka* poetry is 5-7-5-7-7, in *haiku* 5-7-5, and in the *dodoitsu* (or folk song form) 7-7-7-5. *Nōmai* song texts do not conform with much regularity to the five- and seven-syllable groupings, and in many pieces portions of songs are presented in heightened speech. Irregularities occur, such as eight syllables in a unit. The term used to designate a unit with an extra syllable is *jiamari.* Conversely, *jitarazu* refers to a unit which lacks a syllable, such as four instead of five. Both of these alterations are found in the song texts, in addition to divisions of the seven-syllable unit into four- and three-syllable subunits. In counting the number of syllables in these text groupings, it is important to note that a syllable with a long vowel, such as *sō,* is equivalent to two syllables when written in Japanese.

Each of the three song sections distinguished in *nōmai* pieces—*hairi no uta, makudashi*, and *makuzuki*—has a standard melody and is sung at a specific point in a piece to describe the setting, narrate the story, or introduce a particular character. This chapter analyzes each of these song sections, taken from specific pieces, to show their general melodic style. This study is not comprehensive of all *nōmai* song melodies. Only melodies which are used consistently throughout the repertoire have been included. Special *makuzuki* melodies in many pieces are excluded.

Tonal centers established in the transcriptions provided show the relationship between pitches in each of the song melodies. It is important to mention that pitch levels for the songs are not set, but vary according to the pitch level set by the lead or strongest singer. The variety of pitch levels presented in this chapter is greater than normally heard in a performance and is a result of transcribing songs that were sung outside the performance context—that is, solo and without a pitch referent. Songs were recorded out of context to more closely decipher the vocal melody, which is often overpowered in actual performances, particularly when accompanied by the *hayashi.*

## SONG CATEGORIES

### *Hairi no Uta* Song Melody

*Hairi,* derived from the verb *hairu,* meaning "to enter," identifies *hairi no uta* as the standard opening song in the presentation of a *nōmai* dance drama. A sixty-one-beat sample of the *hairi no uta* sung in "Henzai" is studied here. It is representative of the opening song peformed in nearly all of the pieces except for the comic plays (see Appendix Figure A.5).

**Form** The phrase structure of *hairi no uta* varies from piece to piece. In the ceremonial pieces the form—opening-A-B-A-A-interlude-C-D—is standard. Abbreviated versions of this form are sung at the beginning of all the warrior pieces. An example is the abridged form sung in "Shinobu," which includes only four phrases: opening-C-D-closing. There are slight modifications in the melody of this abridged form due to variances in the text, but phrase lengths of the opening phrase and phrases C and D are identical to those in the ceremonial version. The closing phrase, however, is shortened from eleven beats (in the "Henzai" version) to seven beats, and the melody is presented in a rhythmically more complex scheme.

The obscured and corrupted texts of the *hairi no uta* song in the ceremonial pieces are difficult to decipher, but they seem to suggest the invocation of a deity (*gongen* in the case of *nōmai*) for whom the dance is being offered. In the warrior dances, the text of this song section describes the village or location in which the drama takes place.

**Rhythmic Organization** The melody flows at a slow tempo in which a quarter note equals M.M. 58 in the given sample and singers loosely follow the quarter note beat of the *tebiragane* with some delays in the attack on the beat. Several rhythmic motives heard repeatedly are:

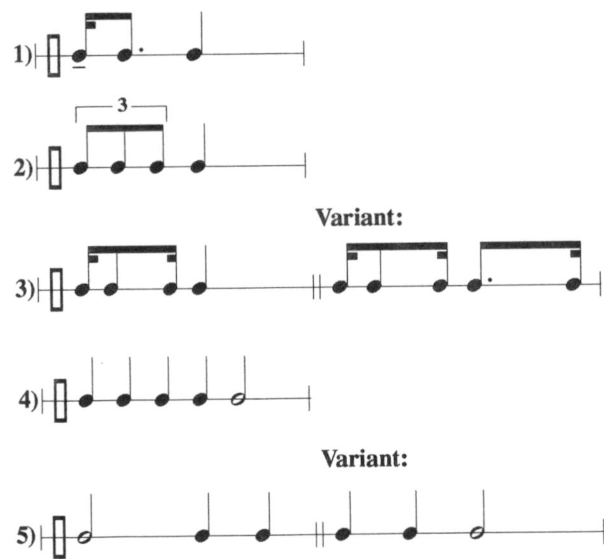


Motive 4 is the rhythm used in the opening phrase. It is repeated between the third statement of A and phrase C. Motive 5 is employed at the end of phrases A and D. Rhythmic contrast is created by the alternate use of shorter note values in motives 1, 2, and 3 and longer note values in motives 4 and 5.

Melodic phrases correspond to the syllabic structure of the text. The text structure of five-, seven-, and eight-syllable groupings delineates phrases that vary in length from six to fifteen beats:

| Phrase | Number of beats | Syllable grouping in text |
|---|---|---|
| Opening | 6 | 5 |
| A | 12 | 5 |
| B | 15 | 7 + 4 |
| A | 13 | 5 |
| A | 13 | 5 |
| Interlude | 6 | 5 |
| C | 6 | 7 |
| D | 6 | 7 |
| Closing | 11 | 7 |

In performance, the actual number of syllables sung in phrases A, B, and C, shown in this chart, is one or two syllables more than indicated in the song books. The syllables *i* (ee), *e* (eh), and *ie* (iye) are sung as standard opening syllables to the beginning texts of phrases A and B. In addition, *e* and *haiya* appear as ending syllables to all statements of phrase A. This results in the addition of one or two syllables to the syllable groupings of 5 and 7 written in the song books. The melody in phrase A serves as the musical setting to five-syllable text lines; phrase B is set to both seven- and four-syllable text lines; and the melodies in phrases C, D, and the closing phrase correspond to seven-syllable text lines. The text of the opening phrase *i-ho-o-ye-re* is traditionally set for *hairi no uta.*[6] This phrase is also sung following the third statement of phrase A before phrase C, which I have indicated above as an interlude. Since this phrase is not indicated in the songbook text, it is presumably a performance practice that has been orally transmitted. The text of the closing phrase is a repetition of that stated in phrase D, but it is set to a different melody. Repetition of the last line of text is standard practice in *nōmai* songs.

From the chart, the correspondence of syllables to the number of beats in each of the phrases show phrase A to be the most melismatic. This is a result of the elongation of vowels at the end of a word, sung in a melismatic style called *umiji.* This technique is heard in all *nōmai* songs. Vowels of the syllables in phrase A are prolonged from one and a half beats to almost four beats. In the opening phrase and phrases C and D, the number of syllables to one beat decreases to an almost 1:1 correspondence. The progression from the melismatic phrases of A and B to the faster syllabic poetic rhythm in phrases C and D creates a momentum that propels the listeners to the end of the song.

**Tonal Organization** The *hairi no uta* melody consists of the following pitches:

The three middle tones outline a *ritsu* tetrachord formed from the nuclear tones, F#1, G#1 and B1. The *miyakobushi* tetrachord is implied by the half-step movement between C# and D, with F# missing at the top. Although pitch D is a weak tone in the implied *miyakobushi* tetrachord, it is an important pitch. It is most often heard at the beginning of phrases, as the highest note in the melodic line, and at the end of phrases at an octave below.

Pitches in the *hairi no uta* melody are arranged in intervals that range from a minor second to an augmented fourth. An unusual feature of this melody is the augmented fourth interval heard on the first beat of phrase A, which I propose is an arbitrarily sung interval. This interval does occur again in the second statement of phrase A, but is disjoined by pitch B. In general, the melodic movement is disjunct with the perfect fourth interval occurring with the greatest frequency (34.6 percent of all intervals) and a major third as the next most frequently sung interval (21.1 percent).

Two melodic motives heard throughout the song include:

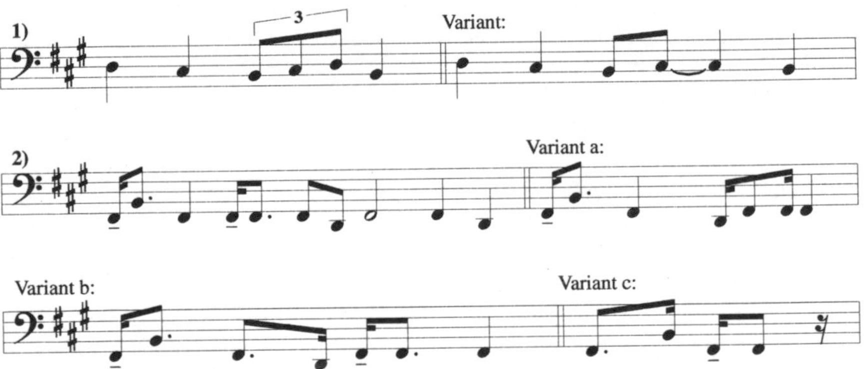


Motives 1 and 2 are companion melodic units that combine to form phrases A and B. The second motive and its many variations also function to end phrases. Variants of these musical ideas offer some diversity within the melody.

No ornamentation occurs in the "Henzai" version of the *hairi no uta* melody. When this song is performed in "Bangaku" and "Torimai," however, grace notes within the tonal material of the melody occur on the first, second, or third beats at the beginning of phrases. Notes are embellished from both above and below, and the intervals formed include a minor second, a minor third, a perfect fourth, and a major sixth:

### *Makudashi* Song Melody—Ceremonial Pieces

A forty-one-beat sample of the *makudashi* melody was taken from the piece "Henzai" (see Appendix Figure A.6). This melody is representative of the melodic setting of the *makudashi* text sung only in the ceremonial pieces "Henzai" and "Okina," since "Torimai" contains lyrics only for the *hairi no uta.* The "Henzai" and "Okina" versions differ slightly due to variances in the text, but the melodic intervals and rhythmic motives employed in both are the same. The *makudashi* melody in "Sanba," the fourth and final ceremonial dance, is a special melody and therefore not included in this analysis.

*Makudashi* is a song sung prior to and sometimes during the stage entrance of a character in a *nōmai* dance drama. The song text introduces the character portrayed by the dancer.

**Form** A complete statement of the ceremonial version of the *makudashi* melody includes four phrases: opening, A, B, and closing. Textual units of five and six syllables subdivide phrases A and B.

| Phrase | Number of beats | Syllable groupings in text |
|---|---|---|
| Opening | 5 | 5 |
| A | 19 | 6+6+5 |
| B | 10 | 6+5 |
| Closing | 7 | 6 |

The correspondence of syllables in the text to the number of beats shows this melody to be less melismatic than the *hairi no uta* melody.

**Rhythmic Organization** The tempo is slow and deliberate, with the eighth note equivalent to M.M. 76. Quarter notes and the sixteenth and dotted eighth note figure predominate. Three rhythmic motives create continuity:

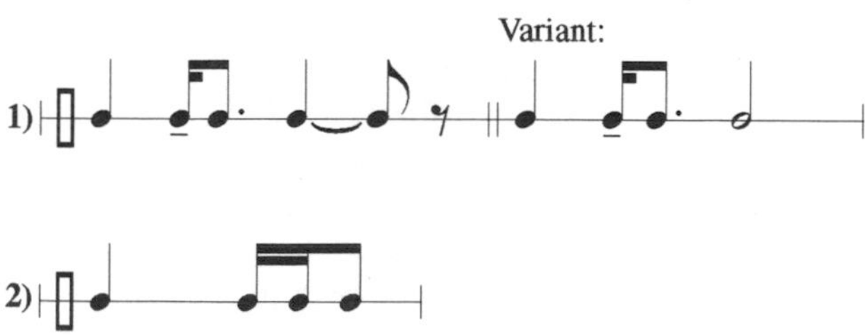

Motive 1 and its variant are employed in the cadential figure at the end of phrases A and B. Motive 2 is sung twice in succession at the beginning of phrase B and motive 3 appears twice in the closing phrase.

**Tonal Organization** The *makudashi* melody is sung on five pitches:

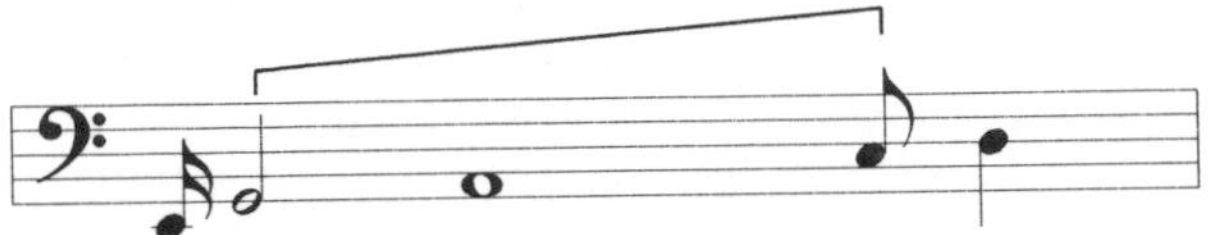

$G^1$, $A^1$, and C outline an independent *ritsu* tetrachord with pitches D and $E^2$ implying an incomplete *ritsu* scale. The melody in the opening phrase and phrase A centers around pitch $A^1$; phrase B fluctuates between pitches $G^1$ and $A^1$; and the melody in the closing phrase shifts between pitches D and $A^1$. Pitch $C^1$ serves as an approach tone to note D in the closing phrase.

The *makudashi* melody sung in ceremonial pieces employs three intervals. Major seconds predominate (62.5 percent of all intervals); perfect fourths occur with the next greatest frequency (20.8 percent), with major thirds next (16.6 percent). The use of a limited number of intervals gives the melody a chant-like quality. The influence of Buddhist chant is evident, and the melodic line is reminiscent of the *kōshiki* hymn, in which a single note is intoned followed by a melodic cadence. In phrase A, pitch A is intoned; in phrase B, pitch G is the primary tone; and the closing phrase is equivalent to an ornamental coda.

There is an alternation of conjunct and disjunct melodic movement. Frequent use of the major second interval creates conjunct movement, while the perfect fourth interval between the nuclear tone A and grace note E forms disjunct movement.

Three melodic motives emerge in unifying the melody:

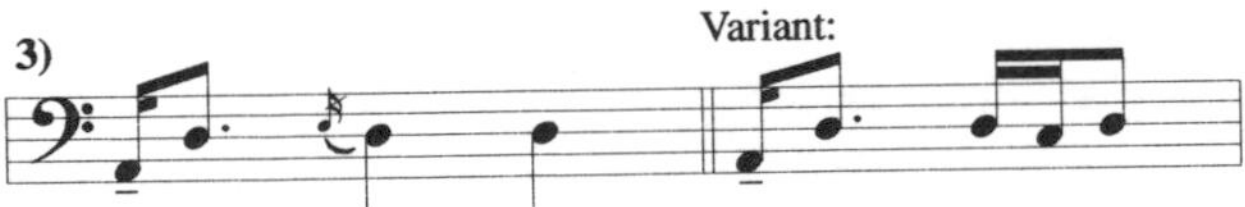


Motive 1 is repeated four consecutive times in phrase A. Motive 2 is a cadential figure that occurs at the end of both phrases A and B, and motive 3 frames the entire melody by being sung as both the opening and closing melodic figure.

Grace notes are the only form of ornamentation used to provide melodic variety. These embellishments approach nuclear tones from a major second above, or a perfect fourth below, or begin with the nuclear tone and ascend a major third before descending to the nuclear tone again, as seen in example 3 below:

### *Makudashi* 1 Melody—Warrior Pieces

A different *makudashi* melody sung in the warrior pieces developed at a later date than the ceremonial pieces. A twenty-three beat sample of this melody is taken from one of the most widely and often performed warrior pieces, "Shinobu" (see Appendix Figure A.7).

The melodic line is more static than the ceremonial version of *makudashi* melodies. As melodic settings to the narration of the stories behind the pieces, it appears that the song melodies in warrior dances were simplified in response to the dominance of the text.

The *makudashi* melody is sung in every warrior piece, either to name the village or to describe the location where the story of the dance drama unfolds. Slight variations of this melody are sung from one warrior piece to another according to the structure of the text: more notes are sung if the text is longer, while notes are omitted if the text is shorter.

**Form** The melody is divided into two phrases. Phrase A corresponds to the first line of text and phrase B includes the second and third textual lines:

| Phrase | Number of beats | Syllable groupings of text |
|---|---|---|
| A | 7 | 7+5 |
| B | 14 | 7+5+7+5 |

The last grouping of five syllables in phrase B is performed in heightened speech. This mode of text presentation is the standard ending of all the song sections in the warrior pieces except for the *hairi no uta.*

**Rhythmic Organization** The tempo of this brief song section is relatively slow, with a quarter note roughly equal to M.M. 63. The rhythmic organization displays an alternation of quarter notes and the figures

which create a momentum and flow necessary to carry the melody.

**Tonal Organization** The tonal material includes four pitches:

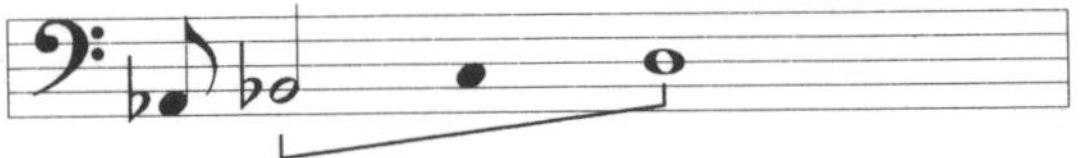

An important feature of the melody is the major third interval between tones B♭[1] and D, rather than a perfect fourth forming a tetrachord, as seen in all of the previous melodies. The major third interval implies the lower half of a *ryō* scale, placing this melody in the previously mentioned *ryōkyoku* classification of Buddhist chant melodies. The melody in phrase A centers around pitch D, while the melody descends in phrase B and fluctuates between B♭[1] and D. Tones C and A♭[1] primarily function as lower neighbors to the nuclear tones D and B♭[1], respectively. This *makudashi* melody is less melodic than the song melodies studied thus far, probably to bring out the narrative aspect of the text by emphasizing its decipherability.

Melodic movement is conjunct. Phrase A, in which pitch D is intoned with an occasional descent to lower neighbor pitch C, is more static than phrase B, where major third intervals create greater leaps in the melody. The melody is unadorned except for the single grace note C, which embellishes nuclear tone D in the beginning of the piece on beat three.

### *Makuzuki* 1 Melody—Warrior Pieces

Among the ceremonial pieces, only "Okina" and "Sanba" have *makuzuki* song sections. "Okina" has a special *makuzuki* melody, and in "Sanba" the *makuzuki* text is presented in heighened speech. In the warrior pieces, however, there is a standard *makuzuki* 1 melody sung in the first half of each piece. The melody analyzed here is taken from the piece "Shinobu" as the representative *makuzuki* 1 melody (see Appendix Figure A.8.). This melody is referred to as *makuzuki* 1 because the *makuzuki* text in the second half of the warrior pieces employs a different melody, later introduced as *makuzuki* 2. The *makuzuki* 1 melody varies slightly in each piece according to the structure of the text.

The *makuzuki* song section is sung as an interlude between dance sections. It serves to narrate the ceremonial or story background of a *nōmai* piece. During the singing of this song, the dancer rests at back stage center. When the *makuzuki* song ends, the *hayashi* plays a bridge into the next instrumental piece and the dancer resumes dancing.

**Form** The form of the *makuzuki* 1 melody is a series of melodic units that corresponds to the syllable groupings of the text. These melodic units are combined into four phrases that are separated by either a half-beat or two-beat rest. Each phrase consists of several melodic units as follows:

| Phrase | Number of beats | Syllable groupings of text |
|---|---|---|
| A | 14 | 7+5+5+7 |
| B | 9 | 7+6 |
| C | 13 | 5+5+5+5 |
| D | 12 | 5+5+5 |

Two factors considered in determining the above phrases were the opening melodic figure, involving pitches E1, A1, and B1, as well as breaks in the text indicated by eighth and quarter note rests. The final text unit at the end of phrase D is performed in heightened speech, which appears to function as a kind of cadence or standardized ending.

The text of this song section introduces the main character of the dance drama by proper name. The armor-clad appearance of the character, ready for battle, is also sometimes described.

**Rhythmic Organization** Patterns of eighth and quarter notes predominate in the melody, creating a steady, chant-like rhythm. The characteristic sixteenth note and dotted eighth note figure is used sparingly in this melody. The tempo is moderately fast, with the quarter note roughly equivalent to M.M. 108. Elasticity in the tempo is created by the alternation of notes surging forward in portions of the melody where the momentum builds, and a slight elongation in the time value of other notes. Rhythm in this melody is dictated by the poetic text, resulting in constantly changing rhythmic sequences.

**Tonal Organization** Three pitches form this rather static melody:

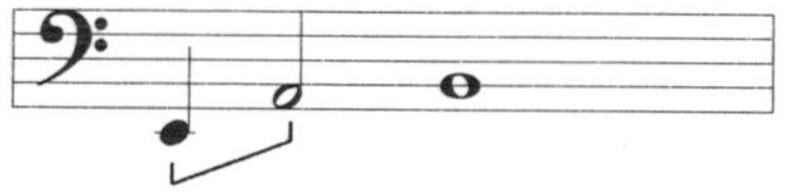

From these three notes one can only discern the importance of the perfect fourth interval formed between pitches E1 and A1, underscoring the importance of this interval in *nōmai* music and traditional Japanese music in general. This version of the *makuzuki* melody is even simpler than the *makudashi* 1 melody for warrior pieces. Again, it is most likely that the narrative importance of the text commanded a less distracting melody.

The melody is intoned on B1 forming a conjunct line, except for the melodic descent to pitch E1, which then ascends to pitch A1 leading back to B1. The melodic figure involving the pitches E1 and A1 serves as a melodic approach to nuclear tone B1, which is sung at the beginning of hemistiches of five or seven syllables. It is one of two melodic motives, shown below, which serve to unify the melody:

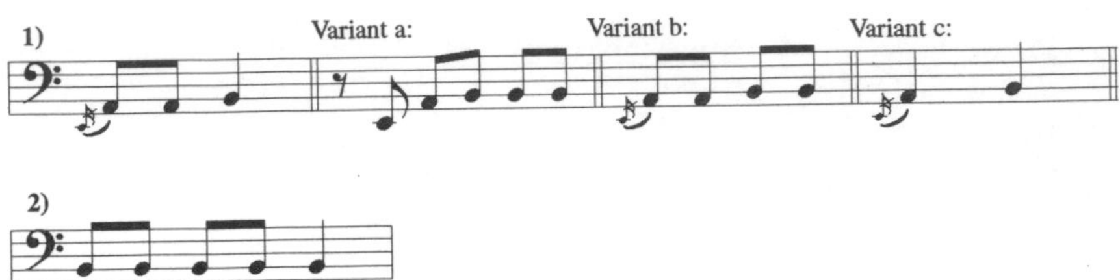


Motive 1 is varied each time it is stated except for variation 1a, which is sung twice in succession in the latter half of phrase A. Motive 2, which corresponds to the text lines of five syllables, occurs twice in succession in phrase B.

Minimal ornamentation of the melody features grace notes used in approaching pitches $A^1$ and $B^1$:

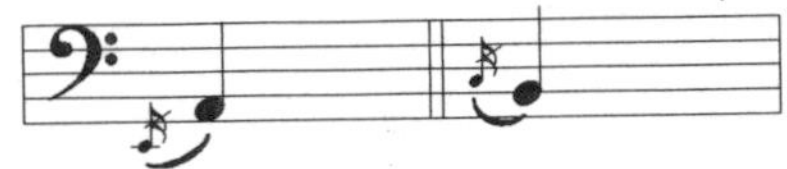

### *Makudashi* 2 Melody—Warrior Pieces

The two halves of a warrior piece are structurally identical; the second half of the warrior dances is a repeat of the format presented in the first half. The first half, called "morning," metaphorically refers to the main character's period of youth.[7] In the second half, called "afternoon," symbolizing the main character's mature years, the dancer dons a courageous-looking mask and enacts a battle scene. Both halves commence with the singing of *hairi no uta.* The melodies of both *hairi no uta* are the same, except for some variation resulting from the differences in text structure of the two songs. The *makudashi* melody in the second half, however, melodically differs from that in the first half, and it is analyzed separately here (see Appendix Figure A.9).

**Form** The *makudashi* 2 melody is comprised of two phrases:

| Phrase | Number of beats | Syllable groupings in text |
|---|---|---|
| A | 8 | 7+5 |
| B | 10 | 7+5+7+5 |

The text is sung syllabically, except for the slight drawing out of vowels on quarter notes at the end of phrase A and at the end of the first 7+5 grouping in phrase B. The lengthier phrase B ends with the final five syllables performed cadentially in heightened speech. The text sung is usually unrelated to the drama and is instead poetry that often describes a season or some natural setting.

**Rhythmic Organization** Similar to that of *makudashi* 1 melodies, the tempo is moderately slow, with a quarter note approximating M.M. 72. Rhythmic contrast is created by the use of sixteenth, eighth, and dotted eighth notes, which build tension and drive the melody, followed by quarter notes that bring resolution and relaxation. The only rhythmic motive that helps to unify this short melody is the sequence heard in the first four beats of both phrases A and B:

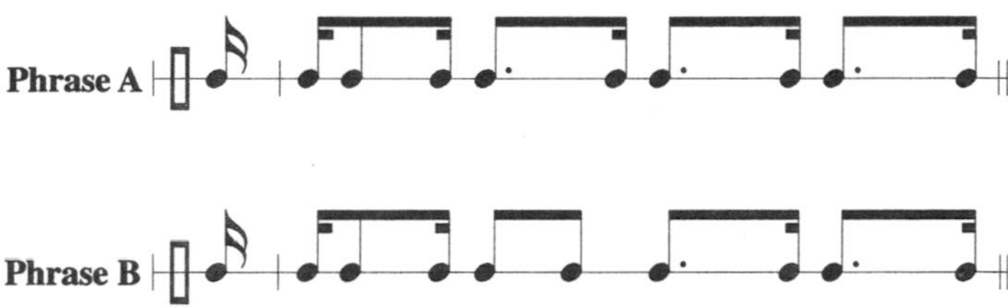


Instead of the usual sixteenth and dotted eighth note figure, its inverted form (dotted eighth and sixteenth note) is featured in this melody. Also, the sixteenth-; eighth-, sixteenth-note figure is a rhythm that this melody shares with the *makudashi* 1 melody.

**Tonal Organization** The *makudashi* 2 melody is built on three basic pitches:

The perfect fourth interval between the nuclear tones G#[1] and C# again proves to be the main feature of this basically three-note melody. Singers intone exclusively on both pitches. In phrase A pitch C# is intoned, with note B functioning as a lower neighbor. In phrase B singers intone on both C# and G#[1]. Pitches A# and F# both occur only once as embellishments surrounding the note G#, but their full quarter note values in phrase B give them some significance. This static melody highlights the storytelling.

Major second, minor third, and perfect fourth intervals are used in the construction of this melody. A majority of the major second intervals occur in phrase A, forming a conjunct melodic line. This contrasts with the minor third and perfect fourth intervals heard in phrase B, which form a more disjunct melodic line.

Ornamentation is minimal. Grace notes are used to approach tones C# and F#[1] from above and a mordent on pitch A#[1] is featured in the middle of phrase B:

### *Makuzuki* 2 Melody—Warrior Pieces

The *makuzuki* 2 melody is the final song section heard in all of the warrior dances. The text describes the heroic battle scene of the warrior featured in a particular piece. This song section, which is usually quite lengthy, is sung to a melody that is repeated for the duration of the text. The following forty-seven-beat example is the basic melody. It accompanies the first three lines of the text (see Appendix Figure A.10.). The melody presented here is repeated in performance in constantly changing combinations, dictated by the structure of the text, until the end of the song.

**Form** One full statement of the *makuzuki* 2 melody, analyzed here, can be divided into three phrases:

| Phrase | Number of beats | Syllable grouping in text |
|---|---|---|
| A | 17 | 5+7+7+7 |
| B | 20 | 7+7+7+7+4 |
| C | 7+ | 7+7 |

Phrases A, B, and C can be subdivided into melodic units that correspond to the syllabic groupings of the text. Phrase A consists of four melodic units, phrase B five melodic units, and phrase C two melodic units. The phrases are determined by the pauses separating them, such as the quarter note rest between A and B and the eighth note rest between B and C. Another delineating factor was the ending melodic pattern played at the end of phrases A and B.

The text identifies and describes the battle in which the main character displays his valor and strength. The battles depicted are well-known events that took place between two powerful clans, the Minamoto and Taira and their allies, during the latter part of the 12th century. Some of the *makuzuki* 2 texts include the geographic location of the battle and names of warriors killed in action.

**Rhythmic Organization** The duration of a quarter note ranges from M.M. 76 to 80 in the moderate tempo of the *makuzuki* 2 melody. A rubato feeling prevails, with a fair amount of rhythmic give and take between notes. Two-beat and four-beat motives rhythmically unify the melody:

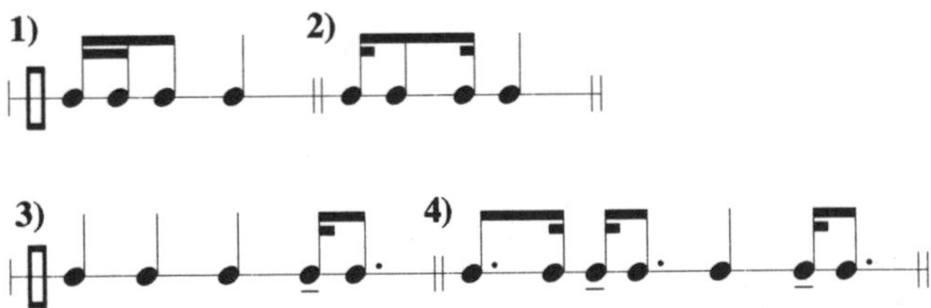


**Tonal Organization** The range of the melody is an octave and a half and the following pitches are employed:

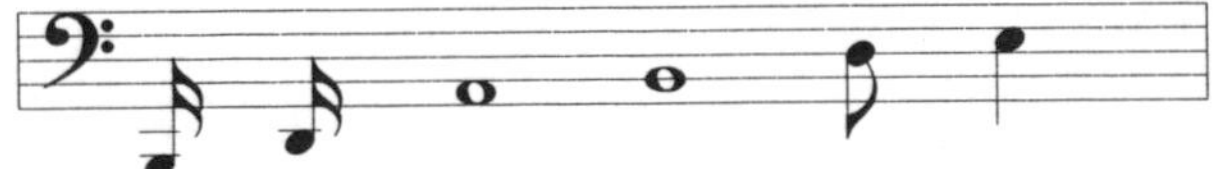

There is no discernible scale used in this chanted melody. Instead, the perfect fourth and minor third intervals play an important role. Pitch $B^1$, the central nuclear tone intoned extensively throughout the melody, skips up a fourth to E or up a minor third to D. Pitches $A^1$ and D form another fourth interval heard as a cadential formula on the last four beats of phrase A and the first beat of phrase B, as well as the last four beats of phrase B and the first beat of phrase C. Pitch $A^1$ also serves as a lower neighbor to $B^1$. Notes $B^2$ and $D^1$ function as octave equivalents to $B^1$ and D, each occurring only once in the given sample. Another note which only occurs once is C; it serves as an upper neighbor to pitch $B^1$.

Disjunct melodic motion alternates with conjunct motion. Disjunct motion is created by leaps of a perfect fourth, major sixth, or perfect octave. This is contrasted with melodic movement of minor and major seconds and minor third intervals. Three melodic motives emerge in the melody:

Melodic motive 1 is sung twice in succession at the beginning of phrase A. Motive 3 is sung as an ending motif in both phrases A and B.

The melody is unadorned, although pitch $B^2$, sung on the second half of the fifth beat of phrase B, can be considered to decorate $B^1$ as an octave equivalent.

## SUMMARY OF ORGANIZING PRINCIPLES

Examination of *nōmai* song melodies generally reveals a tetrachordal melodic structure based on the *ritsu* scale that is characteristic of *kōshiki* Buddhist hymns, *heikyoku* epic songs, and *nō* songs. Since the range of most of the melodies is less than an octave, the independent tetrachord, rather than conjoined or disjoined tetrachords, is dominant. Exceptions to the tetrachordal melodic structure are the *makudashi* 1 and *makuzuki* 1 melodies heard in the warrior pieces. The *makudashi* 1 melody interestingly employs a major third interval as its principal feature, implying a *ryō*-based scalar structure, rather than the *ritsu*. The three-note *makuzuki* 1 song has too few notes to create a tetrachordal structure, although a perfect fourth interval is integral to the melodic movement.

The *hairi no uta* and *makudashi* songs sung for the ceremonial dances employ the mutated division of the tetrachord, with a minor third followed by a major second. The tetrachords of the *makudashi* 2 and *makuzuki* 2 melodies featured in the second half of warrior dances follows the division from high to low of a major second followed by a minor third, characteristic of *kōshiki* melodies. This older tetrachordal structure used in the warrior dance songs may point to their greater age, or at least these songs' resistance to later melodic developments.

Finally, semitones are not common in *nōmai* song melodies, except for the semitone that appears in the *hairi no uta* melody. The rare occurrence of a semitone demonstrates a predominance of the older *ritsu* scale and a retention of the Buddhist chant style that became popular in medieval Japan.

The two classifications of *shōmyō* melodies, *ritsukyoku* and *ryōkyoku*, have been useful in categorizing *nōmai* melodies, since they contain either the perfect fourth or major third interval that distinguish the two classifications.

*Nōmai* songs rhythmically follow the poetic meter of the text rather than a set musical meter. The song texts in general follow the seven- and five-syllable text structures of traditional Japanese poetry and song forms. The songs for the ceremonial pieces tend to be more melismatic than the syllabic treatment of sung texts in the warrior dances.

The melismatic correspondence of the melody to the text, including the elongation and repetition of a vowel at the end of a word, embraces the singing style of Buddhist chant. The melodic progression of the narrative *shōmyō* form, or *kōshiki,* strongly emerges in *nōmai* songs, which are intoned on a single note and end in a melodic cadence, thereby allowing the conveyance of words to take precedence over the melody. The melodic features of *nōmai* songs clearly reflect the Buddhist musical orientation of *yamabushi* who created this genre. The influence of Buddhist chant in *nōmai* songs contrasts with the dominance of Shinto music in *nōmai* instrumental music.

## INTERRELATIONSHIP OF *HAYASHI* MUSIC AND *NŌMAI SONGS*

A number of textures are woven in *nōmai* music by the alternation and various ensemble combinations of the cymbals, drum, flute, and singers. The steady rhythm played by *tebiragane* players, together with the more varied and improvisatory *taiko* part, form the rhythmic layer of *nōmai* music. The highly embellished flute melody flows loosely above the percussion rhythms, creating a second layer of sound and, in sections where the singers enter, the song creates a third layer that is heterophonically related to the flute melody. The musical rhythm of the *hayashi* and the songs are independent, although they do intermittently coincide. A certain fluidity and flexibility prevails in the music as a result of this loose rhythmic correspondence between the percussion, flute, and song.

*Hayashi* music and song sections alternate throughout a piece, but they do overlap at times, such as in the *hairi no uta,* where the singers enter before the *hayashi* part ends (See Appendix, measures 49-60 in Figure A.1). The vocal melody, similar to the flute melody, is an independent line that only loosely follows the rhythm played by the *tebiragane* and *taiko*. Then in the *utagakari* section at the close of a piece, *hayashi* accompaniment, song, and dance unite climactically; the independent rhythms of both the poetic song texts and *hayashi* music create a polyrhythmic effect that is particularly effective in the buildup of tension in this section.

Scales and melodies of the flute part and songs differ completely. Kojima Tomiko argues that this is evidence that they are not intended to be intrisically matched (Kojima 1965: 95). It is probable that the songs were superimposed upon preexistent *hayashi* melodies. While the flute primarily plays in a scale combining the *miyakobushi* and *minyō* tetrachords, the song is predominantly sung in a scale related to the *ritsu* scale. Matching pitches between the flute and vocal melodies is of little concern in *nōmai* music, and bitonality occurs as a result of the two independent melodies. This independence allows singers to choose pitches and ranges that are comfortable for them. The bitonality created in the simultaneous performance of the flute and song melodies, and the absence of matching pitches or intonation between the two, is not unusual in the folk performing arts of Japan. The sonic phenomenon of bitonality and polyrhythm in a single piece is also heard in the classical traditions of kabuki and *nō* theater.

## CONCLUSION

The appeal of *nōmai* music is the spontaneity of its musical features within traditional boundaries. The sequence of music and dance sections within a piece form boundaries to which performers traditionally adhere. Some consistency in rhythm and form required to accompany the set choreography of a dance or ritual being dramatized also creates the need for boundaries. Within this framework, however, variation and flexibility in the flute melodies and rhythms of the *taiko* effect an unpredictable and spontaneous quality. The *nōmai* lineage or musical tastes of a particular village and the skill of individual flute players and drummers dictate variances in the music. The amalgamation of *kagura*-style *hayashi* music with Buddhist-oriented vocal melodies also required flexibility in form and style. In *nōmai*, a balance of tradition, flexibility, and change in the music contributed toward creating a dynamic and free-spirited dance drama.

The Shinto aspect of *nōmai* music is strong. Already discussed in detail in the previous chapter are the instrumentation and melodic and rhythmic elements borrowed from folk *kagura*. Also, although *nōmai* songs are primarily of Buddhist origin, the *hairi no uta* song exhibits some *kagura* influence. *Kami uta* (deity songs) form the basis for the *hairi no uta* songs, since the texts, although obscured, describe the dance of shrine maidens and appear to contain expressions about prolonging life, a link to Shinto. Melodically, the melismatic style of *kami uta* is heard in *hairi no uta*.

Manifestations of Buddhist music are evident in *nōmai*. The influence of *kōshiki* hymns in *nōmai* songs were discussed in detail earlier. Also associated with Buddhism is the use of a conch shell (*horagai*) in the prayer dances "Gongenmai" and "Kanemaki." The *horagai* originated as a musical instrument in Shugendō services. The sound that the *horagai* produces is regarded as the sound of enlightenment itself. The use of the *taiko* drum in *nōmai* is an adjunct to this, since the drum's sound is the second of the two sounds associated with enlightenment. Buddhist musical elements in the music reinforce the religious intent *yamabushi* had in fashioning *nōmai* performances.

The coupling of musical influences from both Shintoism and Buddhism in *nōmai* reflects medieval music practices and is an expression of the syncretism in religious beliefs of the period. The classical theater traditions of *nō* and kabuki benefitted from this dynamic coupling and the musical instrumentation of both forms is evidence of this. *Nōmai* music represents the eclectic artistic joining of Shintoism and Buddhism in Ryōbu Shinto. The coexistence of the two religions eventually led to the coalescence of their ritual music which, through the efforts of *yamabushi*, found form in *nōmai*.

## NOTES

1. *Saibari* are different from the court song genre, *saibara*, which were folk songs set to *gagaku* melodies.

2. *Heike Monogatari* is a medieval epic that tells of the downfall of the Taira (Heike) family. Authorship is attributed to Hamuro Tokinaga.

3. *Gempei Seisuiki* is a historical work in forty-eight volumes, spanning the years 1160 to 1185 and also attributed to Hamuro Tokinaga.

4. *Taiheiki* is a historical work in forty-one volumes attributed to the monk Kojima (d. 1374) of Enryaku temple in Kyoto, covering the period from 1318 to 1368.

5. *Teikyoku* pieces have been retained in the Tendai Buddhist sect, while most all of Shingon chant is *jokyoku*.

6. It is not clear whether these syllables have any semantic meaning or are just vocables.

7. The metaphorical meaning of "morning" and "afternoon" differs from village to village. The above is a description offered by Mr. Ageji in the village of Ōri.

# PART IV

## EPILOGUE

# 9

# *Nōmai* in the 20th Century: Balancing Tradition and Change

*Nōmai* is more than a vehicle for studying musical, dramatic, and sacred practices of medieval Japan; it encompasses more than a nostalgic view of the past as a counterpoint to contemporary life. *Nōmai* is a source of pride and local identity that expresses the worldview of residents in certain small, rural communities in northern Japan. Performances are in the process of becoming a public event; a cultural production that began to attract researchers (like myself), media people, photographers, and tourists in the 1980s. Before introducing changes occurring within this tradition, let us piece together the remnants of a medieval age that make *nōmai* distinct.

## TRADITION

Historically, *nōmai* exemplifies the artistic exchange that took place among social classes in medieval times and the mutual borrowing between court and folk traditions that paved the way for the emergence of *yamabushi kagura*. A number of factors provided an impetus for such exchange. Before the medieval period, the court and the provinces maintained, for the most part, separate performing traditions. The court was the primary patron of *mikagura*, *bugaku*, *gagaku*, and *sarugaku*, while the rural provinces practiced their own arts. The court's gradual decline in power and the attendant inability to support a lavish lifestyle, combined with the growing role of Shinto shrines and Buddhist temples in the provinces, created a shift in job opportunities for performers. As centers of commerce and worship, shrines and temples supplied audiences for a growing number of performances. Requiring entertainment following rituals and ceremonies to appease deities and attract audiences, these institutions provided increased chances for artists not only to perform, but to view other genres, giving way to the dynamic interplay among performing traditions. Increased contact between folk and court performing arts was also due to the exchange of performances between courtiers and the rural population during the imperial court's pilgrimages to holy sites and places of worship, particularly in the Nara and Wakayama prefectures. Last, the ascendance of the provincial warrior class in power and prestige engendered their need for artists to enhance their lifestyle to match that of the court. This need made it possible for artists, for the first time, to emerge from the lower classes. The interchange between the court and folk performing arts was essential for the flowering of a native culture in Japan. The indigenous quality of the folk performing arts added a Japanese cast to imported traditions that prevailed in the court.

The study of *nōmai* reveals the importance of music and dance in medieval religious practices. *Yamabushi*, authors of *yamabushi kagura/shugen nō*, were instrumental in the mixing of sacred practices and beliefs in their efforts to proselytize to the rural population. On their pilgrimages to temples and shrines throughout Japan, particularly those at Shugendō headquarters at Kumano, these ascetic mountain priests experienced the popularity and appeal of performances in drawing audiences. In their efforts to reach the provincial population, they adopted the tactic of inaugurating performances as a didactic tool. In the process of shaping their performances, *yamabushi* incorporated folk forms that would already be familiar to audiences. Their co-optation of folk *kagura* music and dance reflected the medieval tendency of Buddhism to build its base on indigenous beliefs and practices. From a *kagura* base, they added elements of their magicoreligious Shugendō training. The synthesis of Buddhist- and Shinto-based practices in *nōmai* came together quite easily, since many Tendai and Shingon Buddhist practices—magic, divination, and exorcism, as well as the *ennen* dance of long life—originated in folk *kagura*. As a result of the integration, two musical styles were brought together.

*Nōmai* music clearly reflects the religious syncretism of Ryōbu Shinto. As discussed above, Buddhism achieved acceptance among the Japanese by superimposing its deities and concepts onto the Shinto pantheon and ritual framework. The instrumental music and associated dances, instrumentation, and ceremonial songs and their accompanying texts appropriated from folk *kagura* represent the Shinto musical aspects. The Buddhist influence is manifested in the borrowing of musical instruments and the singing and melodic style of *kōshiki* Buddhist hymns for *nōmai* songs. The variance between the instrumental and vocal music is striking when heard simultaneously, serving to enhance the drama on stage. It is parallel to the sonic phenomenon heard in kabuki when the *nōgaku* instrumental ensemble and the *shamisen*-accompanied *nagauta* concurrently sound.

A historical view of *nōmai* also provides theater scholars with some insight into the development of *nō* drama before it reached its zenith under the patronage of the Ashikaga shoguns and in the hands of *sarugaku nō* masters, Kan'nami and Zeami. This is a fertile area of research on which I can only touch briefly. To begin with, both genres developed from *sarugaku nō* in the 13th and 14th centuries in the hands of lower-class performers. *Nō* and *nōmai* went their separate ways in the Muromachi period; *nō* incorporating secular and urbane elements in its efforts to match the aesthetic refinement of the ruling warrior elite, and *nōmai* remaining a plebeian performing genre with *yamabushi* emphasizing its ritual character. As a result of their shared lineage, these dramatic genres overlap in repertoire, performance practices, dance movements, and vocal influences. Repertoire that they have in common includes the ceremonial trilogy, featuring the dances "Senzai," "Okina," and "Sanbasō"; the warrior pieces "Yashima," "Soga Monogatari," "Shinobu no Tarō," "Tomoe [Gozen]," and "Kurama"; the play "Dōjōji," referred to as "Kanemaki" in the *nōmai* repertoire [the basis for the two pieces are different versions of the same story]; and the comic play "Hagoromo," called "Tengyō" in *nōmai* [their differing titles allude to the fact that their stories represent two versions].

The binary structure of the plays in which the second part features dance in a quick tempo is another shared characteristic between *nō* and *nōmai* plays. Shared performance practices include the importance of masking and costumes to signify character and social rank; a minimal use of props that are symbolic, abstract, and conceptual; the use of a male chorus to both sing and narrate; and consideration of the stage as sacred space, requiring ritual purification and respectful protocol. Musically, the two dramatic genres employ a chant vocal style based on *shōmyō*, the rich and sophisticated tradition of Buddhist chant.

## LOCAL IDENTITY AND GOVERNMENT SUPPORT

To performers, *nōmai* is a distinguished tradition of Shimokita Peninsula, and it is a source of cultural and local pride. Performers reveal this pride in emphasizing that the tradition is a distinct genre in itself and not a type of *yamabushi kagura*, as categorized by scholars. The local color of *nōmai* is marked by the performance style of villagers who added their own interpretations of what they considered the original style. The preservation of *nōmai* highlights the cultural tenacity of rural areas of Japan where traditional customs and lifestyles remain strong.

Performers and residents of the thirteen villages in Higashidorimura negotiate their traditional beliefs, as expressed in *nōmai*, within the context of contemporary Japan in a number of ways. First, *nōmai* is an not only an artistic statement, but an expression of a more comprehensive worldview that is closely tied to agriculture as a way of life. Even though there are an increasing number of residents who farm only part-time now, the agricultural foundation of life in these villages endures. Retention of a traditional lifestyle is partly due to the geographic isolation of Higashidorimura and the Tōhoku region in general, where folk performing art and craft traditions continue to flourish. The fact that the bullet train does not reach into this area has kept it somewhat sequestered. The population growth has also eluded this part of Japan as young people often head south to big cities. Despite the fracturing of the population, *nōmai* preparations, rituals, and presentations continue to socially bind residents and perpetuate a spirit of cooperation so important to agricultural communities. Besides the social interaction, *nōmai* unites the villager's collective memories of entertaining deities and making requests for the general health and welfare of the community as have generations before them.

*Nōmai* appears to be preserved primarily through the efforts of the older generation, perhaps as a way to better absorb the changes occurring around them, or to maintain a prescribed way of socially bonding families and individuals. The younger generation, conceivably, consider *nōmai* more as a symbol of the past and how communities sustain a cooperative spirit. But for the young men interested in performing, the tradition serves as a bridge to the area's past that speaks to their deep-seated consciousness of the ties they have to a particular community. If their performances are skillful, they also enjoy fame and recognition as *nōmai* reaches ever-growing audiences that now include both insiders and outsiders of the local area and region. Then there are people with jobs in the nearby city of Mutsu or at the cement factory near Shiriya who face the challenge of integrating *nōmai* into modern life. The lack of time and a less flexible work schedule have quickened their lessening connection to the tradition. The declining interest of the young in *nōmai* is indicative of Higashidorimura's gradual absorption into mainstream society, a course that many rural communities in Japan have travelled.

Local government support is partly responsible for the preservation of *nōmai* in Higashidorimura. In 1980, the federal Agency of Cultural Affairs (*bunkachō*) designated this dance drama as an "Intangible Cultural Asset" (*Jūyō Mukei Bunkazai*) and the Aomori prefectural office declared it as a "Prefectural Intangible Cultural Asset" (Aomori-ken *Jūyō Mukei Bunkazai*). These designations entitle villages that preserve *nōmai* to obtain matching grants from the local government. This arrangement provides each village with fifty percent of the budget allotted for performances. Government support has also been crucial in the formation of the Kyōdō Geinō Hozon Rengokai preservation organization in Higashidorimura founded by Mr. Ōta. The generous support is part of the Japanese government's efforts to promote regional pride and traditional values in communities such as Shishipashi, Ōri, Iwaya, and Shiriya and to increase economic and tourist activity.

The Cultural Properties Protection Law passed in 1950 is the source of governmental involvement in securing and promoting Japan's cultural heritage. Under this law the folk performing arts come under the category of folk cultural properties (*minzoku bunkazai*). The Agency of Cultural Affairs carries out the provisions of the law on the national level within the Ministry of Education. Spurred by this law, the Council for the Protection of Cultural Properties was set up to annually designate important cultural properties in the five categories established by the Agency. Prefectural and local governments under this law have the jurisdiction to designate local traditions as cultural properties. An important arm of the local government in the preservation of the folk performing arts is the board of education (Thornbury 1997: 55,56,149). This is significant because of the recruitment potential this board has in creating programs for students and teachers in building future support and interest in local folk traditions.

The anthropologist William Kelly, in his interpretation of the current politics of heritage in Japan, states that government support is a state policy that engages regional populations in a "national way of life." Simultaneously, however, such support fortifies the local identity of the villagers, limiting their participation in mainstream modern Japan. Kelly describes the oppositionality of the two tendencies as the "crosstalk of public culture" (1990:79-80). The thirteen villages that perform *nōmai* certainly exhibit such crosstalk in their continuing dialogue and negotiations concerning the original *nōmai* style. The reconfiguring of performing traditions is an ongoing phenomenon dictated by the intersection of both insider intentions and outsider interest. *Nōmai* is no exception as outsider interest of scholars, media people, and tourists continues to grow, forcing the sacred nature of this tradition to broaden its sphere and intention. Any study of a folk performing art's survival and retention in Japan today is not complete without discussing the impact of modern life and the accompanying changes on a tradition. The following section touches on such changes affecting *nōmai.*

## CHANGE

Despite *nōmai*'s rich heritage and local government support, modern life and the flight of young people to urban centers challenge its retention. There is a growing problem of maintaining the interest of youths to secure *nōmai*'s existence into the next century. Holding the interest of members of the young men's associations is a challenge to *nōmai* as it competes with a hyped reality viewed on television and the trappings of modern life.

In general, there is a decline in the participation of young men in the traditional men's associations, as evidenced by the small memberships of the Shishipashi *seinenkai*, the Ōri *keishindan*, and the Iwaya *seinenkai*. This drop is indicative of a growing trend in villages throughout Japan. Of the four villages I documented, only Shiriya's young men's association practiced mandatory membership of its inhabitants. How this decrease in membership will impact the future of *nōmai* remains to be seen, but it is an issue of concern to keepers of this tradition.

Concomitant to this decline is the decreasing number of young men being trained, threatening the pool of talent needed to continue *nōmai*'s legacy. Additionally, the rigorous demands of the tradition in learning dance, as well as singing or playing a musical instrument, make it difficult to train young men adequately. The long hours of full time jobs have reduced the amount of time available for rehearsals. For example, many Shishipashi, Iwaya, and Shiriya residents now work at at the Nitetsu cement company, located between Iwaya and Shiriya. Previously, the primary occupations of fishing and farming allowed greater flexibility in scheduling and more available time for *nōmai* rehearsals. Winter was a slack season for fishing and farming, making it the ideal time to prepare and train for the New Year's performances. The amount of leisure time, coupled with the significance of the New Year as an auspicious occasion for renewal, made this time of year the most important for *nōmai* presentations.

Television-viewing is another modern-day source for alterations in the *nōmai* tradition. Shishipashi's Mr. Ōta remarked that "after the war (World War II), when men returned to the village, the performing arts flourished, but then television became popular, drawing the interest of the villagers away from the performing arts." Communities changed the dates of their performances to avoid coinciding with popular programs, such as pro-wrestling.

In 1966, some communities almost surrendered to the diminishing availability of performers until thirteen villages decided to form the Kyōdō Geinō Hozon Rengokai (Federation of the Preservation of Village Performing Arts). The federation holds an annual performance featuring *nōmai* and *kagura* by any community in the district wanting to participate. The event is also an attempt to attract young men by providing a venue that has the potential to bring recognition and prestige to an individual if a performance is well received. The program I attended at the Shiriya Middle School on January 8, 1984, boasted a large audience which filled the assembly hall with standing room only in the back. It was a good turnout and people came from as far as Tokyo to view the performance; others came from the island of Hokkaidō to the north and the city of Hirosaki, a five-hour drive south. A further intent of the combined performance every year is to stimulate competition among the *nōmai* groups. The federation assigns a performance piece to each community, setting a competitive aspect in which villages try to outperform one another. The intent of the competition is an attempt to hold the interest for younger performers, while increasing the entertainment value.

*Nōmai's* transformation into a public event and a broadening of its audience is inexorable as increasing tourism becomes an aspect of potential support. Change in the original intent or style of an art usually accompanies such transformations. Stylistically, for example, there is a trend among some *nōmai* groups to further develop the theatrical effects of the tradition. The increased theatricality is an attempt to attract greater audiences in competing with modern forms of entertainment. The greater theatricality is also possibly meant to draw the attention of younger men in the area who might find *nōmai* more appealing in this enhanced form. At the combined performance of the federation, the village of Horobe's version of the piece "Kurama" was reminiscent of Beijing opera with glittering costumes, dramatic face makeup, and acrobatic stunts. The acrobatics featured in Horobe's performance, however, are more likely a remnant of *dengaku*, an early antecedent of this performing art known for this feature. The performance, in any case, was conspicuous in comparison to the more subdued *nōmai* style of the other villages.

Formation of the federation raises the issue of classicizing folk dramatic forms caught in the throes of change. Mr. Ōta's intent in creating the federation, I believe, was to preserve what he considered the authentic *nōmai* style—elaborate songs and flute melodies and elegant and fluid dance movements accompanied by precise drumming and percussion. The annual performance of the federation is successful in its attempt to maintain *nōmai*, but stylistic changes in costuming, music, and dance are unavoidable in *nōmai*'s efforts to survive. The pull to secularize and theatricalize this tradition is strong with the intent of increasing audiences and drawing in young men as potential performers.

It is a difficult task for communities to preserve *nōmai* even with the assistance of other villages. A local newspaper, *Tōnippō*, ran a story about how Shiranuka, the largest community of Higashidorimura district, recruits even children for *nōmai*'s preservation. Also in that town, a friendship group of 160 people perform *nōmai*, altering the established tradition of men's associations being the primary carrier of the tradition. According to Mr. Hidegoro Nishiyama, the president of the friendship group, "from long ago as many as thirty people practiced *nōmai*, but now we have decreasing numbers of inheritors in this desperate situation" (*Tōnippō* 1984:12). Shiranuka was afraid of losing all its *nōmai* inheritors before

Mr. Nishiyama and other *nōmai* masters began training young boys who are interested. Their source for recruiting the next generation of performers is the *kodomokai* (children's club), consisting of 300 students from the fourth to the ninth grades. Thirty-two boys from this group of 300 were being trained in 1984. Mr. Sōichi Higashida, president of the *kodomokai*, stated that "*nōmai* training not only fosters inheritors of *nōmai*, but contributes to a close communication between adults and children. Some people are afraid that many of the children who are now being trained might leave the village, but even the one or two who stay will help preserve *nōmai*" (*Tōnippō*, 1984: 12). The necessity of preserving *nōmai* has generated innovative ways to train the next generation.

Will women, currently restricted from performing *nōmai*, break through the gender barrier to ensure its survival? The question of whether *nōmai* inheritors will ever include women is difficult to answer. *Nōmai*, *kagura*, and *okajishimai*, all performing traditions in Aomori Prefecture, continue to be limited to men. The Buddhist conception of women and copulation as a worldy desire reinforced a precedent disallowing women from performing *nōmai*. Women in this region perform *mochitsuki odori*, a folk dance that imitates the pounding of rice to make offerings and rice cakes to eat. Their role within *nōmai* is marginal, being primarily a custodial one consisting of making and repairing costumes and preparing food for rehearsals and performances. Strict roles assigned to each gender appear to prevail and *nōmai* remains firmly planted as a men's tradition. If performers continue to dwindle, it will be interesting to see if the gender barrier crumbles and whether men's associations gracefully accept women who step forward to assist in sustaining *nōmai*.

More current research is needed to check on the status of the issues raised here, since this study was conducted fourteen years ago. It is my contention that a shortage of performers continues to be a major obstacle in the retention of *nōmai*. I also imagine that the growing tourist trade in this area is increasingly transforming the sacred, private face of *nōmai* into a more secularized, public event.

## THE BALANCE

The unavoidable changes and adversities facing *nōmai* call for a moment to reflect on the balance needed to maintain the style, performance practices, and sacred intent of the art. The community performances given by villages in the Higashidorimura district serve to sustain the private side, the intrinsic nature of *nōmai* within each, including the sacred custom of making requests for the welfare of its members. Ōri's performance on January 15, 1984 included the *betto*'s ritual of waving a *shakujō* over the heads of villagers in the audience to rid individuals of evil spirits for the coming year. It was a sacred moment as people reverently bowed their heads and the *hayashi* accompaniment of *kai no kudari* filled the air. Such moments are not seen at more public performances.

The public side of *nōmai* includes not only the annual Kyōdō Geinō Hozon Rengokai event, but performances at regional and national folk performing arts festivals, music society meetings, national television (NHK) programs featuring local traditions, and appearances at the National Theater in Tokyo. A performance at the National Theater signals the official recognition of an art tradition that has been designated as a national treasure. These contexts, less personal and less sacred, are *nōmai*'s public face. Perhaps two arenas of performance—private ones tied to communities and ones given in public settings—offer a reasonable compromise to keepers of the *nōmai* tradition as they attempt to retain aspects of their past that still hold value for them today.

# APPENDIX

## MUSICAL TRANSCRIPTIONS

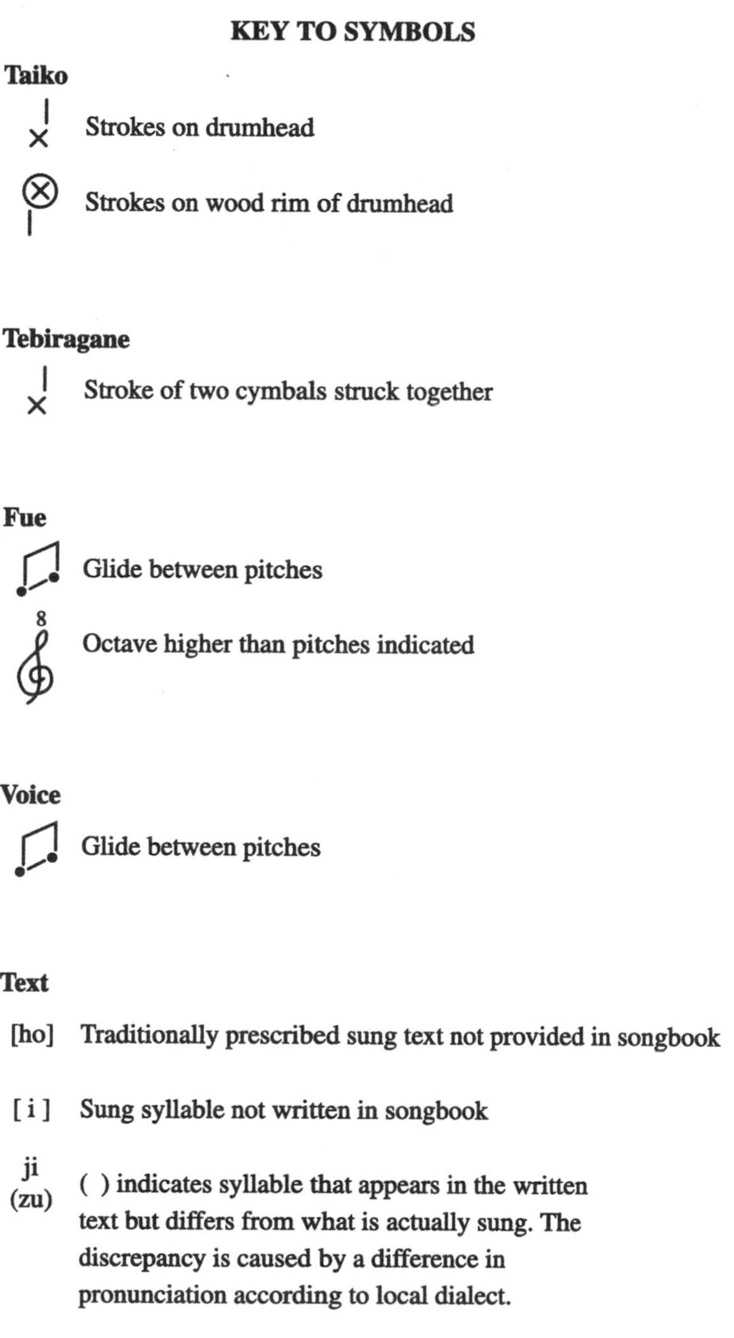

## KEY TO SYMBOLS

**Taiko**

Strokes on drumhead

Strokes on wood rim of drumhead

**Tebiragane**

Stroke of two cymbals struck together

**Fue**

Glide between pitches

Octave higher than pitches indicated

**Voice**

Glide between pitches

**Text**

[ho] Traditionally prescribed sung text not provided in songbook

[ i ] Sung syllable not written in songbook

ji
(zu) ( ) indicates syllable that appears in the written text but differs from what is actually sung. The discrepancy is caused by a difference in pronunciation according to local dialect.

**Figure A.1.** **Gobyōshi no iri**

15
Fue
Basic Fue Melody
Voice
Tebiragane
Taiko
B
5
20

C
25
Fue
Basic Fue Melody
Voice
Tebiragane
Taiko
30
D
5

35
Fue
Basic Fue Melody
Voice
Tebiragane
Taiko
E
40
5

45
Fue
Basic Fue Melody
Voice
Tebiragane
Taiko
5
Bridge section-tempo quickens
F
(Cadential)
50
5
5
I
ho
6
ye
re
e

55
Bridge section–tempo quickens
Fue
Basic Fue Melody
Voice
Tebiragane
Taiko
i
na
no
ka
3
60
(a)
-
yo
ri
The music continues until the dance is completed

**Figure A.2.** **Kiri**

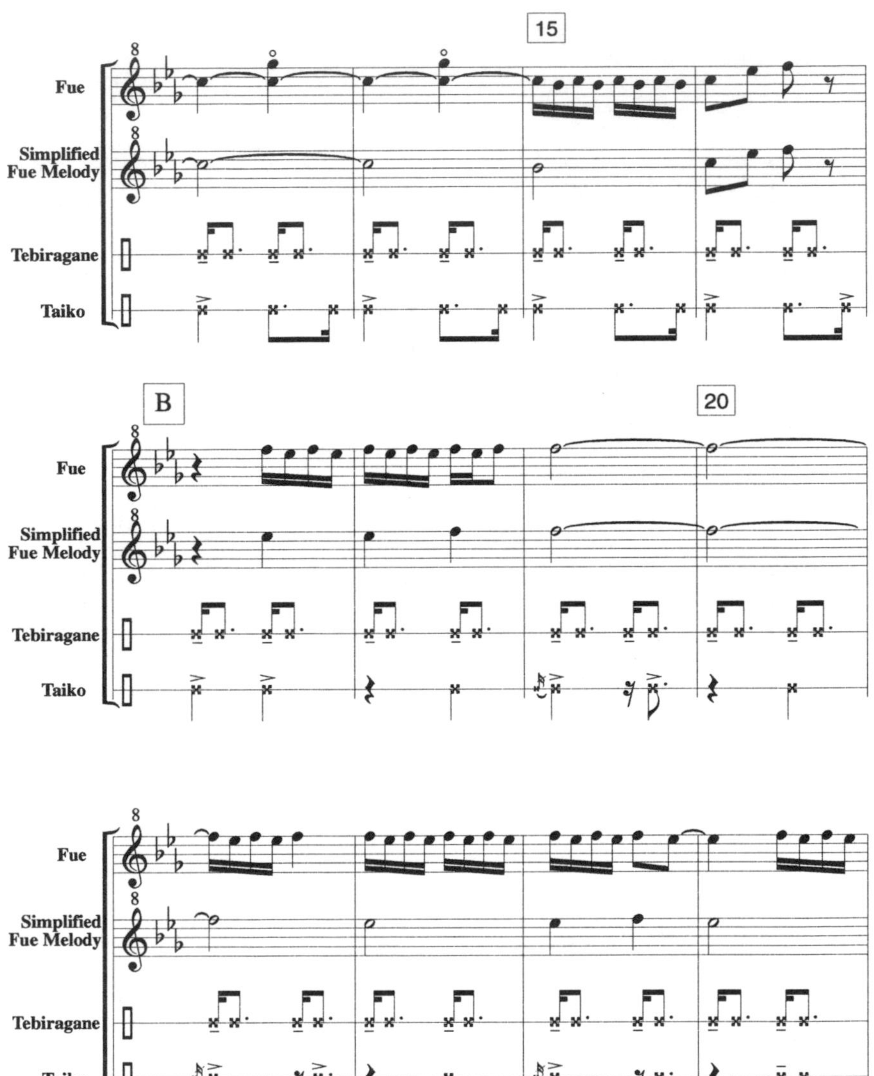
15
Fue
Simplified Fue Melody
Tebiragane
Taiko
B
20
Fue
Simplified Fue Melody
Tebiragane
Taiko
Fue
Simplified Fue Melody
Tebiragane
Taiko

25
C
Fue
Simplified Fue Melody
Tebiragane
Taiko
30
B1
35

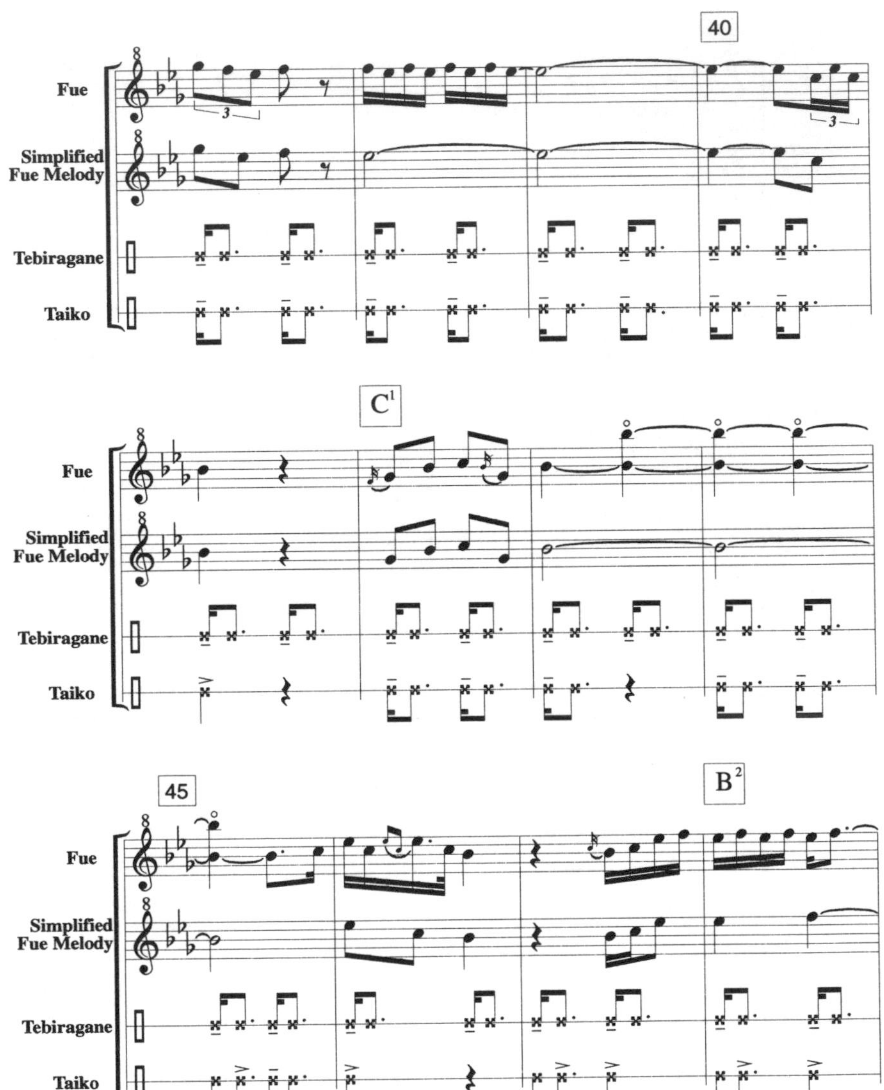
40
Fue
Simplified Fue Melody
Tebiragane
Taiko
C1
45
B2

50
C²
Fue
Simplified Fue Melody
Tebiragane
Taiko
55
6
B³
5
60

70
D1
3
Fue
Simplified Fue Melody
Tebiragane
Taiko
75
Fue
Simplified Fue Melody
Tebiragane
Taiko

Figure A.3. Sagari ha

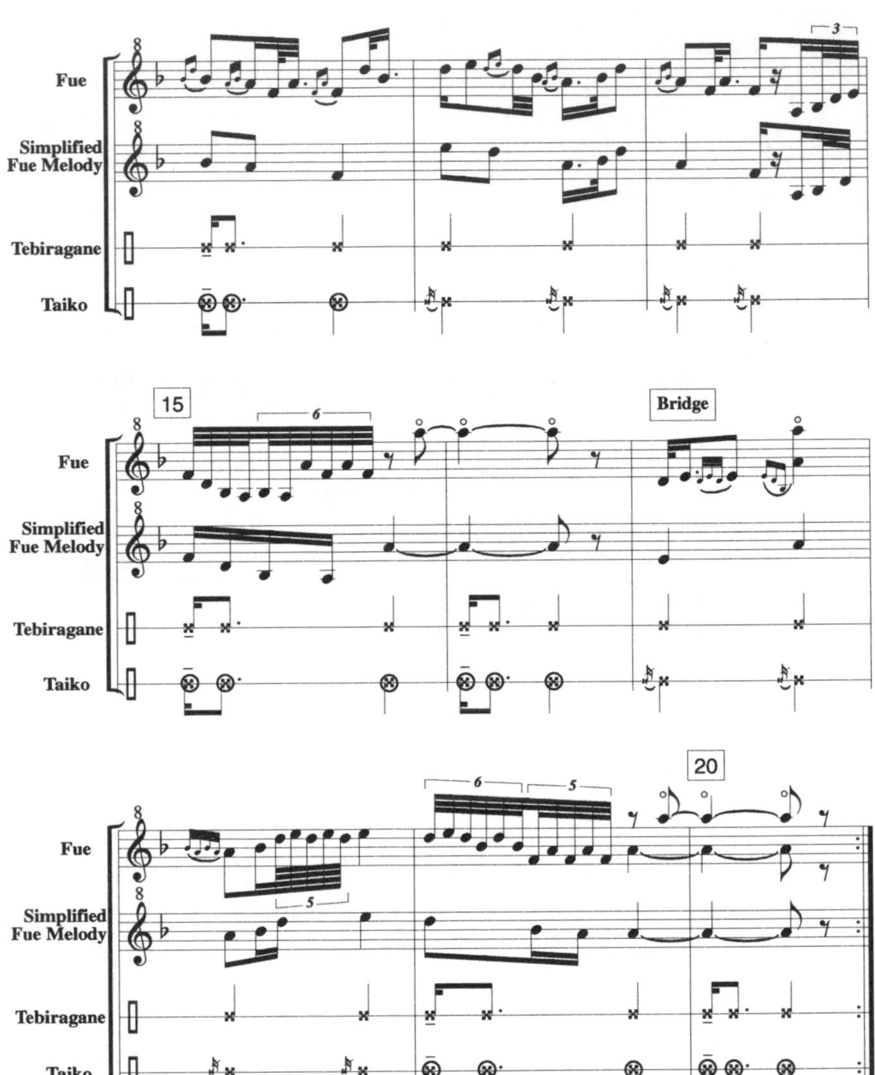
Fue
Simplified Fue Melody
Tebiragane
Taiko
3
15
6
Bridge
20
6
5
5

Figure A.4.
Kai no Kudari
Introduction
♩=108–112
Fue
Simplified Fue Melody
Tebiragane
Taiko
5
A
10

15
Fue
Simplified Fue Melody
Tebiragane
Taiko
B
20
C
6
5
3

25
Fue
Simplified Fue Melody
Tebiragane
Taiko
D
30
Fue
Simplified Fue Melody
Tebiragane
Taiko
A
35
Fue
Simplified Fue Melody
Tebiragane
Taiko

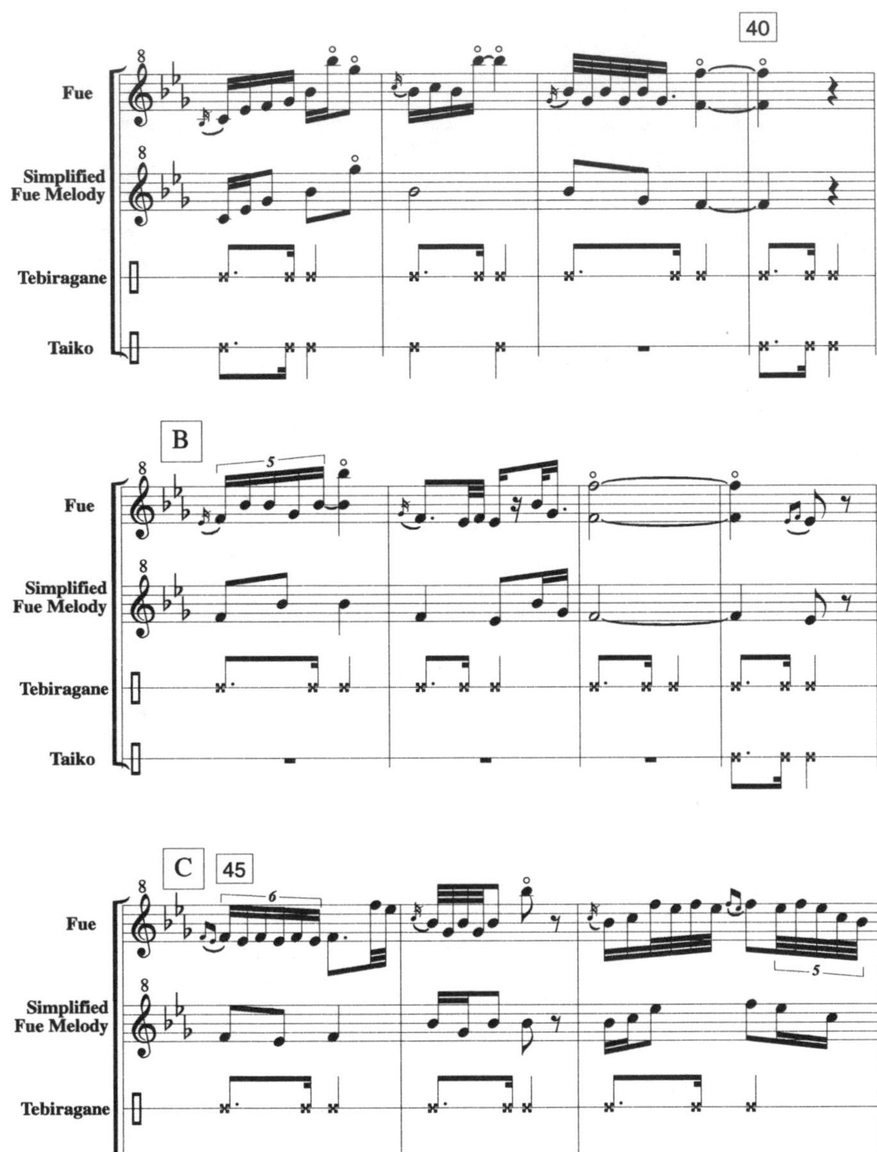
40
Fue
Simplified Fue Melody
Tebiragane
Taiko
B
5
C
45
6
5

50
Fue
Simplified Fue Melody
Tebiragane
Taiko
D
55
A

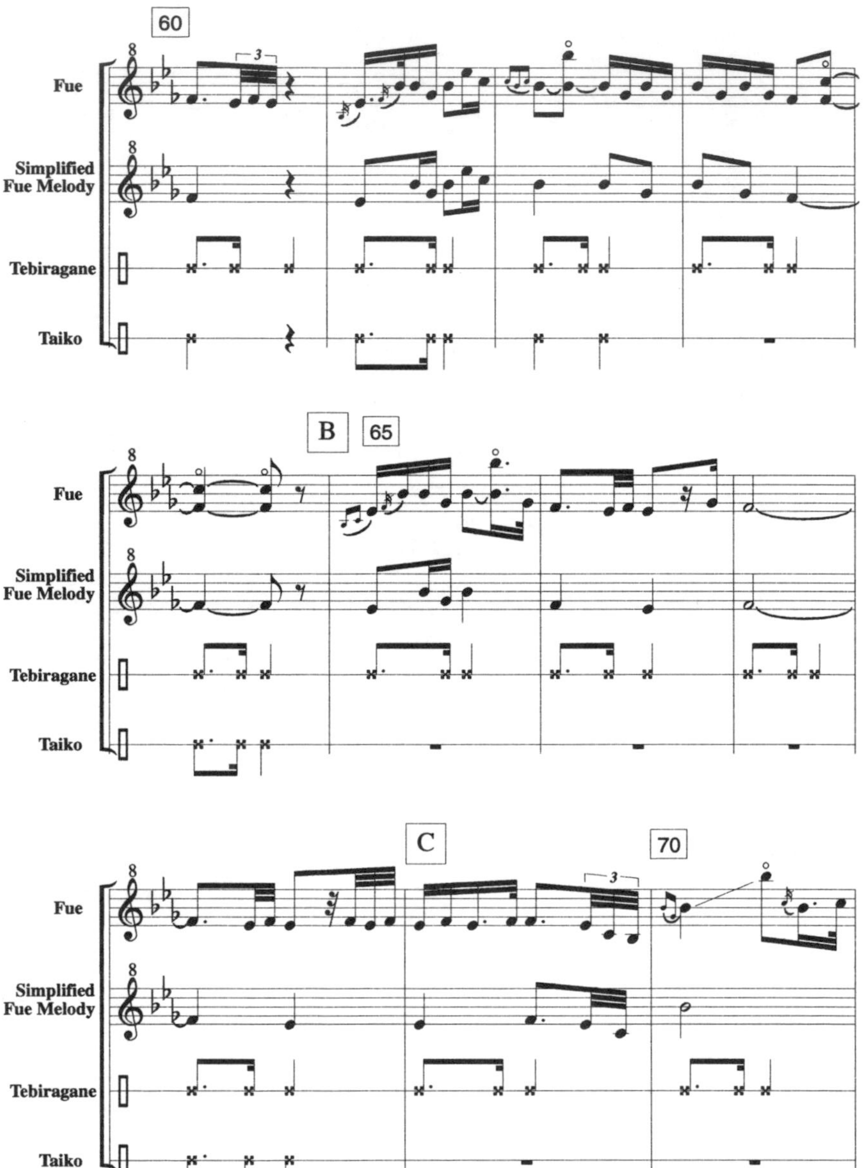
60
Fue
Simplified Fue Melody
Tebiragane
Taiko
B
65
C
70

(music continues to end of dance)

**Figure A.5.** **Hairi no uta—Ceremonial Pieces**

Interlude
C
[ie ho - o ye re] [e] na mo su
D
sa - a shi - gi wa ka - mi no - o mi - i -
Closing phrase
yo - o ka a - na - ka - mi no - o
mi yo - o ka na - a [hai - ya - a]

**Figure A.6.** **Makudashi—Ceremonial Pieces**

**Figure A.7.** **Makudashi 1—Warrior Pieces**

**Figure A.8.** **Makuzuki 1—Warrior Pieces**

**Figure A.9.** **Makudashi 2—Warrior Pieces**

**Figure A.10.** **Makudashi 2—Warrior Pieces (excerpt)**

# Glossary of Japanese Terms

***aruku junjo*** 歩く順序 - "step sequence"; a graphic representation of the choreographic sequence of a dance used by *nōmai* performers as a visual memory aid

***bachi*** 撥 - drumsticks made from paulownia or maple wood

***bangaku*** 番楽 - formerly a guarding dance performed by soldiers; name of the dance performed in the first half of the *nōmai* pieces "Gongenmai," "Torimai," and "Henzai"; this dance is also performed as a separate piece in certain ceremonial contexts

***betto*** 別当 - shrine caretaker; within the *nōmai* context, it is a responsible person of the young men's association who acts as caretaker for the *gongengashira*, which is considered the temporary abode of the *gongen* deity

***biwa*** 琵琶 - a pear-shaped plucked lute with a bent neck, having four or five strings with four or five frets depending on the type, and played with a triangular plectrum.

***bonden*** 梵天 - ritual cut paper offerings attached to a wood stick; the conventional emblem of *kami* in Shinto ritual throughout Japan

***buchi komi*** 打ち込み - a short ritual *nōmai* performance held at the *betto*'s house; this occasion is not public and only is attended by members of a *nōmai* association

***bugaku*** 舞楽 - classical Japanese court dance with instrumental accompaniment (*gagaku* )

***bushimai*** 武士舞 - warrior dances

***byōshi*** 拍子 - see *hyōshi*

***chinkon*** 鎮魂 - complex of beliefs concerning the power of man to invoke and manipulate spirits; funeral rite for the repose of souls of the dead

***chotate eboshi*** ちょたて烏帽子 - headgear, lacquered black and without a brim, worn with court garments by those holding the highest noble rank from the Nara period to feudal times

***chūkyoku*** 中曲 - scale used in Buddhist chant that combines both the *ritsu* and *ryō* scales

***daikagura*** 大神楽 - a grand performance of sacred music and dance held at the Ise Shrine in Mie prefecture

***dengaku*** 田楽 - a rice-planting music and dance ritual that evolved into a variety show of folk dances, jugglery, and acrobatics

***dengaku nō*** 田楽能 - a later, more dramatic form of *dengaku* that included humorous skits and imitative acts

***dōkemai*** 道化舞 - comic, satirical dances

***dōtori*** 頭取 - *taiko* drummer's role as the antagonist in *nōmai*'s comic pieces

***eboshi*** 烏帽子 - headgear, lacquered black and without a brim, which was worn with court garments by nobles, or those holding rank from the Nara period to feudal times; held in place by two cords tied under the chin. The top is bent to one side—to the right for the shogun and to the left for others like the military

***enkyoku*** 宴曲 - songs sung at banquets and parties in the Heian court; *enzui* ("drunken pools") was another name for this song genre which describes the function of these songs

***ennen*** 延年 - originally a Buddhist ceremony of prayer for the prolongation of a high-ranking person's life; later, the general name for the various types of performances given in Buddhist temples after festivals and ceremonies and during the visits of important guests

***ennen nō*** 延年能 - expansion of *ennen* in the latter half of the 13th century by incorporating *shirabyōshi* dance, *bugaku* dance, or plays that emphasized singing

***fue*** 笛 - Japanese bamboo transverse flute

***fujinkai*** 婦人会 - married women's association

***furoshiki*** 風呂敷 - a scarf-like square cloth made of silk or cotton, or sometimes synthetic fiber used for wrapping and carrying things

***gagaku*** 雅楽 - classical Japanese court music

***gakuya*** 楽屋 - a separate backstage area of the *nōmai* stage where the *gongengashira* is enshrined, performers change costumes and ready themselves, and the flute player and singers situate themselves for performance

***gigaku*** 伎楽 - a performing tradition of dance pieces and pantomimes associated with the central Chinese state of Wu and introduced to Japan in the 7th century via Korea

***gireimai*** 儀礼舞 - ceremonial dances

***gobyōshi*** 五拍子 - understood to mean "five beats" by *nōmai* performers

***gobyōshi no iri*** 五拍子の入り - instrumental piece that serves as a prelude to a majority of the *nōmai* dance dramas

***gohei*** 御幣 - sacred wand with strips of white paper; a ritual object used to cleanse a person or people of impurities and sins; sometimes used to invite the descent of the gods and ward off misfortune, especially in exorcism

***gōmin*** 郷民 - village folk

***gongen*** 権現 - (lit. incarnation of Buddha) central deity revered in the *nōmai* tradition

***gongengashira*** 権現頭 - wooden lion's head where the *gongen* deity is believed to temporarily reside

***gongensama*** 権現様 - honorific name for *gongen* deity

***hachimaki*** 鉢巻 - a headband; a kerchief or a slip of cotton cloth tied around one's head

***hairi no uta*** 入りの歌 - standard opening song of *nōmai* dance dramas

***hakama*** 袴 - a divided skirt for men's formal Japanese wear

***hana*** 花 - aesthetic concept in *nō* theatre describing effect of charm and interest characterized by novelty and grace (*yūgen*); in *nōmai* it refers to monetary donations volunteered by audience members, who throw or put the money on stage to acknowledge a particular dancer's skill during his performance

***haniwa*** 埴輪 - clay figures which represented human or animal figures as well as buildings, boats, and other items that were made for ritual use and buried with the dead in ancient Japan during the Tumulus period (3rd-6th centuries)

***hayashi*** 囃子 - *nōmai* instrumental ensemble consisting of a flute, cymbals, and drum

***heikyoku*** 平曲 - music recited to the epic-ballad *Tale of the Heike* with *biwa* accompaniment

***heisoku*** 幣束 - Shinto offering of cut paper

***henbai*** 片陪 - violent stamping intended to drive away evil spirits or *kami*; derived from rituals introduced to Japan by Taoist priests

***hijiri*** 聖 - ascetics who synthesized ideas from religious Taoism that included mountain retreats and a special diet to promote their becoming sacred wizards (*shinsen*)

***hiragana*** 平仮名 - one of two sets of Japanese syllabary writing; usually used for writing inflectional endings and words not represented by Chinese characters (*kanji*)

***horagai*** 法螺貝 - a conch shell trumpet

***hōshigen*** 法師元 - *sarugaku* performers who were low-ranking Buddhist temple officers

***hyōshi (-byōshi)*** 拍子 - meter; time; rhythm; measure; a musical time pattern; refers to a rhythmic framework (meter) rather than just "beat"

***hyottoko*** ひょっとこ - a masked comic character in folk dances

***imayō*** 今様 - popular songs of the ancient court

***inkyōsama*** 隠居様 - older manifestation of the *gongen* deity often enshrined together with the younger *gongensama*

***jukkai shugyō*** 十界修行 - a Tendai Buddhist concept built on a ranking system of ten worlds; a hierarchy of ten stages divided into six preliminary stages and four enlightened states

***juzu*** 数珠 - a string of Buddhist rosary beads

***kado uchi*** 門打ち - a practice performed on New Year's day in which a group of *nōmai* musicians and dancers make their rounds to each house in their village to perform primarily "Gongenmai" to pray for a prosperous and healthy coming year

***kagura*** 神楽 - Shinto music and dance

***kai no kudari*** 甲斐の下り - *nōmai* instrumental piece accompanying dance in the piece "Bangaku," as well as ritual processions in transporting the *gongen-gashira* from its storage place to the *betto*'s house, then to the *nōmai* performing space and back again into storage

***kaji kitō*** 加持祈祷 - Buddhist term which denotes prayer that draws on the strength of Buddha

***kakegoe*** 掛け声 - punctuated shouts or sounds of drummers or other musicians that functions to keep time or encourage dancers.

***kami*** 神 - deity; divinity; ancestors of the Japanese people who have been deified; natural objects or phenomena that have been deified

***kami gakari*** 神懸り - divine inspiration; divine possession

***kamidana*** 神棚 - ("deity shelf") a shelf that serves as an altar to a specific deity, on which an object representing that deity is placed

***kami uta*** 神歌 - deity song; early *kagura* song

***kane no o*** 鐘の緒 - cloth or straw bell cord found at entrances to shrines or temples, which is pulled to make the bell it is attached to sound

***kata*** 型 - a set [traditional] form; traditionally prescribed postures and poses used in dance dramas

***katana*** 刀 - a Japanese long sword used by samurai. It has a gently curved blade with a single edge, a long hilt and a guard.

***keishindan*** 敬信団 - reverence society

***kiri*** 切 - *nōmai* instrumental piece that accompanies warrior dances and dance in the latter half of certain ceremonial pieces

***kitōmai*** 祈祷舞 - a ritual dance of exorcism considered to be a type of prayer dance

***kōjakumai*** 幸若舞 - a type of acrobatic dancing

***Kojiki*** 古事記 - [Record of Ancient Matters] a story that relates mythological stories and historical events of ancient Japan; one of the most valuable sources of information on the ancient history, religion, and culture of Japan

***kōshiki*** 講式 - one of two new forms of Buddhist psalmody that emerged as a result of Buddhist reforms at the end of the 12th century; hymns that are didactic in nature and are sung as praises to deities and ancestors; considered narrative *shōmyō* since emphasis is placed on conveying the words, rather than the efficacy of tones sung

***koto*** 琴 - a Japanese thirteen-string board zither; strings are tuned with bridges placed under each and are plucked by three finger plectra placed on the thumb, forefinger, and third finger of the right hand

***kouta*** 小唄 - lit. a short song; a Japanese traditional song or ballad sung to the accompaniment of the *shamisen* and may accompany traditional dances

***kōwakamai*** 幸若舞 - a narrative art with a small element of dance that was popular in the 16th and 17th centuries; narratives tell of the valor of famous warriors and of well-known battles especially between the Taira and Minamoto families

***kusemai*** 曲舞 - a dance performed to the melodic recitation of historical narratives

***kyōgen*** 狂言 ("crazy words") - one style of traditional drama reflecting everyday and social conditions, often making use of mime and comical situations

***mai*** 舞 - dance; a horizontal, quiet, dignified circling dance

***makubiraki*** 幕開き ("curtain opening") - first New Year's *nōmai* performance

***makudashi*** 幕出し - song sung prior to and sometimes during the stage entrance of a character in a *nōmai* dance drama

***makuosame*** 幕納め - ("curtain closing") final New Year's *nōmai* performance

***makuzuki*** 幕付き - song section that is sung as accompaniment to dance or in between dance sections of *nōmai* dance dramas

***mikagura*** 御神楽 - Shinto music and dance for Imperial court ceremonies

***miko*** 巫女 - originally referred to women who practiced techniques of spirit possession; it now refers to shrine maidens who assist Shinto priests and also perform sacred Shinto dances at shrines

***mikomai*** 巫女舞 - one of two main styles of female Shinto dances still performed at shrines in Kyoto, Nara and Ise

***minyō*** 民謡 - refers to both a musical scale and a tetrachord upon which the scale is built; the tetrachord is characterized by the interval of a minor third between the lower nuclear and intermediate tones and a major second between the intermediate and upper nuclear tones; heard mostly in folk songs and children's traditional game songs

***miyakobushi*** 都節 - refers to both a musical scale and a tetrachord upon which the scale is built; the tetrachord consists of a minor second interval between the lower nuclear and intermediate tones and a major third between the intermediate and upper nuclear tones; heard primarily in *koto*, *shakuhachi*, *shamisen*, and *biwa* music, including music of the kabuki theater

***mochi*** 餅 - rice that is pounded into a glutinous consistency and then shaped into small, round cakes

***modoki*** 擬き - mimicry or an explanatory device prevalent in the form of comic parody; also refers to a main performance that has been modified to a level of popular understanding—often expressed as a type of comic relief

***monomane*** 物真似 - (lit. imitative) a realistic presentation of characters in a drama

***montsuki*** 紋付き - formal kimono bearing the family crest

***nagauta*** 長唄 - lit. a long song; a long epic song or ballad chanted to the accompaniment of *shamisen*, often with drums and flute added, for dances performed in the kabuki theater

***naorai*** 直会 - socialized eating and drinking

***nō*** 能 - classical dance drama that reached the peak of its development in the 14th century and continues to be performed today

***nōmai*** 能舞 - folk dance drama performed by thirteen villages on Shimokita Peninsula in northern Japan

***odori*** 踊り - dance; dancing; originally a vertical, jumpy, and rather violent dance in spirit quelling rituals of ancient *kagura*

***ōgi*** 扇 - a Japanese folding fan

***oiwake*** 追分 - a Japanese folk song genre; a packhorse driver's song

***okajishimai*** 岡獅子舞 - a divergent form of *nōmai* practiced by the villages of Horobe and Iriguchi

***onnamai*** 女舞 - dance performed by women characters; it involves taking a step forward, pausing for one beat, taking a step with the opposite foot, and pausing for another beat

***ritsu*** 律 - refers to both a musical scale and the tetrachord upon which the scale is built; the tetrachord consists of intervals a major second between the lower nuclear and intermediate tones and a minor third between the intermediate and upper nuclear tones; occurs mostly in Japanese court music and Buddhist chant, including folk songs it influenced

***ryo*** 呂 - a musical scale heard in Japanese court music and Buddhist chant, including folk songs it influenced

***sagari ha*** 下がり破 - *nōmai* instrumental accompaniment for women characters portrayed in the dramas, and for dance sections in the first half of the ceremonial pieces "Okina" and "Henzai"

***sanbyōshi*** 三拍子 - term meaning "three-beat" used by *nōmai* performers to describe the music of *okajishimai*; term is ambiguous in meaning since the music it describes is in duple meter, and instead is meant to convey that the music is played in a faster tempo

***sangaku*** 散楽 - a variety of performing acts, including jugglery and acrobatics, magical tricks, songs and dances, puppetry, and acts of burlesque, brought from China as early as the 7th century

***sangaku shinkō*** 山岳信仰 - indigenous religion whose beliefs and activities are associated with mountains considered sacred

***sarugaku*** 猿楽 - a theatrical art which included music, dance, drama, and comic mimicry performed for commoners beginning in the 10th century, primarily at temples and shrines

***sarugaku hōshi*** 猿楽法師 - *sarugaku* performers who served as low-ranking sextons of Buddhist temples (synonymous with *hōshigen)*

***sarugaku nō*** 猿楽能 - a later manifestation of *sarugaku* that incorporated more realistic acting and the urbane forms of *shirabyōshi* and *kusemai* dance.

***seinenkai*** 青年会 - young men's association

***serifu*** 台詞 - speech, words, one's lines; in *nōmai* plays this term refers to dialogue

***shakuhachi*** 尺八 - a Japanese end-blown flute

***shakujō*** 錫杖 - priest's staff; the top of the staff is made of metal, on which metal rings are affixed, serving as a rattle; derived from the Khakkhara of Indian Buddhism and was used as a magical implement for protection and exorcism

***shamisen*** 三味線 - a Japanese three-string plucked lute; strings are plucked with a triangular-shaped ivory plectrum (*bachi*)

***shime daiko*** 締め太鼓 - a double-headed drum shaped like a Western snare drum

***shinchiku*** 新築 - ritual of exorcism performed for the dedication of a newly constructed house

***shinobue*** 篠笛 - a Japanese transverse bamboo flute

***shirabyōshi*** 白拍子 - a type of dance in which rhythm was the sole accompaniment; a plebeian dance form which became widespread after the middle of the 12th century among lower-class female entertainers

***shishigashira*** 獅子頭 - wooden lion's head

***shishimai*** 獅子舞 - lion's dance, in which a wooden lion's head is manipulated as part of the choreography

***shitamai*** 下舞 - refers to the first half of the piece "Gongenmai" in which a white fan is held by the dancer and in this capacity is also called "Bangaku"; also is used to refer to the second half of warrior dances, a section of dance accompanied by instrumental music with no singing

***shōmyō*** 声明 - Buddhist chant

***shugen nō*** 修験能 - repertoire of ceremonial dances that *yamabushi* developed into a dramatic form

**Shugendō** 修験道 - esoteric Buddhist sect that combined Shinto, the mystical leanings of Shingon and Tendai Buddhism, Confucianism, and religious Taoism

***shugenja*** 修験者 - Shugendō practitioner

***shushi*** 呪師 - esoteric Buddhist priests who practiced magic, divination, and exorcism in official Buddhist rites

***suzu*** 鈴 - a bell tree rattle; an important instrument in *mikomai* dances

***taiko*** 太鼓 - double-headed barrel drum

***tamashii*** 魂 - the life force of a person; ancient Shinto concept

***tamashizume*** 鎮魂 - funeral rite performed to secure or restrain within the body the life force of a person to prevent its departure

***tebiragane/kane*** 手平鉦/鉦 - hand-held cymbals made from a metallic mixture that includes iron; it is an accompanimental instrument heard in folk music throughout Japan and in many *kagura* forms

***te odori*** 手踊り - (lit. hand dance) regional folk dances, in which hand and arm movements are prominent

***torimono*** 採り物 - offerings that serve to attract a deity to descend and dwell within the object being offered during a ritual dance

***ujigami*** 氏神 - a tutelary god; the god who protects the local area or shrine; the god worshipped as an ancestor's spirit

***utagakari*** 歌掛かり - musical section in which the instrumental ensemble and singers perform simultaneously in accompanying dance; this coupling increases the tension and leads to the climax of a *nōmai* dance drama

***yagatame*** 屋固め - event in which a newly constructed home is dedicated with the performance of a ritual, called *shinchiku*

***yamabushi*** 山伏 - mountaineering ascetic priest of the Shugendō religious order

***yamabushi kagura*** 山伏神楽 - dance drama developed and originally performed by *yamabushi*

***yōkyoku*** 謡曲 - lyrics delivered in a chanting form in the libretto used in *nō* drama as accompaniment to dance

# Bibliography

Abe, Itaru
1973 *Kyū Nanbu ryōki ni okeru yamabushi kagura denshō to fue sōhō no saishū kōsatsu* [On the Collection of Materials on the Mtn. Priest Tradition and Flute Styles in the Nanbu Region—A Consideration]. Hachinohe, Aomori Prefecture, Japan: n.p.

Anesaki, Masaharu
1963 *History of Japanese Religion* (With Special Reference to the Social and Moral Life of the Nation). Rutland, Vermont, and Tokyo: Charles E. Tuttle Co.

*Aomori ken chimei jiten* [Aomori Prefecture Geographical Name Dictionary]
1979 Aomori Prefecture, Japan: Aomori Hōsō Kabushiki Gaisha [Aomori Broadcasting Company].

Araki, James T.
1978 *The Ballad-Drama of Medieval Japan.* Rutland, Vermont, and Tokyo: Charles E. Tuttle Co.

Beardsley, Richard, John W. Hall, and Robert E. Ward
1959 *Village Japan*, Second Edition (revised). Chicago and London: University of Chicago Press.

Befu, Harumi
1971 *Japan: An Anthropological Introduction.* San Francisco: Chandler Publishing Co.

Berberich, Junko Sakaba
1984 "Some Observations on Movement in Nō." *Asian Theatre Journal*, volume 1, no. 2, pp. 207-216.

Blacker, Carmen
1975 *The Catalpa Bow—A Study of Shamanistic Practices in Japan.* London: George Allen and Unwin.

Blau, Hagen
1966 *Sarugaku und shushi.* Wiesbaden: Otto Harrassowitz.

Bouchy, Ann-Marie
1976 "Kagura and Ascetics." *Ōtsugunai yamabushi kagura.* Yoshihiro Tanaka, ed. Nagoya: Matsuri Society.

*A Cultural Dictionary of Japan*

1979 Momoo Yamaguchi and Setsuko Kojima, eds. Tokyo: The Japan Times, Ltd.

Danielou, Alain

1980 "Ethical and Spiritual Values in Music." *The World of Music*, vol. 22, no. 2, pp. 3-8.

*A Dictionary of Buddhist Terms and Concept*

1983 Tomohiro Matsuda, ed. Tokyo: Nichiren Shoshu International Center.

Earhart, H. Byron

1970 *A Religious Study of the Mount Haguro Sect of Shugendō: An Example of Japanese Mountain Religion.* Tokyo: Sophia University.

1974 *Japanese Religion: Unity and Diversity*, Second Edition. Encino and Belmont, California: Dickenson Publishing Company, Inc.

Embree, John F.

1941 "Some Social Functions of Religion in Rural Japan." *The American Journal of Sociology*, vol. 47, no. 2, pp.184-189.

Fairchild, William P.

1962 "Shamanism in Japan."*Folklore Studies*, vol. 21, pp. 1-122.

Foley, Edward

1984 *Music in Ritual: A Pre-Theological Investigation.* American Essays in Liturgy 1. Washington, D.C.: Pastoral Press.

Garfias, Robert

1965 *The Tōgaku Style of Japanese Court Music: An Analysis of Theory in Practice.* Ph.D. Dissertation in Music. Los Angeles: University of California.

Geertz, Clifford

1973 *The Interpretation of Cultures: Selected Essays.* New York Basic Books.

Gorai, Shigeru

1972a "Minkan geinō kaidai" [Folk Performing Arts—Introduction], *Minkan geinō*, vol. 17, *Nihon shomin minzoku seikatsu shiryōshūsei.* Tokyo: Sanichi Shōbō.

1972b "Minkan kagura" [Folk Shinto Music and Dance]. *Minkan geinō,* vol. 17, *Nihon shomin minzoku seikatsu shiryōshūsei.* Tokyo: Sanichi Shōbō.

Gotō, Hajime
1975 *Nōgaku no kigen* [The Origin of Nōgaku]. Tokyo: Mokujisha.

Grainger, Roger
1974 *The Language of the Rite.* London: Darton, Longmann, and Todd.

Grimes, Ronald L.
1985 *Research in Ritual Studies: A Programmatic Essay and Bibliography.* Metuchen, New Jersey: Scarecrow Press.

Hall, John Whitney
1971 *Japan—From Prehistory to Modern Times.* Tokyo: Charles E. Tuttle Co.

Harich-Schneider, Eta
n.d. "Buddhist Music." *The Music of Japan,* vol.4, UNESCO Collection—A Musical Anthology of the Orient. Barenreiter Musicaphon BM 30 L 2015 [Record Notes].

*Heike Monogatari* [The Tale of the Heike]
1975 Hiroshi Kitagawa and Bruce T. Tsuchida, eds. 2 volumes. Tokyo: University of Tokyo Press.

*Higashidorimura minzoku chōsa hokokusho* [A Report on the Folk Customs of Higashidorimura]
1980 4 volumes. Aomori Prefecture, Japan: Higashidorimura Board of Education.

*Higashidorimura no nōmai* [*Nōmai* in Higashidorimura]
1984 Aomori Prefecture, Japan: Higashidorimura Board of Education.

Hoff, Frank
1977 "The 'Evocation' and 'Blessing' of Okina: A Performance Version of Ritual Shamanism." *Alcheringa Ethnopoetics,* New Series, vol. 3, no. 1, pp. 48-60.

1978 "Song, Dance, Storytelling: Aspects of the Performing Arts in Japan." *East Asia Papers,* no. 15. Ithaca, New York: Cornell University China-Japan Program.

Honda, Yasuji

1954 "Denshō kayō no nembutsu chō" [The *Nembutsu* Melody of Traditional Songs]. English Summary. *Toyo Ongaku Kenkyū*, no. 12-13, pp. 8-10.

1960-61 "Kamigakari." *Engeki hyakka daijiten*, vol. 3, Waseda Daigaku Engeki Hatsubusukan, ed. Tokyo: Heibonsha.

1962 *Minzoku geinō* [Folk Performing Arts]. Tokyo: Shakai Shisō Kenkyūkai Shuppanbu.

1966 *Nihon no minzoku geinō* [Folk Performing Arts of Japan]. Tokyo: Kijisha.

1974 "Yamabushi kagura and bangaku: Performance in the Japanese Middle Ages and Contemporary Folk Performance." Frank Hoff, transl. *Educational Theater Journal*, vol. 26, no. 2, pp.192-208.

1976 "Yamabushi kagura," in *Ōtsugunai yamabushi kagura*. Yoshihiro Tanaka, ed. Nagoya: Matsuri Society.

1977 "Nō no hassei—mikomai kara nō e." *Bungaku* (March), vol. 45, pp. 269-281.

1983 "Reflections on Dance, its Origins, and the Value of Comparative Studies." *Dance as Cultural Heritage*, vol. 1 [Dance Research Annual 14], Frank Hoff, transl. New York: CORD, Inc., pp. 99-104.

Honda, Yasuji, Kasho Machida, Haruo Misumi, and Tomiko Kojima

1967 "Min'yō to minzoku geinō" [Folk Song and the Folk Performing Arts]. *Toyo ongaku sensho*, compiled by Tōyō Ongaku Gakkai, vol. 1. Tokyo: Ongaku no tomosha.

Hori, Ichiro

1968 *Folk Religion in Japan: Continuity and Change*. Joseph M. Kitagawa and Alan L. Miller, eds. Chicago: University of Chicago Press.

1972 *Japanese Religion: A Survey by the Agency for Cultural Affairs*. Hori Ichiro, Ikada Fujio, et al., eds., Abe Yoshiya and David Reid, transl. Tokyo: Kodansha International, Ltd.

Imamura, Teizo and Kyoshi Okukawa

1947 *Nōmai*. n.p.

Immoos, Thomas

1969 "The Birth of Japanese Theatre." *Monumenta Nipponica*, vol. 24, pp. 403-414.

1977 *Japanese Theatre*, Hugh Young, transl. London: Cassell [1974] and Collier Macmillan Publishers, Ltd.

Inoura, Yoshinobu

1963 *Nihon engeki shi* [History of Japanese Theatre]. Tokyo: Shibundō.

Inoura, Yoshinobu and Toshio Kawatake

1981 *The Traditional Theater of Japan*. New York and Tokyo: Weatherhill, Inc.

*Japanese Religion: A Survey by the Agency for Cultural Affairs*

1981 Ken Arai, et al., eds. Tokyo: Kodansha International.

*Kabuki jiten*

1983 Kunihiko Shimonaka, ed. Tokyo: Heibonsha Ltd.

Kageyama, Haruki

1973 *The Arts of Shinto*, vol. 4 of *Arts of Japan*, transl. and adapted with an introduction by Christine Guth. New York and Tokyo: Weatherhill/Shibundō.

Kakinoki, Goro

1975 "A Comparative Method on Japanese Melodic Styles in Structural Formulae." *Asian Music*, vol. 1-2, pp. 60-87.

Ka´rpa´ti, Ja´nos

1990 *Kagura: Japanese Shinto Ritual Music*. Hungaroton HCD 18193 [Record notes].

Kato, Shuichi

1979 *A History of Japanese Literature—The First Thousand Years*. David Chibbett, transl. Tokyo/New York/San Francisco: Kodansha International, Ltd.

Keene, Donald

1966 *Nō - The Classical Theatre of Japan*. Tokyo: Kodansha International, Ltd.

Kelly, William

1990 "Japanese No-Noh : The Crosstalk of Public Culture in a Rural Festivity." *Public Culture: Bulletin of the Project for*

*Transnational Cultural Studies*, vol. 2, no. 2, (Spring), pp. 65-81. Philadelphia: The Project [University of Pennsylvania].

Kirby, Ernest Theodore

1973 "The Origin of Nō Drama." *Educational Theatre Journal*, vol. 25, no. 3, pp. 269-284.

1976 "Shamanistic Origins of Popular Entertainments." *Ritual, Play, and Performance—Readings in The Social Sciences/Theatre*, Richard Schechner and Mady Schuman, eds., pp. 139-149. New York: The Seabury Press.

Kishibe, Shigeo

1962 "Japanese Music" [Seminar notes of lectures given at University of Los Angeles].

Kobayashi, Kazushige

1981 "On the Meaning of Masked Dances in Kagura." *Asian Folklore Studies*, vol. 40, no. 1, pp. 1-22.

Koida, Saiya

1981 "Shimokita no nōmai: Shishipashi no "Kanemaki." *Minzoku geinō taikai kiroku* [Proceedings of the Folk Performing Arts General Assembly of the 23rd Hokkaidō Tōhoku Block Public Performance], pp. 21-26. Iwate Prefecture: Iwate Prefecture Board of Education.

Koizumi, Fumio

1958 *Nihon dentō ongaku no kenkyū* [A Study of Traditional Japanese Music], vol. 1. Tokyo: Ongaku no tomo sha.

1977 "Musical Scales in Japanese Music." *Asian Musics in an Asian Perspective*. Tokyo: Heibonsha Ltd. Publishers.

*Kōjien*

1984 Izuru Shinmura, ed. Third Edition. Tokyo: Iwanami Shoten.

*Kojiki* [Record of Ancient Matters]

1981 Basil Hall Chamberlain, ed. Rutland, Vermont, and Tokyo: Charles E. Tuttle Co.

Kojima, Tomiko

1965 "Higashidorimura nōmai no ongakuteki kōzō" [The Musical Structure of Higashidorimura Nōmai]. *Jinrui kagaku*, vol. 17, pp.88-108.

1967a "Shimokita no minzoku ongaku" [Folk Music of Shimokita]. *Shimokita*, Kyū Gakkai, ed., pp. 330-332. Tokyo: Heibonsha.

1967b "Shimokita no geinō ken" [The Sphere of Performing Arts in Shimokita]. *Shimokita*, Kyū Gakkai, ed. Tokyo: Heibonsha.

Langer, Suzanne K.
1976 *Philosophy in a New Key: A Study in the Symbolism of Reason, Rite, and Art,* Third Edition. [1942] Cambridge: Harvard University Press.

Lombard, Frank Allison
1928 *An Outline History of Japanese Drama.* London: Allen and Unwin.

Malefijt, Annemarie de Waal
1968 *Religion and Culture: An Introduction to Anthropology and Religion.* New York: The Macmillan Co.

Malm, William P.
1974 *Japanese Music and Musical Instruments.* Rutland, Vermont: [1959] Charles E. Tuttle Co.

Markham, Elizabeth J.
1982 *Saibara: Japanese Court Songs of the Heian Period.* Cambridge and New York: Cambridge University Press.

*Minzokugaku jiten* [Folk Studies Dictionary]
1985 Minzokugaku Kenkyūsho [Folk Studies Research Institute], ed. Tokyo: Tokyo dō Shuppan.

Miyake, Hitoshi
1978 *Shugendō: Yamabushi no rekishi to shisō* [Mountain-based Asceticism: History and Thought of Buddhist Mountain Priests]. Tokyo: Kyoikusha.

Murakami, Toshio
1943 *Shugendō no hattatsu* [The Development of Shugendō]. Tokyo: Unebi Shobō.

Nakamura, Yasuo
1971 *Nō: The Classical Theater.* Don Kenny, ed. New York and Tokyo: Walker/Weatherhill in collaboration with Tankosha Publishers, Kyoto.

Nelson, Andrew Nathaniel

1974 *Japanese-English Character Dictionary*, Second Revised Edition. Rutland, Vermont, and Tokyo: Charles E. Tuttle Co.

*New Japanese-English Dictionary*

1974 Kō Masuda, ed., Fourth Edition. Tokyo: Kenkyūsha.

*Nihon Kokugo Daijiten*

1972 Compiled by Nihon Daijiten Kankōkai, 20 volumes. Tokyo: 1974 Shogakukan.

*Nihon Koten Bungaku Daijiten*

1973 Ichiko Teiji and Noma Kōshin, eds., 6 volumes. Tokyo: Iwanami Shoten.

Nose, Asaji

1953 "The Antecedent Arts of the Nō." *Nōgaku zensho*, Toyoichirō Nogami, ed., vol. 2, no. 1.

O'Neill, P.G.

1958 *Early Nō Drama: Its Background Character and Development 1300-1450.* London: Lund Humphries.

1972 *Japanese Names* [A Comprehensive Index by Characters and Readings]. New York and Tokyo: John Weatherhill, Inc.

Ortolani, Benito

1995 *The Japanese Theatre: From Shamanistic Ritual to Contemporary Pluralism.* Revised Edition. Princeton, New Jersey: Princeton University Press.

1984 "Shamanism in the Origins of the Nō Theatre." *Asian Theatre Journal*, vol. 1, no. 1, pp. 166-190.

Ōta, Zennosuke

1980 *Nōmai—mikansei setsumei* [Nōmai - Explanations (Incomplete)]. Higashidorimura, Aomori Prefecture, Japan: Higashidorimura Kyōdō Geinō Hozon Tsuaukai.

Papinot, E.

1972 *Historical and Geographical Dictionary of Japan.* Rutland, Vermont, and Tokyo: Charles E. Tuttle Co.

Penner, H.

1985 "The Concept and Forms of Ritual." *The Encyclopedia Britannica*, vol. 26, Macropaedia. 15th Edition. Chicago: Encyclopaedia Britannica, Inc.

Piggott, Francis

1893 *The Music and Musical Instruments of Japan.* London: B.T. Batsford.

Raz, Jacob

1981 "Chinkon: From Folk Beliefs to Stage Conventions." *Maske und Kothurn*, vol. 27, no. 1, pp. 15-18.

1983 *Audience and Actors: A Study of Their Interaction in the Japanese Traditional Theatre*. Leiden: E.J. Brill.

Reischauer, Edwin O.

1970 *Japan: The Story of a Nation.* New York: Alfred A. Knopf.

Sansom, G.B.

1978 *Japan: A Short Cultural History*, Second Revised Edition. Stanford, California: Stanford University Press.

Sasamori, Takefusa

1969 *Temari-uta (Japanese ball-bouncing game song): An Analysis with Emphasis on Rhythm.* Master's Thesis. Music Department, University of Hawaii.

Saunders, Dale E.

1960 *Mudra. A Study of Symbolic Gestures in Japanese Buddhist Sculpture*. New York: Pantheon Books.

Swanson, Paul L.

1981 "Shugendō and the Yoshino-Kumano Pilgrimage: An Example of Mountain Pilgrimage." *Monumenta Nipponica*, vol. 36, no. 1, pp. 55-84.

Tamba, Akira

1981 *The Musical Structure of Nō*. Translated from the French by Patricia Matore. Tokyo: Tokai University Press.

Tazawa, Yutaka, Saburo Matsubara, Shunsuke Okuda, and Yasunori Nagahata

1990 *Japan's Cultural History: A Perspective.* Tokyo: Ministry of Foreign Affairs.

Thornbury, Barbara E.

1997 *The Folk Performing Arts: Traditional Culture in Contemporary Japan.* Albany: State University of New York Press.

*Tōnippō*

1984 "Geinō no sato—Shimokita-gun, Higashidorimura" [Village Performing Traditions—Higashidorimura, Shimokita County], vol. 1, article 33156-33161 (April 1-6).

Ueda, Masāki "Chinkon to henbai." *Nihon no koten geinō*, vol. 10, pp. 97-98.

Wolz, Carl
1965 *Bugaku, Japanese Court Dance, with the Notation of Basic Movements and of Nasori.* Masters Thesis. Dance Department, University of Hawaii.

Yamaji, Kōzō
1983 "Early Kabuki Dance." *Dance as Cultural Heritage*, vol. 1 (Dance Research Annual 14), Frank Hoff, transl., Betty True Jones, eds., pp. 105-112. New York: CORD, Inc.

Yanagita, Kunio
1911 "Odori no ima to mukashi" [Dances of Ancient Times to the Present], in *Jinruigaku Zasshi* [Journal of Anthropology], vol. 27, no. 1-5.

*Yōkyoku Taikan* [A Comprehensive Study of Nō Texts]
1930-34 Kentaro Sanari, ed. 7 volumes. Tokyo: Meijishoin.

Zeami, Motokiyo
ca. 1404 *Kadensho* [Writings on the Tradition of (Creative) Flowering]. Reprint with corrections. Chūichi Sakurai, Shūseki Hayashi, Rokurō Satai, and Bin Miyai, transl. Kyoto: Sumiya-Shinobe.

# Index

## About the Author

SUSAN M. ASAI is a music professor at Northeastern University in Boston.

ISBN 0-313-30698-2
90000>
EAN
9 780313 306983
HARDCOVER BAR CODE